Baptism and the
Anglican Reformers

Baptism and the Anglican Reformers

G.W. Bromiley

Ⓒ

James Clarke & Co

James Clarke & Co.

P.O. Box 60
Cambridge
CB1 2NT
United Kingdom

www.jamesclarke.co
publishing@jamesclarke.co

Hardback ISBN: 978 0 227 17868 3
Paperback ISBN: 978 0 227 17867 6
PDF ISBN: 978 0 227 17870 6
ePub ISBN: 978 0 227 17869 0

British Library Cataloguing in Publication Data
A record is available from the British Library

First published by The Lutterworth Press, 1953
This edition published by James Clarke & Co., 2023

To
Stuart Barton Babbage

Contents

Abbreviations

AR	J Strype, Annals of the Reformation
B.P.S	T. Beza, A Brief and Pithy Summe
B.R.	British Reformers Series
B.R.N.	Bibliotheca Reformatoria Neerlandica
C.D.	Canons and Decrees of Trent
C.R.	Corpus Reformatorum
C.T.	Catechism of Trent
D.A.	Dosker, The Dutch Anabaptists
D.C.R.	Kidd, Documents of the Continental Reformation
E.B.I.	W. Goode, The Effects of Baptism in the case of Infants
E.E.D.	C. Burrage, The Early English Dissenters
E.M.	J. Strype, Ecclesiastical Memorials
E.R.	H. Hart, Ecclesiastical Records
H.D.	A. Harnack, History of Dogma II
J.	Cranmer, Works, Ed. Jenkins
K.B.	The King's Book
L.E.P.	Hooker, The Laws of Ecclesiastical Polity
P.B.O.	H. Gee, The Elizabethan Prayer Book and Ornaments
P.M.	Puritan Manifestos
P.S.	Parker Society Series
Q.R.C	T. Beza, Quaestionum et Responsionum Christianarum Libellus
R.D.	H. Heppe, Die Dogmatik der evangelisch
S.	Aquinas, Summa
S.P.R.	Seconde Parte of a Register
S.S.	W. Barlow, The Summe and Substance of the Conference
T.B.	J. de la Servière, La Théologie de Bellarmine
W.A.	Luther, Werke, Weimarer Ausgabe

Preface

The recent revival of interest in the sacrament of Holy Baptism suggests that the time is now ripe for a fresh study of the contribution made to this subject by the Anglican Reformers. For the most part such a study will be largely an essay in historical theology. To that extent it may appear to be rather remote from contemporary needs and contemporary issues. The modern outlook has enlarged. New problems have arisen. In theology, as in life as a whole, new situations have emerged for which the old solutions do not appear to suffice. But while all that is true, it is also true that we cannot afford simply to ignore the lessons of the past. An inquiry into the teaching of any age, and especially of so formative an age as that of the Reformation, is not merely useful but essential if we are to understand the present situation, to see it in its interconnection with the past, and to bring to the study of it the stimulus which is given by contact with the great thinkers of a great epoch. The field of investigation is restricted, but a large area of intellectual activity is opened up. Some of the controversies may be petty and tiresome in detail, but high and abiding principles are always involved.

Apart from the general value, which is of course the value of all history, the investigation has a particular interest because much of the material has a direct as well as an indirect bearing upon the problems which still confront us. There are the general problems like infant baptism and "indiscriminate" baptism, both of which were discussed in the Reformation periods, and on both of which valuable insights may be gained by a consideration of the arguments then advanced. Indeed, many of the points which may seem to us to be startling and novel will be found to be the old ones dressed up in the speech and thought forms of a new age. Again, the study has a considerable ecumenical interest, since it touches on the wider problems of the status and standpoint of the Anglican communion both within itself and in relation to other churches. Naturally, this aspect is of greater interest to members of that communion, but the problems of one communion cannot be of only local interest, especially when that communion has preserved a certain continuity in liturgy and order while accepting the Reformed reconstruction in doctrine.

From this standpoint there are two main questions involved; that of the ultimate truth of the confessional teaching in the light of present-day criticisms, and that of loyalty to the actual formulation as the established rule of faith, and the limits of legitimate interpretation of that formulation. In a sense, of course, both questions are primarily questions of the domestic discipline of the Church of England, and in the prevailing doctrinal as well as liturgical confusion in that church any contribution towards the elucidation of the confession has an obvious value. But the questions are also wider questions of intercommunion. There are many Anglicans who like to see in their church a possible bridge-church between the "Catholic" and "Evangelical" communions. In point of fact, however, there is a danger that it may become an island-church, with communion neither on the one side nor the other. On the one side its orders and liturgy are rejected by the Church of Rome, and on the other it refuses to make doctrinal affiliation a ground of fellowship with non-episcopal churches. Inter-communion will be possible only as dogmatic issues like that of baptism are honestly faced, and if it is found that in these matters the Anglican fathers and the confessions which they issued involve a substantial identity in doctrine with the other Protestant churches, then a big step will be taken towards the re-establishment of those brotherly relations which were assumed and accepted in the sixteenth century.

It is with this hope, and with the desire that light may be shed upon our understanding of the great sacrament of baptism, that the present modest contribution is made to the discussion of the subject.

Introduction

The impression has sometimes been gained that the Anglican Reformers had no great interest in the doctrine of baptism. Their concern about the eucharistic question is evident, for it was largely over the "sacrament of the altar" that the decisive battle of the English Reformation was fought. And there can be no doubt, of course, that it was the second sacrament which did attract the greater notice. Yet it must not be supposed that they entirely neglected the first sacrament, or that they took over the traditional teaching with very little change. It is true, no doubt, that a comparison of the baptismal office with the parallel service in the Church of Rome will reveal not a few points of similarity, but the fact that there is an inevitable agreement in certain matters must not blind us to the fact that the Reformers themselves may have been conscious of fundamental cleavages at others. Such a consciousness arose out of a detailed consideration of the whole question.

In point of fact, the baptismal question was forced upon the Anglican no less than the Continental reformers by extraneous circumstances, and they had no option but to think out the doctrinal questions involved. For one thing, the very discussion of the doctrine of the Lord's supper carried with it inevitably a study of the parallel sacrament of baptism, for although the two sacraments were seen to differ in nature, and purpose, and application, they were also seen to correspond closely to one another in their general character and operation: to be, in fact, identical in constitution and principle. This point emerges clearly in Cranmer's *True and Catholic Doctrine*,[1] in which he illustrates his teaching on the one sacrament by generally accepted views in relation to the other.

But again, as the sacrament of remission and regeneration, baptism was very closely connected with justification. As Luther's *Sermon on Baptism* makes clear, it was because he had won through to an evangelical understanding of justification that he came to a new study and a deeper apprehension of the meaning of baptism. It was no accident that Romans 6

---

1. Cranmer, P.S., I, p. 64.

formed an integral part of the great epistle of justification. And the relationship between baptism and justification was clearly perceived by the Anglican Reformers too: indeed, it could hardly be otherwise when a traditionalist like Stephen Gardiner asserted bluntly that we are all justified "in the sacrament of baptisme before we could talke of the justification we strive for".[2] At this point the sacramentalist and evangelical conceptions confronted each other in all their starkness. The maintenance of a Reformed doctrine of justification depended upon a rethinking of the meaning and efficacy of baptism.

The question pressed even more acutely. The emergence of Anabaptism, which insisted that baptism is merely a sign of individual conversion and the new birth, made it imperative that the Reformers should either accept this more radical view or give good reasons for its rejection. The challenge was a seribus one, for in Wittenberg the Zwickau prophets were carrying all before them prior to the return of Luther,[3] and in Zürich Zwingli was at first a friend of Grebel and Manz, and sympathized with their teaching.[4] But although much of the opposition to the Anabaptists was on social grounds, and because of their uncomfortable ideas of church and state, in the long run the Reformers had to oppose them because they could not agree that their crucial doctrine of adult baptism was well founded either biblically or theologically. In a word, the Anabaptist attack did involve a profound and serious wrestling with the whole meaning and efficacy of baptism.

Now it is true that during the Reformation period Anabaptism never assumed any serious proportions in England. It was confined almost exclusively to the Eastern counties, and those convicted of the error were mostly of Dutch or German extraction. A first proclamation was issued against Anabaptists after the Münster tragedy of 1534,[5] and quite a number were arraigned in 1535, of whom some were pardoned, some executed.[6] A commission was appointed to root them out in 1538, and their books were proscribed in 1539, but there was no serious danger. During the reign of Edward, Ridley and Latimer were sent to Kent to deal with more Dutch Anabaptists. Some English adherents also appeared, notably Joan Boucher, who held the common Anabaptist view that Christ did not take flesh from the Virgin;

---

2. Letters (ed. Muller), p. 407.

3. D.C.R., pp. 94 f.

4. *Ibid.*, pp. 450 f.

5. Smith, *The Anabaptists*, p. 192.

6. Foxe, V, p. 44.

the courtier Robert Cooke, who "denied both baptism and original sin";[7] and a certain Michael Thombe, who claimed that "the baptism of infants is not profitable because it goeth without faith".[8] It was suspected that the Papists employed emissaries to spread the heresy.[9] Great pains were taken to refute it, both in the 42 Articles and in various individual writings, mostly translations from the Continental reformers.[10] The proclamation against the Anabaptists was revived under Elizabeth. A few were expelled in 1562, but their numbers must have been small, for in 1567 Jewel could claim that there were none at all in England. There was a fresh outbreak, especially of Familism, during the period after 1574. It must be remembered, however, that in the later sixteenth century the term Anabaptism was a useful term of abuse applied indiscriminately but quite wrongly to the Separatists[11] and even the Puritans.[12] It has still to be shown that the number of native Anabaptists was ever very large.

But while the fewness of English Anabaptists may be admitted, this does not mean that the Anglican Reformers could ignore the Anabaptist menace. The zealous protagonists of the new doctrine had constantly to be watched and their propaganda encountered. Persecuted in all countries and by all parties,[13] they were always on the look-out to effect an entry. Although the arm of the State could be called in to check their activities, a theological bulwark was also needed against their teachings. The Anglicans had in fact no option but to examine and refute the Anabaptist doctrine of baptism, and this necessarily involved a consideration of baptismal doctrine as a whole.

For these three reasons, then, the Reformers were forced to reckon radically and seriously with the subject of baptism. And even on the surface there is a sufficient unanimity of opinion to make possible a general survey and presentation of their teaching. That there should be a certain amount of minor disagreement was inevitable, for the questions involved were both complex and difficult. But in spite of the variations

---

7. Strype, *Cranmer*, II, p. 96.

8. E.M., II, 1, p. 111.

9. Strype, *Cranmer*, II, p. 192.

10. E.g. Bullinger's *Holsome Antidotus* and Calvin's *Shorte Instruction*.

11. E.E.D., I, pp. 41 f.

12. Cf. Whitgift, P.S., III, p. 576.

13. Smith, *op. cit.*, pp. 168 f.

in detail, it is still the case that, when the baptismal doctrine of the Anglican Reformers is considered, it does form a most definite and by no means negligible whole. It forms a whole which may be related without difficulty to the larger whole of Reformation teaching in general. It forms a whole which stands over against the traditionalist whole in sharp and uncompromising hostility.

I

The Sacrament

(1) General Concept

The Reformers inherited the sacrament of baptism from the medieval church, but in this as in other matters they were anxious to test the accepted usage by the supreme rule of Holy Scripture. For that reason they were led to some extent to consider the foundations of the rite even from the linguistic stand-point. Of course, too much must not be expected of them in this direction. The Reformers had learned the need for a great carefulness in exegesis, but they had no gratuitous linguistic or historical interest. They were not scholars even in the sense that Erasmus was a scholar. Certainly they did not share the enthusiasm for the historical method, or the faith in it, which have characterized the more modern period. Their interest was for the most part engaged only where grammatical inquiry might determine a disputed doctrinal point.

In these circumstances the paucity of purely linguistic discussion can hardly surprise even if it may disappoint us. There had been definitions even in the older theology. Thomas, for instance, had granted that the word baptism could be used for any kind of washing, but he had alleged three reasons for giving to the general term a specific Christian connotation: first, because baptism as it is practised in the church is more than a washing; second, because the sacrament of baptism is a particular use of water; and third, because the baptismal "word" is added to the element.[1] The Tridentines were merely following Thomas when they explained that the Greek word may be used for any kind of ablution, but "that with the ecclesiastical writers it denotes that ecclesiastical use which belongs to the sacraments".[2]

Of the Reformers abroad it was Luther who was primarily interested in the linguistic aspect. In an early sketch he contrasted Christian baptism with the ceremonial washings of the Jews and the Johannine rite, linking the three in a quasi-evolutionary theological scheme.[3] Again, in his *Sermon on Baptism* he discussed the derivation of the two terms *mersio*

---

1. S., III, qu. 66.
2. C.T., II, 2, qu. 3.
3. W.A., VI, p. 472.

and *touff,* connecting the latter with *tief* and pointing out that in both cases the root-idea is submersion under the water.[4] Once again, the linguistic study was occasioned by more strictly dogmatic considerations, and subordinated to them.

It was the same dogmatic concern which prompted the parallel inquiry of Zwingli into the use of the term "baptism" in the New Testament. Not very convincingly, he attempted to distinguish four different senses: the baptism of water, the baptism of the Spirit, the baptism of teaching, and the baptism of faith and profession.[5] With a different intention, some of the Anabaptists tried to press the fact that the term "baptism" has a wider and more general connotation: their deduction being that Christian baptism does not differ in kind or efficacy from similar washings amongst the Jews and Turks. Rogers noted that the Bannisterians held a view of this type.[6] But this early if tendentious effort at a comparative study was decisively rejected by the Reformers.

The Anglicans had singularly little interest in the question of origin or derivation. The matter was not discussed at all until the publication of the Rhemish New Testament. Even then it arose only in a wider context, for Fulke used the example of baptism to show that the originals often justify the non-ecclesiastical rendering of ecclesiastical terms: "This word *baptisma* signifies by ecclesiastical use the sacrament of holy baptism, yet you are enforced Mark 7 to translate *baptismata* 'washings'."[7] The reference was purely polemical in purpose. By and large we may say that the. Reformers were satisfied with the traditional interpretation. The word "baptism" signified "washing", but in the Christian church it was applied specifically to the sacramental washing, holy baptism. No very significant doctrinal point appeared to be at issue in this connection, and having no historical interest except in the service of doctrine, they did not see any great necessity to press the matter more closely.

In the form in which it interested the theologian, baptism was the rite which has been handed down from the earliest days of Christianity as the first and initiatory sacrament. But the ranking of baptism as a sacrament raised a preliminary question in which the Anglican teaching especially still demands clarification. In the Middle Ages the number of acknowledged sacraments had been fixed as seven. Of course, it had always been seen that in the early church the term "sacrament" was used

---

4. W.A., VI, p. 727.
5. C.R., IV, p. 219.
6. Rogers, P.S., p. 278.
7. Fulke, P.S., I, p. 110.

in an extended sense,[8] but after some disputing the Schoolmen had laid it down that there are seven particular signs appointed by God as special means of grace. For all seven the divine institution was expressly claimed[9] and the authority of Scripture and the Councils as well as tradition was alleged in favour of this particular number.[10] It was not pretended, of course, that all seven were of equal rank. Baptism, communion and penance were singled out as "generally necessary to salvation", and even of these communion was exalted as the most excellent[11] to all the seven the term sacrament was applied even in its more rigorous sense.

Earlier critics of the medieval system do not seem to have taken up this point, for Wycliffe could still refer to seven sacraments in his *Trialogus*.[12] But in the first days of the Reformation Luther boldly singled out the three pre-eminent sacraments and contended that they alone were sacraments of the Gospel instituted by the Lord Himself. The others could be termed sacraments in a loose sense, but not strictly or properly. Even of the three, baptism and communion were of higher dignity than penance.[13] The Reformed school took up the same point, but more radically still, for Zwingli would admit only two evangelical or dominical sacraments[14] and the Anabaptists were of the same mind, except for those like Franck who rejected all sacraments as mummery and childish play.[15] Calvin made a clear distinction between sacraments in general and those sacraments which are the divinely appointed means of grace.[16] Of the latter there are only the two, although as it was practised by the apostles confirmation might also be regarded as a temporary sacrament.[17] The various Reformed confessions all made it clear that in the stricter sense there are "twa chiefe sacramentis onelie instituted by the Lord Jesus", as the Scotch confession puts it.

In England Henry VIII had of course defended the seven sacraments in his rash assault upon Luther, who as he saw it had destroyed all the sacraments except baptism.[18] The question did not arise seriously until

---

8. Cf. Calvin, *Instit.*, IV, 14, 18.
9. C.D., VII, Bapt. Can. 1.
10. C.T., II, 2, qu. 14.
11. C.D., VII, Sac. Can. 2-3.
12. *Trialogus*, p. 156.
13. R. Seeberg, *Die Lehre Luthers*, p. 315.
14. C.R., III, p. 761.
15. D.A., p. 188.
16. *Instit.*, IV, 14, 19-21.
17. *Comm. Acts*, II, p. 209.
18. *Assertio*, pp. 46, 183.

1536, when a great debate was held upon the subject in Convocation.[19] Stokesley headed a considerable traditionalist party in support of the view that "the rites of confirmation, and of orders, and of annealing, and such other, ought to be called sacraments, and to be compared with baptism and the supper of the Lord", but Cranmer himself favoured only the two sacraments, and he introduced the Scot Alesius as a chief speaker in the discussion. According to Alesius, a true sacrament must be of divine institution, and must have both a visible form and an invisible grace, which the Master of Sentences had equated with the remission of sins. Only the two main sacraments answered to these tests. Cranmer followed up the debate with a questionnaire on the Scriptural evidence, and in his own reply he stated: "I find not in the Scripture, the matter, nature and effect of all those which we call the seven sacraments, but only of certain of them, as baptism."[20]

In the reign of Edward VI the Reformed view quickly established itself. Three sacraments could still be asserted in the Lutheran *Cranmer's Catechism*,[21] but Hooper saw only two sacraments "with their proper promises, and proper commandments",[22] and Nowell claimed that "Christ instituted only two sacraments in his church".[23] This teaching evidently filtered down to the rank and file, for under Mary the "error" was sufficiently important to be noticed in the official interrogatory, and although there were a few like Elizabeth Thackvel and Kathleen Hut who "could not tell what a sacrament is",[24] Iveson and many others answered that "there be in the catholic church of Christ two sacraments only".[25]

The Elizabethans adopted the same position, as we may see from Jewel's statement in the *Apology*: "We acknowledge that there are two sacraments properly so called: for so many we see were delivered by Christ, and approved by St. Ambrose, St. Augustine, and the ancient fathers."[26] The two decisive tests of the true sacraments were the element and the institution, as Jewel pointed out in his larger *Treatise of the Sacraments*.[27]

It is in the light of statements such as these that the Article (25) has to

19. Cf. J., II, pp. 16-17; Foxe, V, p. 381.
20. G. Burnet, *A History of the Reformation in the Church of England*, III, p. 69.
21. *Cranmer's Catechism*, p. 184.
22. Hooper, B.R., p. 215.
23. Nowell, P.S., p. 85.
24. Foxe, VIII, p. 450.
25. Foxe, VII, p. 307.
26. Jewel, P.S., II, p. 12.
27. *Ibid.*, p. 1103.

be understood, and the statement is clear and definite. There are only two sacraments of the Gospel generally necessary to salvation. The five other rites are perhaps sacramental in a loose sense, but they are not sacraments according to the strict and proper meaning of the term. Some are states of life which have a sacramental aspect. Others are based on apostolic customs which may still be turned to a profitable use, although not in any way obligatory. The words "commonly called sacraments" indicate, perhaps, a willingness to ascribe a wider sacramental significance to these rites or states, but they can hardly be construed to mean that the five are after all true sacraments by popular consent. The point is made much more fully and with complete clarity in the *Homily on Common Prayer and the Sacraments* approved in Article 35.

Baptism, then, was one of the two evangelical sacraments for which element, institution and promise could all be claimed. It was in this theological context that the Reformers sought to understand its real basis and meaning. As they saw it, they were not dealing with a human and historical rite, venerable only by reason of its associations and antiquity, but with a divinely appointed means of grace. Baptism was a visible sign with an invisible signification and grace.

It was by reason of this divine aspect that in common with earlier writers the Reformers emphasized the twofold and even threefold use of the term in apostolic and patristic writings. The distinction had already been clearly made by Thomas, for in spite of the possible objection from Ephesians 4:5 Thomas had contended strongly for a threefold baptism, pointing out that the baptism of blood and the baptism of the Spirit had always been accepted as full equivalents for water-baptism.[28] could not be regarded as a fourth equivalent, since the fire of Matthew 3:2 was merely symbolical of the Holy Spirit.[29]

Wycliffe in the fourteenth century had tried to press the distinction in an evangelical direction, claiming that "ther ben three baptisingis: the firste ... in water, the tother ... with blood, but the thridde baptising, moost needeful and moost worth, is purging of the Hooli Goost".[30] Some of his followers carried the emphasis almost to a denial of the external act. Swinderby argued that the water of John 3:5 does not signify real water any more than does the fire of Matthew 3:2 real fire,[31] and

---

28. S., III, qu. 66, 11.
29. C.T., II, 2, qu. 8.
30. Arnold, *Select English Works*, II, p. 4.
31. Foxe, III, p. 168.

John Pyke maintained that there is no baptism but of the Holy Spirit.[32] The same view was to appear again amongst the Anabaptists.

The Reformers were not sidetracked into this depreciation of the external washing, but they accepted the general distinction between the baptism of water and the baptism of the Spirit. Zwingli broke new ground when he claimed that there is a baptism of teaching and faith as well as of water and the Spirit. But the other Reformers did not develop this analysis. For the most part they were content to see only the twofold baptism, of water and the Spirit.[33]

In England a considerable stress was laid upon the threefoldness of baptism. Tyndale set the fashion by making the Johan- nine link of water, blood and Spirit.[34] He was followed by Becon, who emphasized the fact that without the inward baptism of the Spirit, which is the true baptism, "the outward baptism of the water profiteth nothing",[35] a good Zwinglian assertion. Elsewhere Becon mentioned the three baptisms of the Spirit, blood and water, of which three "the baptism of water is the most inferior".[36] Ultimately, however, the three were only the different moments of the one baptism, "of divers diversely taken".[37] Sandys made a similar distinction between the outward washing and the inward cleansing,[38] and Jewel contended for a threefold baptism, the outward water being a witness to the cleansing death and resurrection of Christ and also to the purgation of the life-giving Spirit.[39]

The Reformers did not attempt to separate between a so-called water-baptism for repentance and a Spirit-baptism for regeneration and inward filling. Certain texts of the New Testament can be and have been read in this way. An almost inevitable result is either to deny water-baptism altogether or to depreciate its importance by linking up the Spirit-baptism with confirmation, of which it becomes the otherwise obscure inward grace. The earlier practice of taking baptism and confirmation together has sometimes been advanced in favour of this view.[40] But what the Reformers were contending for was not the twofoldness of baptism and confirmation, but the twofoldness of

32. E.M., I., 1, p. 190.
33. Cf. *Instit.*, IV, 15, 8; Bullinger, P.S., IV, p. 251.
34. Tyndale, P.S. II, p. 209.
35. Becon, P.S., II, p. 218.
36. *Ibid.*, p. 225.
37. *Loc. cit.*
38. Sandys, P.S., p. 302.
39. Jewel, P.S., II, p. 1107; III, p. 470.
40. Cf. E.C. Ratcliffe in *Theology*, LIX, No. 315.

baptism itself. Baptism was a human act, a washing in water: but it was also a divine act, the inward washing and regeneration of the Spirit. The two acts might not coincide in time, but both were necessary to constitute baptism in the full sense. It was this conception which underlay the clear-cut division of Tyndale between "those who are baptized in the flesh and those who are baptized in heart".[41] The same view may be found in such varied writers as Hooper,[42] Cranmer,[43] and the Elizabethan Lake,[44] all of whom demanded both an internal and external baptism, but insisted upon the primacy of the baptism of the Spirit. If the baptism of blood played only a minor part in these discussions, the reason was that the question usually arose in relation to the alleged necessity of the sacrament. The concern of the Reformers was to show that it is not the external rite which alone or primarily constituted the sacrament.

The fact that baptism was an act of God as well as an act of man implied necessarily its divine origin. Historically, the rite could no doubt be traced back to Jewish and even pagan sources, but the human antecedents were not of great interest to the sixteenth-century theologians. What mattered to them was the divine authorization and authority, from which the sacrament derived its true signification and force.

At this point, as at so many others, the traditionalists and the Protestants were in substantial agreement. The main controversy arose in relation to the time of institution, which had always been a thorny point. Thomas had contributed an early and thorough discussion of the problem. In support of the favourite conception of an institution in Matthew 28 he saw three main arguments: first, that baptism derives its power only from the passion; second, that the mandate of Christ is necessary to its efficacy; and third, that it has been binding only since the passion. But Thomas himself inclined to the view that its institution dates from the baptism of Christ Himself, according to the teaching of Augustine. He conceded that it did not become obligatory until after the passion.[45]

The detailed argumentation of Thomas was not repeated by all theologians, but the traditionalists of the sixteenth century insisted

---

41. Tyndale, P.S.I., p. 357.
42. Hooper, P.S., I, p. 74.
43. J., IV, p. 29.
44. Sermons, p. 174.
45. S. III, qu. 66, 2.

upon the divine institution, as we may see both from the Canons[46] and also from the Catechism of Trent.[47] To the question of origin the answer of Thomas was given: "The sacrament was instituted by the Lord, when he himself, having been baptized of John, gave to the water the virtue of sanctifying. ... After the resurrection of our Lord, he gave to the apostles the command: Go and teach all nations, baptizing them."[48]

The Reformers had no great interest in the time of institution, except in so far as they claimed an identity with the baptism of John, but they all laid emphasis upon the fact of the divine institution. Luther spoke of God or Christ as the true author of baptism.[49] Zwingli referred to the sacraments as bequeathed to us by Christ.[50] Calvin inveighed strongly against those who usurped the divine prerogative by adding new sacraments: "Foolish men forge various sacraments at their pleasure, but as the word, which is the soul, is not in them, they are idle and unmeaning shadows."[51] It was largely because Christ alone can institute a sacrament that Calvin claimed Him as the author even of John's baptism. In different ways the confessions all referred to the divine institution. The *Confession of Faith in the name of the Church of France* spoke of baptism as a treasure which God has placed in the church.[52] Knox made the divine institution the test of a true sacrament, and derived the continued observance of baptism from the divine mandate.[53]

The English writers did not add anything new, but they made the usual points with impressive unanimity. Wycliffe already had pointed out that "God hath ordeigned, in tyme of his both lawes, how man shuld have sacramentis to make him able for this traveil".[54] He had found in Matthew 28 the authority for a continued use of baptism.[55] In the earlier Reformation formularies, the *Ten* and *Thirteen Articles*,[56] and the *King's Book*,[57] reference was made to the divine institution, and Cranmer mentioned it again in his *Answer to the Men of Devon*.[58] Frith, Hooper and Becon all stressed the point, Becon claiming that "God the Father did first institute this holy

46. Schaff, *Creeds*, p. 207.
47. C.T., II, 2, qu. 20.
48. *Ibid.*, qu. 21.
49. W.A., VI, p. 530.
50. C.R., III, p. 761.
51. *Harm. Evang.*, p. 385.
52. Calvin *Tracis*, II, p. 153.
53. Knox, I, p. 198, Cf. the *Ordoure of Baptisme.*
54. Arnold, II, p. 258.
55. *Trialogus*, p. 156.
56. Cranmer, P.S., II, p. 474.
57. K.B., p. 41.
58. Cranmer, P.S., II, p. 176.

sacrament with John".[59] At a later date the Reformed view was propagated in Bullinger's *Decades*,[60] and Hooker described baptism as "a sacrament which God hath instituted in His church".[61]

The argument from the divine institution was used by Bonner in Mary's reign as an argument against certain confessors who refused to accept "Papist" baptism. Thomas Haukes, for example, was told that baptism is commanded by the Word of God. Haukes did not deny this, but with Knox he could not agree that Papist baptism is the "trew baptisme whilke Cryst Jesus did institute".[62] The Separatists followed the same line of reasoning when they refused to be baptized in the established church, for it was one of their aims to have the sacrament administered "purely, onely, and all together according to the institution and good words of the Lord Jesus."[63] The one doctrine of the divine institution underlay both the demand for conformity and the refusal to conform.

The various official formularies all found a place for the doctrine. It was mentioned in Article 25, and in the Baptismal Office the words of institution were recited from Matthew 28. It is interesting that in the opening prayer there is perhaps an echo of Augustine's view in the words: "Who by the baptism of Thy well-beloved Son in the river Jordan didst sanctify water to the mystical washing away of sin", a phrase which was hotly contested by the Puritans. There was a further reference to the divine institution in the sacramental section later added to the Catechism.

Naturally, in the sixteenth century there was no question of applying historico-critical tests to the evangelical narratives. The verse in Matthew 28 was the main proof of a divine authorization, although it was supported by apostolic practice. Yet it must be remembered that the belief was of a piece with the general theology of the Reformers. According to their view, Christianity is not a human religion, but a divine revelation. It is not the culmination of a spiritual search, but the transscendent gift of God in the unique word and work and person of the divine Son. If this is the case, it is irrelevant to seek to understand the Christian mysteries in terms of their possible natural or historical development. The important thing concerning them is the fact that they have been divinely given.

---

59. Becon, P.S., II, p. 2C3.
60. Bullinger, P.S., IV, p. 352.
61. L.E.P., V, 60, 3.
62. Knox, I, p. 19.
63. E.E.D., II, p. 13.

It was because baptism was thought of as divinely given that it could be described in terms of what it was believed either to signify or to effect. At a later stage we shall have to study more closely both the signification and the effect, but already we may notice some of the terms by which it was defined and described. The terms do, of course, indicate the various effects or meaning ascribed to it, for, as the Reformers constantly insisted, the early writers commonly called the signs by the names of that which was signified.

On the traditionalist side the *Catechism* of Trent assembled many of the definitions used by earlier writers. It described baptism as the sacrament of faith, an illumination, a purgation, a planting, and a burial.[64] In the later Greek and Russian symbols it was referred to as a washing, and as the extirpation of original sin.[65] Elsewhere it had been called our regeneration, and the gateway or door of the Christian life.[66]

As will appear later, the Reformers had a particular interest in the signification of the sacrament, and they summed up the various meanings in the descriptive titles which they applied to it. Luther defined baptism as a conjunction of word and water, the water being the water of life which is rich in grace, the bath of regeneration.[67] In the *Confession of Seventeen Articles* it was described as a holy and mighty thing, a bath of regeneration and spiritual renewal.[68] Again, baptism was a divine covenant of grace given under a visible form.[69] Melanchthon had much the same thought in mind when he styled it the sign of a divine promise.

The covenantal aspect was particularly prominent in Zwingli, for whom baptism was essentially a pledge or initiatory sign.[70] Baptism was the covenant sign of the people of God, and it served as their badge of allegiance.[71] The Anabaptists developed this idea, interpreting the external rite as a public confession and witness.[72] On this view, the human aspect tended to become much more pronounced, and baptism was no longer defined in terms of its inward grace.

---

64. C.T., II, 2, qu. 4.
65. Schaff, *Creeds*, pp. 373 f.
66. Cf. *Catholic Encyclopedia*, Art. Baptism.
67. W.A., XXXIV, 1, p. 88;Wernle, *Luther*, p. 257.
68. Wernle, *op. cit.*, p. 286.
69. Seeberg, *op. cit.*, p. 317.
70. Wernle, *Zwingli*, p. 202.
71. *Ibid.*, p. 204.
72. C.R., IV, p. 218 (Hübmaier).

With Calvin the emphasis shifted, for while he rejected sacramentalist conceptions he certainly maintained a high doctrine of the sacraments. One of the titles which he frequently applied to both sacraments was that of a "visible word", a testimony to the grace of God.[73] But he could also call the sacrament an instrument by which God Himself acts.[74] Baptism was still an initiatory sign, but it pointed not merely to our entrance into the church, but to our insertion into Christ.[75] Like the Lord's supper, it was a mark or badge of the Christian profession and fraternity,[76] but it was also a badge and attestation of the divine grace and seal of the divine promise.[77] Stressing as he did the divine as well as the human aspect, Calvin could easily refer to the sacrament in terms of its signification, as a spiritual washing and sign of regeneration. The Confessions and the later Reformed theologians concentrated upon the two aspects, covenant and regeneration: thus Knox described baptism as "a holie syne and seale of God's promesses",[78] and Heidegger entitled it the sacrament of regeneration.

It would be tedious to list in detail the various Anglican definitions, which for the most part followed the same lines. Tyndale, for example, described baptism as a witness, as the bond and seal of the covenant,[79] and as "the sign of repentance (or, if they will so have it called, penance), washing and new birth".[80] For Frith it was a token of grace and free mercy, the fountain of the new birth.[81] The covenantal aspect found a place even in the *King's Book*, and for the majority of writers baptism served as "a testimony to God's promise", "a certain pledge of his love", "a seal and covenant", "a confirmation and heavenly token", "an evidence and sealed charter", "a substantial covenant and agreement". But it could also be described as "a certain entry by which we are received", "a cleansing away of sin", "the fount of regeneration", "life", "salvation", "the forgiveness of sins", "the power of God to resurrection". Amongst less common definitions we may mention that of the *King's Book*, which equated baptism and justification,[82] Cranmer's reference to baptism as a receiving of the Holy Ghost and putting Christ upon us,[83] Becon's

---

73. J. Beckmann, *Vom Sakrament bei Calvin*, p. 45.
74. *Tracts*, II, p. 340.
75. *Instit.* IV, 15, 1.
76. *Tracts*, II, p. 214.
77. *Harm. Evang.* p. 384; *Tracts*, II, p. 153.
78. Knox, IV, p. 172.
79. Tyndale, B.R., p. 407.
80. *Ibid.*, P.S., II, p. 161.
81. Frith, B.R., pp. 92-4.
82. Cf. Cranmer, P.S., II, p. 133.
83. *Ibid.*, I, p. 64.

description of it as the seal of righteousness,[84] and Whitgift's as the seal of faith,[85] the two latter being combined in Bullinger's "seal of the righteousness of faith".[86] Jewel quoted Tertullian to the effect that baptism may rightly be regarded as a sacrifice, but his main concern was to refute false ideas of the sacrifice of the mass.[87]

The definition given in the Article is rather disappointing, as such statements usually are. In an attempt to be comprehensive it seems to fail in precision. But a comparison with the individual descriptions will show that it is not quite so vague as sometimes suggested. Baptism is a sign of profession and mark of difference – this includes rather than refutes the Sacramentarian view. It is also a sign of the new birth – the normal Reformed interpretation. It is an instrument to graft into the church – the idea of initiation or entry. And it is the seal of the divine promise of forgiveness and adoption – as in all the Protestant teaching. The term "instrument" has attracted some attention, but it is not without parallel in Reformation writings abroad.

With regard to the definitions as a whole, three points may be made. First, they all remain within the general tradition of the church. More modern definitions like Quick's "sacrament of the divine Fatherhood" would have sounded strangely in the Reformers' ears. The new feature was perhaps the greater insistence upon profession and covenant. Second, the sacrament was interpreted in terms of the word. Just as the word might be described as the word of life, so baptism might be described as the water of regeneration; not as the source or cause, but as the sign and means. Finally, in its full sense the sacrament included the thing signified as well as the sign. That is why the Reformers could give even to the external sign the title of the internal grace, not as itself the reality, but as the sign of the reality. The language of sacramentalism could be used, but in a purified and evangelical sense.

The fact that baptism was classified as the first of the two dominical sacraments inevitably suggested a certain comparison with its sister-sacrament, the Lord's supper.

The point is not quite so academic as it may appear, for in the sixteenth century the "sacrament of the altar" was accorded a position of absolute pre-eminence in the sacramental hierarchy, as containing

---

84. Becon, P.S., II, p. 217.
85. Whitgift, P.S., III, p. 113.
86. Bullinger, P.S., IV, p. 323.
87. Jewel, P.S., II, p. 893.

not grace only, but the very author of grace.[88] It was on this ground that Gardiner objected to Cranmer's coupling of baptism and the supper in their eucharistic debate.[89]

But from the very first the Reformers swept away all distinctions of rank between the evangelical sacraments. This was true even of Luther, who in spite of his doctrine of consub- stantiation could find in the two sacraments the one grace of incorporation and a common necessity of faith.[90] On the Reformed side both Bucer and Calvin used the doctrine of baptism as an aid to their eucharistic teaching, Bucer with the aim of conciliation,[91] Calvin with the desire to arrive at a true doctrine of the presence.[92]

In England the comparison was taken up by not a few writers, as, for example, Nowell,[93] but it was Cranmer who made greatest use of it, and here again for the purpose of reaching a true doctrine of the presence. According to Cranmer, no greater reverence ought to be paid to the bread and wine than to the water, for the presence and "shewing" of Christ are the same in both sacraments.[94] The same comparison was used by Ridley and Glyn,[95] and in his controversy with Watson, Cheke attempted to prove it from the Fathers.[96]

There were several interesting discussions of the relationship during the Marian period. Bradford was challenged on the matter by two friars, but he silenced them by quoting 1 Corinthians 12.[97] Philpot pressed the comparison as an argument against private masses: "If a priest say these words over the water, and there be no child to be baptized, those words only pronounced do not make baptism. The pronunciation only is not enough, unless the words be therewithal applied to the use, as Christ spoke them. So is the supper."

> *Harpsfield*: "Nay, that is not like; for '*Hoc est corpus meum*' is an indicative proposition, showing a working of God in the substance of bread and wine."
> *Philpot*: "It is not an indicative proposition, but also imperative or commanding: Take ye, eat ye."
> *Morrow-Mass Priest*: "Many must then be baptized, if the commandment be followed."

---

88. T.B., p. 353.
89. J., III, p. 242.
90. Hamel, *Der junge Luther*, pp. 57, 151.
91. Hastings, Eells *Martin Bucer*, p. 72.
92. *Tracts*, II, pp. 564-5.
93. Nowell, P.S., I, p. 214.
94. J., III, pp. 10, 61 f., 242.
95. Foxe, VI, pp. 452 f.
96. Strype, *Cheke*, pp. 101 f.
97. Bradford, P.S., I, p. 82. Cf. p. 533.

But Philpot could reply with the scriptural example of the eunuch.[98] The same comparison was used by less eminent sufferers like Woodman,[99] and Foxe himself quoted a sermon of Aelric in which the two sacraments were treated as parallel.[100]

The Elizabethans followed the same lines, and they arrived at some curious conclusions. Certain Puritans, for example, claimed that no more than the surplice should be worn at communion, since the communion does not give higher or better things.[101] Others argued that deacons ought to administer either both sacraments or none and Cartwright detected a false distinction between the sacraments in the disciplinary ruling upon this point.[102] In essentials, however, Anglicans and Puritans were well agreed.

It may be noted that the Reformed use of the comparison was almost exclusively controversial, but behind the polemical application there was a point of real theological importance. The sacraments are different in detail and use, but they are one in essential nature. Both are instituted by Christ to proclaim His redemptive work and to be a means of grace in the church. To create a false distinction between the sacraments is not merely to disturb sacramental theology, but to confuse the whole witness and operation of the Spirit.

Baptism was not in any way subordinate to the Lord's supper, but it was certainly subordinate to the Gospel itself: that is, not to the word of the Gospel, Holy Scripture and scriptural preaching, but to the promises of God as they are given in and with Jesus Christ. This point was made by Calvin when he maintained that the gift of baptism, adoption, is prior to baptism itself.[103] Another way of putting it was to say, as Frith did, that the election precedes the sacraments.[104] The fulfilment of a sacramental scheme does not evoke but rather attests the election. It was perhaps for this reason that Tyndale saw a need for preaching as well as baptism,[105] for behind both word and sacrament he discerned both the same promise and the same Christ.

Cranmer approached the matter differently, and at a deeper level. For him the Gospel was not merely the covenant or the election, but Jesus Christ Himself. It was the office of both word and sacrament to exhibit

---

98. Foxe, VII, p. 637.

99. *Ibid.*, VIII, pp. 351 f.

100. *Ibid.*, V, p. 286.

101. P.B.O., p. 39.

102. Whitgift, P.S., III, p. 59. Cf. *A Pleasaunte Dialogue*, p. 28.

103. *Instit.*, IV, 14, 22; *Tracts*, I, p. 73.

104. Frith, B.R., p. 92.

105. Tyndale, P.S., I, p. 253.

Christ, which they did, not by a corporal but by a spiritual presence: "For Christ after one sense is exhibited in all these three, in His word, in baptism, and in the Lord's supper, that is to say, spiritually".[106] Other Anglicans laid stress upon the primacy of "the promise of eternal joy", "the free grace and mere mercy of God", and the divine covenant,[107] for, as Rogers made clear, the means of grace are subordinate both to the grace itself and to the Lord of grace.[108]

A point of no little importance was involved in the discussion, as we may see in the little passage-at-arms between John Smith and Bishop Bonner:

> *Smith*: "I pray you, my lord, show me, are we saved by water or by Christ?"
> *Bonner*: "By both."
> *Smith*: "Then the water died for our sins. ... The water is unto me a preacher, not a Saviour."[109]

The position of Smith was in effect the same as that of Calvin, who accused his opponents of "passing by Christ, and fixing their confidence of sanctification on the elements".[110] But the doctrine could be used against the Anabaptists too, for if children are heirs of the Gospel promises, as Philpot and Bullinger argued, they ought not to be refused the sign of the promises, for the Gospel is more than baptism.[111] Calvin used much the same line of reasoning when he pointed out that the gift of adoption is prior to baptism.[112]

The point was comparatively trifling in itself, but great issues were involved. The subordination of the sacrament to the Gospel meant at bottom its subordination to Christ Himself. It meant a subordination of the sign to the thing signified. It meant a subordination of the individual decision of faith to the prior election and salvation of God. The sacrament was a means of grace, but it could not supplant the grace. And that grace was Christ.

(2) Signification

For many years prior to the sixteenth century the detailed meaning of the sacrament of baptism had hardly been considered except in relation

---

106. Cranmer, P.S., I, p. 156.
107. Hooper, P.S., I, pp. 128-30; Becon, P.S., II, p. 216; Jewel, P.S., II, p. 1105.
108. Rogers, P.S., p. 250.
109. Foxe, P.S., p. 352.
110. *Tracts*, II, p. 340.
111. Philpot, P.S., p. 276; Bullinger, P.S., IV, p. 389.
112. *Tracts*, I, p. 99.

to the effects. If the question was raised at all, it could be answered briefly by an enumeration of the spiritual benefits, as, for example, in the comprehensive statement of Cyril of Jerusalem: "Baptism is a ransom for the captives, the remission of sins, the death of sin, the regeneration of the soul, a bright garment, a holy and indissoluble seal, a carriage to heaven, the enjoyment of paradise, the pledge of the kingdom of heaven, the grace of adoption."[113] In both Lombard and Thomas the signification of baptism was closely interconnected with the effects. Baptism did not merely signify, but actually effected a conformity with Christ in His death and burial and rising again.[114] The *Catechism* of Trent contained a short passage in which it brought out the various truths clearly intimated in baptism, but again it saw in the sacrament a means to effect these realities in the individual life.[115] The word, matter and ceremonies all helped to portray not merely the inward meaning but also the actual effects of that which was done.[116]

With the coming of the Reformation there was a noticeable shift of emphasis away from the effects to the signification. The Reformers did not deny an effect, but just as they related the sacrament itself to the word, so they related the work of the sacrament to the meaning. Not without some cause, they complained bitterly of the gross ignorance of the signification of baptism which prevailed under the traditionalist regime. The common people understood that the rite was necessary, but for what purpose and with what meaning they had little or no conception: "They believe, How that the very plunging into the water saveth them, therefore of the promises they know not, nor what is signified thereby. Baptism is called 'volowing' in many places in England: because the priest saith, 'Volo, say ye'."[117] The use of the Latin was a chief reason for the ignorance, for otherwise the service might to a very large extent have been self-explanatory.

When the Reformers themselves considered the sacrament, they developed its signification in great detail and with no little power. For them, baptism was a significant sign: the very sign itself indicated the thing signified. And the meaning was of the utmost importance, for it was only as the meaning was understood that the sacrament could have its effect. Signification and effect were again related, but at a new and a

---

113. Cf. Cary, *Testimonies of the Fathers*, Art. XXVII.
114. Lombard, IV, *Dist.* 4 C; S., III, qu. 66.
115. C.T., II, 1, qu. 8.
116. *Ibid.*, qu. 11, 13; II, 2, qu. 10.
117. Tyndale, P.S., I, p. 276.

deeper level. It was not that the signification merged into the effect, but rather that it was necessary to the effect. The effect itself was produced in and through the meaning.

In the first instance, and at its very simplest, baptism was obviously a ceremony of initiation, a reception into the church which is the society or family of God. This aspect is perhaps clearer in the case of the adult baptisms of the New Testament and the mission field, but infants too are formally received into the congregation by way of baptism. That is why baptism is a sign of entry, and also of the divine covenant.

On the purely human level this initiation was an entrance into the external church, with all the privileges and responsibilities that that entailed. Nowell had this in mind when he spoke of baptism as a "certain entry",[118] and Latimer put it clearly when he said that baptism serves "to know a Christian from a Turk, or a heathen".[119] It was perhaps something of the same thought which underlay the prayer of thanks-giving in the Baptismal Office: "that it hath pleased thee to incorporate him into thy holy church", and also the expression in the Article: "grafted into the church": although obviously statements such as these had a wider and a deeper reach. The Anabaptists, with their separatist views of the church, tended to magnify this aspect.

On a higher level the initiation was into the church as the family of God, or the body of Christ. The sacramental entry taught clearly the divine adoption and sonship. Baptism was not merely the historical sign or badge of external church-membership. It was an entry into the people of God. That was why in the Baptismal Order at Zürich prayer could be. offered for incorporation into Christ.[120] That was why Calvin could speak of baptism as an "incorporation into Christ, an entry into the divine Sonship".[121] That was why Knox could refer to our being "receyved in baptism into his familie and congregation",[122] and define baptism itself as the "syne of our entrance into the house-hold of God our Father".[123] Bullinger used a sentence very like the English Article: "Baptism is a visible sign and seal of our ingrafting into the body of Christ."[124] In England itself Becon stated the matter

---

118. Nowell, P.S., p. 207.
119. Latimer, P.S., II, p. 133.
120. D.C.R., p. 423.
121. Beckmann, op. cit., p. 61; Niesel, Die Theologie Calvins, p. 209.
122. Knox, IV, p. 172.
123. Ibid., p. 123.
124. Bullinger, P.S., IV, p. 399.

almost in the words of the Catechism: "Baptism declareth evidently unto me that whereas before I was an heathen, now I am become a Christian, a son of God, a member of that holy congregation";[125] and again, "Baptism is a continual sign that we be by adoption the sons of God and heirs of everlasting glory".[126]

This thought of incorporation or adoption opened up a whole world of theological meaning; repentance and faith on the one side, forgiveness, regeneration and identification with Christ on the other. But behind all these things adoption meant the divine election of grace in Jesus Christ. In the first instance adoption was not by a human decision, but by the divine favour. Baptism, therefore, was a testimony to the grace of God and an assurance of the divine election and promises. The point is important, because it underlies the Reformed defence of infant baptism, and marks off the Reformed understanding from humanistic and Pelagian interpretations.

But the election of God meant the love of God, and baptism could be regarded as an objective assurance of that love. In the words of Becon: "Baptism declareth evidently unto me, that God doth so dearly love and favour me ...",[127] or of Coverdale, "In baptism we have an undoubted true token and evidence of the grace of God".[128] In this emphasis the English writers were wholly at one with the Continental, for Luther had found in baptism a constant assurance of the divine favour,[129] and Calvin looked upon it as "the outward attestation of the divine benevolence".[130] Many of the confessions and of the later theologians made the same point.[131] If baptism was an entrance into the divine family, that entrance was possible only as a work and gift of grace in Jesus Christ. Baptism, therefore, points us to the love of God as the ultimate ground of adoption, and since that love endures, it has the character of a testimony, not to our own faith, which may vary, but to the divine grace which cannot change. The understanding of baptism as a testimony or assurance has rightly been described as one of the great contributions of the Reformers to an understanding of the sacrament.[132] It has a particular importance in that it links up baptism directly with fundamental doctrines.

---

125. Becon, P.S., II, pp. 203-4.
126. *Ibid.*, III, p. 173.
127. *Ibid.*, II, pp. 203-4.
128. Coverdale, P.S., II, p. 86.
129. W.A., IV, p. 529.
130. *Catechism of the Church of Geneva*, p. 83.
131. Cf. D.C.R., p. 671; R.D. Bapt.
132. Hastings' E.R.E. Art. Baptism.

But if baptism assures us of the divine favour in Jesus Christ, it carries with it the further thought of the forgiveness of sins. And if the whole action of baptism suggests initiation, the matter of baptism surely signifies cleansing. It is only as the sinner is cleansed that he can also be received: and both adoption and remission are by the one grace in Jesus Christ. Baptism, therefore, testifies to the inward purgation of the soul by the atoning work of Jesus Christ.

From a very early period, and on the New Testament basis, baptism had always been understood as a cleansing, although in Scholastic and Tridentine theology the stress was upon the effect of cleansing rather than the signification.[133] Wycliffe had brought out the point more fully and clearly: "Bodily baptizing is a figure, how mennis soulis shuld be baptisid fro synne both originall and actual. ... Baptisme is a tokene of waishing of the soule fro synne ... bi vertu taken of Cristi's deth."[134] It was not greatly stressed by Luther and Melanchthon, who preferred to think of remission in terms of death and resurrection, but the Reformed school constantly referred to baptism as a washing or cleansing. Calvin, for example, in his exegesis of John 3:5 claimed that water means "nothing more than the purification and invigoration which is produced by the Holy Spirit",[135] and in the *Genevan Catechism* he described water as "a figure of the blood that cleanses".[136] The identification of cleansing with the blood of Christ forms the point of contact between the interpretation in terms of washing or remission and the interpretation in terms of death and resurrection. As Beza put it: The signification of baptism is the aspersion or sprinkling of the death and passion, in remission of all our sins."[137] And Calvin equated the spiritual washing with the new righteousness which we have in Christ.[138] In the confessions the external washing in water was usually related to the inward washing by the blood and Spirit of Christ: the common interrelationship of water and Spirit and blood.[139] Both in their individual statements and also in their confessions the Anabaptists favoured the same teaching.[140]

---

133. Cf. S., III, qu. 66.
134. Arnold, II, p. 328.
135. *Comm. on John*, 3, 5.
136. *Catechism of the Church of Geneva*, pp. 86-7.
137. B.P.S., p. 47.
138. *Harmony Evang.*, p. 385.
139. Cf. *Heidelberg Catechism*, LXIX; *Belgic Confession*, XXXIV.
140. Cf. B.R.N., IV, p. 44, E.E.D., II, p. 196.

Almost all the English writers interpreted baptism as in some sense signifying the inward cleansing of the soul from sin. Even Tyndale mentions this aspect,[141] and Nowell gives to it a central importance: "As the uncleannesses of the body are washed away with water, so the spots of the soul are washed away (in baptism) by forgiveness of sins."[142] Hooper identified the water of the baptism with the cleansing blood of Christ,[143] and Becon related it both to the blood of Christ and also to the purifying Spirit.[144] But the inward purgation was clearly understood to be metaphorical, for Cheke and Grindal maintained against Watson that there is no washing in the strictly literal or grammatical sense, i.e., the soul is not a "substance" which can be literally cleansed from defilement or pollution.[145]

Obviously this whole idea of a baptismal washing linked up with the common conception of a twofold or threefold baptism, the external by water, the internal by the blood or Spirit. From the scriptural point of view, the verse in 1 John 5 underlay much of the work done on this aspect of baptismal interpretation, and there was an evident relationship to the ancient doctrine that martyrdom, or a special work of the Spirit, can supply the lack of water-baptism. Baptism was the external representation of that internal cleansing which is related on the one hand to the death of Christ and on the other to the operation of the Spirit applying that death to the individual.

Cranmer and Ridley both emphasized the fact that the outward washing pictures to us the inward, and Cranmer claimed that the water may be honoured not for what it is but for what it signifies and represents.[146] Jewel linked the cleansing work of the Spirit very closely to His activity in regeneration,[147] but with Sandys[148] he also saw a clear interconnection with the blood: "The signification and the substance of the sacrament is to show us how we are washed with the passion of Christ. ... The water doth signify the blood of Christ."[149]

Many of the Reformers commented on the peculiar aptness of the divinely chosen matter of the sacrament. This point was made by Knox: "That lyke as water outwardlye doth wash away filth, so by baptism we are cleansed in soul".[150] Bullinger popularized the idea in his *Decades*:

---

141. Tyndale, P.S., II.
142. Nowell, P.S., p. 208.
143. Hooper, P.S., II, p. 46.
144. Becon, P.S., II, p. 199, III, p. 616.
145. Strype, *Cheke*, pp. 101 f.

146. J., III, pp. 10, 49; Ridley, P.S., p. 275.
147. Jewel, P.S., I, p. 474.
148. Sandys, P.S., p. 275.
149. Jewel, P.S., II, pp. 1100, 1101.
150. Knox, IV, p. 188.

"The very sign resembleth the thing signified. Water cleanseth filth and quencheth thirst. So also it representeth the grace of God when it cleanseth His faithful ones from their sins, regenerateth and refresheth us with His Spirit."[151]

The Baptismal Office contained several suggestive phrases in development of the whole thought of cleansing. Prayer was made for the "washing and sanctifying of the Holy Ghost". Allusion was made to the water and blood which flowed from the side of Christ. And God was requested to sanctify the baptismal water to the mystical washing away of sin. In spite of Puritan objections, these phrases clearly reflect the Reformed conception of a twofold cleansing, and the common interrelating of water, blood and Spirit.

Baptism as a cleansing plainly linked up with adoption on the one side, but on the other it linked no less plainly with the death and resurrection which are the basis of remission. The inward cleansing was a cleansing in the blood of Christ, which pointed away at once to the atoning death of Christ. It was also a cleansing by the Holy Spirit, who is the Lord and Giver of life. Therefore behind the whole conception of cleansing there stood the deeper conception of a dying and rising again which were represented in the baptismal act. With Romans 6 as their starting-point, the Reformers found here their most profound and powerful interpretation.

It must be emphasized that in the first instance this dying and rising again was the dying and rising again of Christ Himself. The symbolism was this. The baptized person was not merely washed in water, but he went under the water and emerged again to a new life. And this act of submersion and re- emerging proclaimed and actualized the basic facts of the Christian Gospel, that Christ died for our sins according to the Scriptures, and that on the third day He was raised again according to the Scriptures.

This understanding was not in any sense new. It had been proclaimed by Paul himself in Romans 6, and passages could easily be multiplied from both the Fathers and the Schoolmen to show that baptism was commonly taken to be a picture of "that baptism wherewith Christ had had to be baptized, and of His joyful resurrection". Even the *Catechism* of Trent could see in baptism a reminder of the death and passion of Christ.[152]

---

151. Bullinger, P.S., IV, p. 329.
152. C.T., II, 1 qu. 8.

And on the side of reform Wycliffe had drawn attention to this aspect: "And so this water that we ben putte inne is token of Cristis tribulacioun fro his bygynnyng to his deth ... the baptising of us in this water betokeneth biriynge of Crist. ... Oure takyng up of this water betokeneth the rysinge of Crist fro deth."[153] It is not merely that the water represented the atoning blood of Christ, but that the whole action of baptism represented His death and resurrection. The images are parallel, but they demand a different application of the symbolism and can hardly be developed side by side.

The interpretation was a common one, but it had hardly been worked out with any fullness until the time of Luther. Indeed, Luther was more interested in the picture of our identification with the death and resurrection of Christ than with that of the death and resurrection of Christ Himself. However, he did hint fairly clearly at this aspect as well, for the believer can die and rise again with Christ, only as Christ Himself died and rose again. The criticism of Stange, that at most we can establish only an allegorical or typical connection between baptism and the death of Christ,[154] is surely wide of the mark. As Luther saw, baptism is meaningless apart from the death of Christ. And in any case Christ Himself regarded the passion as the true baptism of which the sacrament is the significant sign. Baptism was in fact a proclamation of the objective work of Christ, and not merely a sign of subjective experience. The ground gained by Luther was maintained by the other Reformers, for even the Anabaptists had some inkling of this aspect,[155] and Calvin asserted plainly that we are baptized into the death of Christ.[156] If there were few specific references in the confessions it was because most of them understood baptism in terms of cleansing and regeneration rather than death and resurrection.

The Anglican Reformers followed closely the teaching of the Continentals in this respect. In the main they saw a picture of the death of Christ by implication rather than directly. "We are baptized to believe in the death of Christ, and to die with him", as Tyndale put it;[157] or in the words of Becon, "Baptism doth declare unto me that I am buried with Christ".[158] There was a similar incidental reference in the

---

153. Arnold, II, p. 258.
154. D.C. Stange, *Der Todesgedanke in Luthers Tauflehre, Zeitschr. für system. Theol.*, 1928, IV, p. 800.
155. L. von Muralt, *Glaube und Lehre der schweizerischen Wiedertäufer*, p. 35.
156. *Mutual Consent*, p. 148. Cf. C.R., IV, p. 284.
157. Tyndale, P.S., I, p. 359.
158. Becon, P.S., II, p. 205.

Lutheran *Cranmer's Catechism*, but the *Reformatio Legum* was more explicit: "By our going under the water and rising again out of it, the death and burial of Christ are commended to us, and his raising again and restoration to life."[159] In the Abbey disputation which took place shortly after the accession of Elizabeth, this aspect was emphasized by the Reformed party. As living sermons of the death and resurrection of Christ, the sacraments bring before us that which has been done on our behalf as well as represent to us that which we ourselves have to do.[160] As Cooper was later to put it, "baptism is primarily a representation of death",[161] and Hutchinson is even more explicit: "It is a figure of the death of Christ."[162]

It might be objected that the Reformers were simply reading into the ecclesiastical rite an interesting but imported and artificial significance. Even on the historical level, however, the objection can hardly be sustained, for as practised by the Jews and in the Mystery religions baptism has always had some connotation of death and renewal. On the evangelical level the objection has even less ground, for the sacraments cannot be understood in isolation from the whole message and witness of the Gospel, and the Gospel is the Gospel of reconciliation by the life and death and resurrection of the Incarnate Son. The story of the divine work of redemption is therefore drawn out from the sacrament rather than imported into it.

But the sacrament is a picture not merely of the atoning work of Christ, but also of the entry of the believer into that work. This was, of course, a main insight of Romans 6. The argument of the passage is this: Submersion beneath the baptismal water represents an identification in faith with the death and burial of Christ, and re-emergence an identification in faith with His resurrection. For a proper enacting of the sign it seems that a full immersion is required, as Luther emphasized, but the placing of the baptized person under the water does partially at least fulfil the sign.

The theme of identification with the death and resurrection of Christ clearly underlay the great service of adult baptism in the early days of the church, when conversion was a most definite and meaningful step from the pagan to the Christian life. It was implicit in all the older theology, although in the Middle Ages the emphasis came to rest more upon regeneration than resurrection. Wycliffe had seized clearly and fully

---

159. *Reformatio Legum*, p. 29.
160. Burnet, *op. cit.*, III, 3.
161. Cooper, *Private Mass*, p. 203.
162. Hutchinson, P.S., p. 115.

upon this aspect of the sacrament: "The baptising of us in this water betokeneth ... how we ben biried with him fro synne that rengneth in this worrld. Our takynge up of this water betokeneth ... how we shulden rise goostli in clennesse of newe life."[163] But it was only with the new realization of the need for personal repentance and faith which came with the Reformation that the force of the symbolism could again be understood and the idea expounded with greater fullness and clarity.

It was Luther, of course, who gave prominence to this meaning of baptism, and he related it directly to his evangelical understanding of sin, repentance, and faith in Christ. For Luther, baptism was first of all a destroying of sin, a drowning of the old man and his sinful works.[164] The old Adam was plunged beneath the baptismal waters and done away. But baptism was also a rising again of the new man, the man of faith who is fashioned after the likeness of Christ and able to do works of righteousness which are pleasing to God.[165] Baptism, therefore, signified a spiritual death and resurrection, a death and resurrection which are fulfilled in faith. By faith the baptized are dead already to sin, and have entered already upon that new life which is in the grace and power of Jesus Christ.

A possible criticism of Luther's exposition is that the very richness of his perception introduced into it a certain confusion of the imagery.[166] This is particularly the case in his interconnection of the water and death. On the one hand, submersion in the water is referred to as a death *in* sin, the water representing the sin which overwhelms and destroys us. But on the other hand, it is referred to as a death *to* sin, the water representing the death by which sin itself is destroyed. Yet the contradiction is more apparent than real, for one of the lessons which Luther clearly perceived and taught is that sin is self-destructive.[167] It overwhelms the man of sin, but because man can rise to a new life in Christ, who died for sin, its ultimate fate is simply to destroy itself. A discrepancy has also been noted in Luther's conception of the baptismal renewal, for in some works he identified it with the giving of the new name, in others with the re-emergence from the water.[168] But once again, there was no necessary or essential contradiction.

The Lutheran understanding of baptism found favour with the

---

163. Arnold, II, p. 258.
164. W.A., II, p. 727.
165. *Loc. cit.*
166. See Stange, *op. cit.*, pp. 758 f.
167. W.A., II, *loc. cit.*
168. Stange, *loc. cit.*

Anabaptists, who naturally equated the baptismal death and resurrection with their adult repentance and faith. To quote the words of Grebel, "Scripture tells us that baptism signifies ... that we are dead and ought to die to sin, and that we should walk in newness of life".[169] The Council of Schlatten had a similar statement in its conclusions,[170] and the Dutch Anabaptists pointed out that in baptism we are buried with Christ in the font.[171] But the Reformed school also took up the point. If he did not press it Zwingli referred to Romans 6,[172] and Calvin found in the baptismal sign an assurance "that we are so united to Christ as to be partakers of all His blessings".[173] Calvin was careful to relate this teaching to the Protestant understanding of justification. By faith, we die and rise again in a moment,[174] but in discipleship we have to enter into the death and resurrection of Christ progressively: "Baptism indeed tells us that our Pharaoh is drowned and sin mortified ... but only so as not to have dominion over us."[175] Beza, too, described baptism as "the mortification and sepulture, or burying of our old man",[176] and the *Genevan Catechism* explained the symbolism in detail: "A figure of death is set before us when water is poured upon the head, and the figure of a new life, when, instead of remaining under the water, we only enter it for a moment as a kind of grave out of which we instantly rise."[177]

The Anglican statements all bore clearly the imprint of Luther. This was particularly the case with Tyndale, whose writings often read like free translations or adaptations of the works of Luther.[178] Tyndale identified baptism primarily with repentance: "Baptism is a sign of repentance signifying that I must repent of evil, and believe to be saved therefrom by the blood of Christ."[179] But the baptismal repentance was more than an inward and individual experience. It was an identification with the redemptive action of Christ Himself: "The plunging into the water signifieth that we die. And the pulling out again signifieth that we rise again with Christ into that new life."[180] The same thought was

---

169. Muralt, *op. cit.*, p. 34.
170. *Ibid.*, p. 35.
171. B.R.N., IV, p. 44.
172. C.R., IV, p. 245.
173. *Instit.*, IV, 15, 5-6.
174. Cf. John, 5:24.
175. *Instit.*, IV, 15, 11.
176. B.P.S., p. 47.
177. p. 86.
178. Cf. Jacobs, *The Lutheran Movement in England*.
179. Tyndale, P.S., III, p. 171.
180. *Ibid.*, I, p. 253.

tersely expressed by Frith: "We are dead with Christe from syne, we are risen with Christe from our synes."[181]

There is evidence that this Lutheran understanding took deep root in England even during the earlier and tentative period of the Reformation. It found utterance not only in the book *The Summe of the Holye Scripture*, from which many heretical propositions were extracted and condemned by Warham,[182] but also in the *Book of Ceremonies*,[183] and even in the *King's Book*, which had a reference to Romans 6.[184] Rather strangely, the catechisms of Edward's reign hardly mention it, and the Article speaks only in terms of regeneration. But the teaching was popularized in *Cranmer's Catechism*,[185] and there was a full exposition in the *Reformatio Legum*.[186] The Prayer Book, like the Reformed orders of Zürich, Geneva and Scotland,[187] had many forceful passages on the theme, especially in the prayer of thanks-giving after baptism, and in the exhortation to the godparents: "That as He died, and rose again for us, so should we who are baptized, die from sin, and rise again unto righteousness." The same line of thought was preserved in the seventeenth-century collect for Easter Even.

The individual theologians did not all have an equal interest in the interpretation, although in one way or another all of them referred to mortification and regeneration. Thus in Hooper we find only the one brief reference: "Baptism is a sacrament or sign ... that the baptized creature should die from sin",[188] and Cranmer spoke only of the spiritual regeneration signified in baptism,[189] rather after the manner of Bullinger's *Decades*.[190] In Sandys,[191] Jewel,[192] and Rogers,[193] there are similar short allusions to "the new spiritual birth", "the resurrection to a clean life", and "the new birth of Christ", but without any detailed exposition.

Becon, on the other hand, made a great point of this aspect of the sacrament. He found in baptism an objective testimony to our spiritual renewal: "Baptism doth declare unto me that I am dead unto sin ... that I have crucified the old man and put off the old Adam, that I am buried

---

181. Frith, B.R., p. 93.

182. Cf. folio iii.

183. E.M., 1, 2, pp. 411 f.

184. K.B., p. 45.

185. *Cranmer's Catechism*, pp. 184 f.

186. *Reformatio Legum*, p. 29.

187. Cf. D.C.R., p. 423.

188. Hooper, P.S., I, p. 74.

189. Cranmer, P.S., I, p. 304.

190. Bullinger, P.S., IV, p. 251.

191. Sandys, P.S., p. 253.

192. Jewel, P.S., III, p. 470.

193. Rogers, P.S., p. 276.

with Christ. Baptism preacheth unto me not only the mortification of the flesh, but also the vivification of the spirit, that I should put on the new man, walk in a new life." Elsewhere he described baptism as "a token of our regeneration,[194] of the mortification of our flesh, of our burial with Christ, of our resurrection unto new life".[195] Amongst the Elizabethans Cooper may also be singled out for notice. He was not a theologian of eminence, although the Marprelate Tracts gave an unwelcome notoriety to his conduct. In his attack upon the private mass he showed that the external sign of baptism is given the name of its internal signification, the Apostle Paul describing it as a death and burial.[196]

There can be no question that the Anglican Reformers shared the common Reformation understanding at this deeper Pauline level. The impulse came mainly from Lutheran sources, but in this as in so many other matters there was no essential difference between the Lutheran and the Reformed view. Indeed, there was no actual opposition to the teaching of tradition, for the Reformers simply made explicit something that was for the most part only implicit in the accepted teaching. If there was a difference at all, it was mainly a difference of emphasis. The Reformers gave prominence to the signification, the traditionalists to the effect. But on neither side was the emphasis exclusive.

A final point may be briefly mentioned. The suggestion has been made that perhaps the apostle Paul took over his interpretation of baptism from the Mystery religions, applying it to a simpler and more straightforward rite practised by the original disciples. But this was a possibility which quite apart from its historical merits or demerits the Reformers could not even consider. And in principle they were surely right. For it is not merely that they accepted the plain letter of the Bible, or that they knew for themselves the soul-shattering experience of Paul. It is rather that they perceived the centrality of the death and resurrection of Jesus Christ to the whole Gospel as it is foreshadowed in the Old Testament and actualized in the New. Behind the Pauline understanding there stood the very core of the evangelical message, the Messianic baptism in the self-offering of Jesus Christ on the Cross. To that extent, even on historical grounds, the Reformed view cannot be treated simply as an allegorical or mystical reinterpretation in terms of extraneous beliefs and practices.

---

194. Becon, P.S., II, p. 205.
195. *Ibid.*, III, p. 616.
196. *Private Mass*, p. 203.

Baptism, therefore, was the sacrament of conversion or regeneration, the action of dying to sin and rising again to righteousness. And that death and resurrection was the work of a moment. But just as justification could not be separated from its outworking in daily conduct, so the action of baptismal regeneration could not be separated from the process of baptismal renewal. Baptism was the sacrament of the new birth, but it was also the sacrament of the new life. It spoke of the beginning of the Christian life, the end of the man of sin and the beginning of the man of faith. But it also spoke of the continuance of the Christian life, the putting off of the old man and the putting on of the new. The symbolism was still the same: a death and a resurrection. But the application was now to the whole life of the believer from the first day to the last. Baptism had in fact a meaning which could never be exhausted in this life.

In spite of his preoccupation with the doctrine of justification, Luther maintained a fine sense of proportion at this point. In his *Sermon on Baptism* he showed a clear grasp of the ethical signification of the sacrament: "The whole of this life is a spiritual baptism which continues until death. He who is baptized is sentenced to death. The spiritual birth and the increase in grace and righteousness begins truly in baptism, but it goes forward until death, and indeed to the last day."[197] He made the same point in the *Smaller Catechism*: "Baptism signifies that the old Adam in us, with all sins and evil lusts, ought to be drowned by daily sorrow and repentance, and that a new man should daily come forth, and rise up, living eternally before God in righteousness and holiness".[198] Luther worked out this theme with great power. He saw in baptism a call to discipline, fasting being a means to further the work of baptism by the mortification of the flesh. Baptism was also a key to the understanding of suffering, for the tribulation of a Christian was another means to further the baptismal mortification: "Thus it follows that baptism makes sufferings, and even death itself, useful and helpful."[199] In the light of baptism, an early death was a blessing for the Christian believer: "The shorter the life, the more rapid the fulfilment of baptism."[200]

On the Swiss side there was hardly the same depth or originality as with Luther, but the ethical challenge of baptism was clearly perceived.

---

197. W.A., II, p. 728.
198. W.A., XXX, 1, p. 312.
199. W.A., II, p. 734.
200. W.A., VI, p. 535.

Zwingli described baptism as a pledge which engages us to live according to the rule of Christ.[201] Calvin went deeper, and saw that "we are baptized for the mortification of our flesh, which is begun in baptism, is prosecuted every day, and will be finished when we depart from this life to go to the Lord".[202] Similar passages could be quoted from the *Genevan Catechism*[203] and also from the liturgy of Knox, which claimed that regeneration "stands chiefli in these two points, in mortification, that is to say, a resisting of the rebellious lustes of the fleshe, and in newness of life, whereby we continually stryve to walk in that pureness and perfection wherewith we are cladd in baptisme".[204] The Anabaptists shared the same insight, as we may see from the writings of Grebel,[205] the articles of Schlatten,[206] and the Dutch *Corte Instrucye*.[207]

In England Wycliffe had been teaching as early as the fourteenth century that baptism "techith us how we shulden live here so": seeing that "sin is dead" "we shulde kepe us fro synne after."[208] Instructed by Luther, Tyndale revived this understanding in the early days of the Reformation, finding in baptism a call to die with Christ,[209] and seeing in affliction a means to baptismal mortification: "Tribulation is our right baptism."[210] It was in this sense that baptism could be identified with the whole process of penitence, and "the mortifying of our unruly members and the body of sin."[211] But this meant that baptism was a call to serious and life-long warfare: "We have enough to do all our life long to tame our bodies, and to compel our members to obey the Spirit, and not the appetites; that thereby we might be like unto Christ's death and resurrection, and might fulfil our baptism, which signifieth the mortifying of sin, and the new life of grace."[212]

There was a steady emphasis upon this ethical connotation during the period of Lutheran infiltration. We find it not only in writers like Frith,[213] but also in such varied productions as the *Summe of the Holye Scripture*[214] and the *King's Book*.[215] Perhaps the most forceful statement of all was in the so-called *Cranmer's Catechism*, which was of course the translation of a Lutheran work: "For baptysme, and the dyppyng into the

---

201. C.R., IV, p. 245.
202. *Instit.*, IV, 15, 11.
203. D.C.R., p. 569. Cf. p. 423.
204. *Knox's Liturgy*: Baptism.
205. Muralt, *op. cit.*, p. 34.
206. *Ibid.*, p. 35.
207. B.R.N., IV, p. 44.
208. Arnold, II, p. 258.
209. Tyndale, P.S., I, p. 245.
210. *Ibid.*, p. 138.
211. *Ibid.*, p. 426.
212. *Ibid.*, p. 500.
213. Frith, B.R., pp. 93 f.
214. Folio i.
215. K.B., p. 45.

water, doth betoken that the olde Adam, with al his synne and evil lustes ought to be drowned and kylled by daily contrition and repentance: and that by renewynge of the holy gost we ought to ryse with Christ from the death of synne and to walke in a neu lyfe."[216]

Naturally the later Reformers did not all lay the same stress upon this aspect. Cranmer and Ridley never even mentioned it, but then they never wrote on baptism as such. The same is true of such writers as Calfhill, Sandys, Hutchinson and even Coverdale. Jewel preferred to expound baptism in terms of cleansing, as also did Bullinger in the *Decades*. Rogers had to follow the Article, and he did not find any scope for the development of this theme. Of the others Nowell made a brief reference to baptism as the sacrament of mortification,[217] and Hooper argued that the baptized must die from sin, which includes the process of obedience as well as the act of faith.[218] Becon was more explicit. As he saw it, baptism was the sign of mortification and vivification. It was a clear summons to battle. It reminded us "that we ought valiantly to fight against the Devil, the world and the flesh, to mortify all unclean lusts, to die unto sin, and to rise again new men".[219] Latimer as the preacher of righteousness felt most strongly the ethical force of baptism, and he too saw in it a challenge "to wash away the old Adam, and to put on Christ, to receive him with a pure heart, and to study to go forward in all goodness, according unto his will and commandment".[220] But perhaps the clearest expression of all is to be found in the Liturgy. We have already alluded to two of the passages which make this general point, the prayer of thanks-giving and the exhortation, but in addition we may cite the sentence-prayers before administration, the prayer of reception, and the concluding words of the exhortation, which demand a "continual mortifying of all our evil and corrupt affections, and daily proceeding in all virtue and godliness of living."

At this point, again, there was nothing essentially new in the reformed interpretation. What the Reformers said was implicit in all the earlier writings. But they did say it with a new force and freshness. And they saw clearly the link between the ethical and the evangelical aspects. Baptism was a challenge, but it was not a challenge in the void. It was

216. *Cranmer's Catechism*, p. 192.
217. Nowell, P.S., p. 208.
218. Hooper, P.S., I, p. 74.
219. Becon, P.S., II, p. 508.
220. Latimer, P.S., II, p. 133.

a challenge on the basis of the divine act of redemption in Christ. It was a challenge that the new life which had been begun with Christ in faith should be continued with Christ in obedience. It was a challenge that the identification with Christ which had begun in the new birth should be continued in the new life. And that meant penitence, suffering and even death. At the deepest level, baptism enabled the Reformers to understand and even to affirm the afflictions which come upon us in this life. Baptism was a repetition of the Cross, an entry into the death and resurrection of Christ. And although that entry could be effected in a moment, in faith, it called for a life-long self-crucifixion in obedience and discipleship.

But however sincerely the challenge was accepted, the repetition or entry could never be completed in terms of this life. Its completion demanded death as well as tribulation. And in the last analysis that death had to be physical as well as spiritual and moral. The Christian life began with the act of faith, it continued with the process of daily renunciation and consecration, but it could be consummated only with the final replacement of the temporal by the eternal. The meaning of baptism extended, therefore, to the very end of the life of the Christian on earth and to its fulfilment in the new life in heaven. There could be no final identification with Christ apart from the death of the flesh and the participation in His resurrection. As the Tridentines put it: "Baptism gives no obscure intimation of eternal life also."[221] The signification of baptism was not only evangelical and ethical: it was also eschatological.

Luther again was the thinker who opened up this theme and developed it with the greatest daring and profundity. Already he had shown that the process of mortification and renewal can never be completed during life on earth, but now he went further: "The meaning of baptism, the death or drowning of sin, can never be fully worked out in this life, only with the death of the body and complete dissolution."[222] As the sign of our death and resurrection with Christ, baptism exhausted itself only with the final agony of death and the joy of the resurrection. And there was no contradiction between this eschatological aspect and the ethical, as some writers have tried to maintain.[223] From the very first, baptism spoke of the irruption of the world to come into the present sinful world.

---

221. C.T., II, 1, qu. 8.
222. W.A., II, p. 728.
223. Stange, *op. cit.*

Even with the act of faith the baptized passed from the temporal order to the eternal. The ethical challenge was simply a call to realize in terms of the temporal order that which already is by faith, and one day will be by sight. The consummation involved a literal dying to sin, but, as Luther saw, in the gracious providence of God even death had become in Christ a servant and not an enemy or master. Death was the result of sin, but it was also that which destroyed sin. It had no bitterness in itself: death was bitter only because sin is not willingly destroyed. And when its work was completed, when sin was finally destroyed in the body, the way was opened up for the fullness of resurrection: "Sufferings and death cannot but help forward the work of baptism ... sin does not die willingly, and that is why it makes death so bitter and terrible. But merciful and mighty is God, for sin brought death, and with its own work it is itself destroyed."[224]

This eschatological understanding of baptism underlay the whole Reformed interpretation, but it never appeared again with quite the same depth or power as in Luther. Zwingli hardly referred to it at all, and there are only scattered references in the works of the Anabaptists.[225] Calvin had in mind the Lutheran teaching when he pointed out that "the work of baptism will only be finished when we depart from this life to go to the Lord",[226] but he did not develop the theme as Luther had done, and the confessions for the most part ignored it. The same is true of the English writers, who in spite of their dependence upon Luther and their interconnecting of baptism with tribulation and death seldom linked up the sacrament unequivocally with the final dissolution and resurrection. There are in fact only five passages in which the eschatological significance emerges with any clarity. One of these is in *Cranmer's Catechism*,[227] which is not strictly an Anglican writing. A second is in the writings of Becon, in which he related baptism to the divine covenant: "If thou will believe and be baptized, he will give thee everlasting life freely."[228] The approach here is obviously quite different from that of Luther, although it brings out the same eschatological bearing of baptism. A third is the incidental remark of Cranmer, when in quite a different connection he asked: "What Christian man will say ... that baptism representeth not unto

---

224. W.A., II, p. 734.
225. Cf. Muralt, *op. cit.*, p. 34; D.C.R.,p. 451.
226. *Instit.*, IV, 15, 11.
227. *Cranmer's Catechism*, pp. 184 f.
228. Becon, P.S., II, p. 573.

us the high state of our glorification, and the perfect redemption of our bodies in the general resurrection? "[229] A fourth is the claim of Hutchinson that "Christian men were baptized over dead men's graves, in the primitive church, in token that the dead should rise again".[230] And the last is the clear and forcible petition in the post- baptismal thanksgiving, that as the baptized person "is made partaker of the death of thy Son, he may also be partaker of His resurrection; so that finally, with the residue of thy holy church, he may be an inheritor of thine everlasting kingdom."

It is a matter for regret that more attention was not paid by some writers at least to this interesting aspect of baptismal signification. There was no breach of reformed solidarity at the point. The truth probably is that for the Reformers regeneration, justification and sanctification were the controverted and controversial topics. About the eschatological meaning of baptism there could be little quarrel with anyone, for not even the most rabid sacramentalist could pretend that baptism effected already a literal dissolution of the body, and resurrection to glory. From the evangelical standpoint, however, the suggestions of Luther have an outstanding value. They open up the way to a genuine understanding of suffering and death, at any rate in the life of the Christian. It is, therefore, all the more unfortunate that in post-Reformation theology the disruptive and seemingly interminable Pœdobaptist controversies have blocked the way to advance along these more interesting lines, and that in England, at least, a reviving sacramentalism has again concentrated attention upon the effect of baptism rather than the meaning. The opportunity of a thorough weighing of the eschatological bearing has so far never recurred.

(3) Types

The consideration of the meaning of baptism leads on naturally to the subject of types and analogies. For the most part these were drawn from the Old Testament. It must be remembered that in the sixteenth century the Bible was regarded as a single and divinely inspired book. Similarities between the New Testament sacrament and Old Testament signs or events could not therefore be dismissed as in any sense fortuitous or incidental. On the other hand, analogies were not to be

---

229. Cranmer, P.S., I, p. 176.
230. Hutchinson, P.S., p. 138.

selected arbitrarily or at will. The New Testament itself had pointed to the two outstanding types: the apostle Peter to the Flood, and the apostle Paul to the Red Sea and the Cloud. In this field as in so many others the Reformers were not in any way revolutionaries. From a very early period reference had been made to the common Old Testament figures of baptism. Tertullian, for example, had pointed to the Deluge, the Red Sea and the Rock as the main types of baptism. Again, in the Middle Ages Thomas had discussed the sense in which the Cloud and the Red Sea prefigured the sacrament in certain respects.[231] At the Council of Trent four main types were ultimately recognized: the Deluge, the Red Sea, the cleansing of Naaman and the pool of Bethesda. The circumcision and the baptism of John could also be included in the list,[232] and many other analogies were perceived, some of them possibly more fanciful than real.[233] On the traditionalist side it was always emphasized that the type is only a figure or shadow, whereas the sacrament itself is the reality.[234]

The Continental Reformers accepted the common teaching, but with a concentration upon the two outstanding signs, the Deluge and the Red Sea. Luther did make a naturalistic comparison with physical generation,[235] but his main interest was in the Flood, which taught so clearly the message of destruction and renewal proclaimed in the sacrament.[236] Zwingli, on the other hand, was not greatly interested in types, but he broke new ground by identifying Christian baptism with both circumcision in the Old Testament and the baptism of John in the New.[237] The only types allowed by Zwingli were the two mentioned in the epistles, to which a reference was preserved in the Zürich Baptismal Order.[238] Calvin followed the example of Zwingli, but with a rather fuller treatment of the two "adumbrations of mortification and ablution among the people of Israel[239] For his successor Beza the Ark represented the church shut up into Christ in baptism, and the Red Sea was a descent into the water followed by a triumphant emergence to new life.[240] It was admitted by some of the later dogmaticians that immersion seemed to

---

231. S., III, qu. 70.
232. C.T., II, 2, qu. 9.
233. Cf. *Catholic Encyclopedia* Art. Baptism.
234. Cf. Chrysostom, *Hom.* XXIV, *De Bapt. Christi.*
235. Stange, *op. cit.,* p. 800.
236. W.A., II, p. 729.
237. C.R., IV, p. 260.
238. D.C.R., p. 423.
239. *Instit.,* IV, 15, 9.
240. Q.R.C., 101.

be demanded by the baptismal types, but in favour of other modes they could advance the Old Testament figure of sprinkling.[241]

The reformed position had been anticipated in England by Wycliffe, who had perceived a clear connection between the types and their fulfilment, and had found in the Cloud and the Red Sea the most significant types: "Beleve techeth Cristene men that signes of the Olde Law weren tokenes of oure signes now, as thei ben tokenes of the bliss of hevene. The cloude that ledde them in desert upon daies, as Goddis lawe tellith, figuride the water of Cristis side, by whiche we ben baptisid now. Crist was deed before that water cam of the cloude of his bodi to baptise men, etc."[242] In the first period of the Reformation Tyndale took up the point, finding in the Ark, the Red Sea and the Cloud the only true figures of baptism.[243] As Tyndale saw it, the purpose of these figures was to help us to a better understanding of the sacrament by revealing the pattern of God's work of redemption. He did not try to work out the typological details, which can easily lead to a certain confusion, but probably regarded the pictures as in a broad way self-explanatory.

Rather strangely, Becon did not display any great interest in the types, and Hooper made only a passing reference to baptism as our Red Sea. Philpot, however, seized upon such figures as the Red Sea, the crossing of Jordan and circumcision as arguments against the Anabaptists. It was his contention that "the apostles did attemperate all their doings to the shadows and figures of the Old Testament". But infants as well as adults passed through the Red Sea and the River Jordan. Hence we may conclude that infants were baptized by the apostles.[244] The argument may appear to be somewhat fanciful, but it illustrates two important points: first, the Reformers' belief in the unity of Scripture, and second, their conception of church development in terms of conscious rather than unconscious growth. Even from the purely human and historical angle it is surely true that the apostles must have been greatly influenced by Old Testament practices and precedents.

A strange instance of the way in which typology could be applied is to be found in Woodman's disputation with Langdale. Against the claim of Langdale that faith is given in baptism, Woodman cited the example of Jacob who "had faith before he was baptized".

---

241. R.D., Bapt.
242. Arnold, II, p. 258.
243. Tyndale, P.S., I, p. 426.
244. Philpot, P.S., p. 277.

> *Langdale*: "You speak of the old law. Jacob was not
> christened, but circumcised."
> *Woodman*: "Peter brought in Noah's flood, which was a long
> time before Jacob and Esau, to prove baptism."[245]

Like Philpot, Woodman believed in an essential unity of the Bible, so that he saw no incongruity in illustrating New Testament doctrine by an Old Testament example. The point will emerge more clearly when we consider circumcision.

Amongst the later writers Hutchinson saw a distinction between the "temporal" sacraments of the Old Testament, circumcision, the Red Sea and the Cloud, and the continual sacrament of the New, the laver of regeneration.[246] This was perhaps another way of stating the traditional view that what was type and shadow in the Old Testament had become the reality in the New. The Reformed understanding of the types was popularized in Bullinger's *Decades*, in which there was a full and clear exposition.[247] It will be remembered that the *Decades* became almost a standard text-book in Elizabethan England.

Like the Zürich order, and the majority of the Lutheran offices, the Prayer Book service retained the reference to the Ark and the Red Sea in its introductory prayer. A point of interest is that the Lutheran allusion to the destruction of Pharaoh and all his hosts (representing the old man) was omitted in the 1552 revision. There is no reason to suppose that the change indicates any shift in interpretation. The phrase was perhaps felt to be liturgically inappropriate, or possibly it was desired to stress the fact that primarily and ultimately the types are pictures of redemption. The closing petition elaborated the type somewhat fancifully in relation to the Christian life: "That he, being delivered from thy wrath, may be received into the ark of Christ's church, and ... may so pass the waves of this troublesome world, that finally he may come to the land of everlasting life. ..."

In general, the Reformers used the Old Testament types with restraint and discrimination. They confined themselves to those which had apostolic sanction, and they applied them within the context of that death-resurrection theme which was basic to their whole understanding of baptism. If there was a richness in their interpretation of the types, it was not due to imaginative inventiveness, but rather to the depth of

---

245. Foxe, VII, pp. 357 f.
246. Hutchinson, P.S., p. 219.
247. Bullinger, P.S., IV, pp. 329, 364.

their insight into the signification of the sacrament. The legitimacy of their use of types may perhaps be questioned on a purely historical understanding of Christianity and Holy Scripture, but if we accept the Christological and revelational reference of the Old Testament, that use is both valid and meaningful.

The Deluge and the Red Sea were the outstanding types of baptism, but there was one sign which prefigured the sacrament even more closely: the covenant-sign of circumcision. As we have seen, the older theologians always pointed to circumcision as one of the pre-eminent types of baptism. The comparison was an obvious one, for, like baptism, circumcision was both a sign of the covenant and also a sign of entry or initiation. But the Schoolmen had also drawn attention to what they considered to be the great differences between circumcision and baptism. As Lombard put it, baptism had replaced circumcision, but it was superior to it, being "common to all, and more perfect, and more fully charged with grace".[248] It was true that circumcision did mediate a certain grace, but Thomas pointed out that this grace was restricted, and only in so far as circumcision is a sign of future faith in the passion of Christ. The passion had given to baptism a much superior virtue and efficacy.[249] The relationship between the various signs was carefully considered at Trent, which first marked off religious signs from the purely natural or conventional, and then singled out the signs of the New Law by reason of their inherent capacity to accomplish that which they signify.[250] It was because of this that baptism had to be differentiated from circumcision, and circumcision classified merely as a type or shadow of baptism.[251] The canon relating to this point was not passed without considerable discussion, but the objections were finally overruled. The real distinction was neatly stated by Bellarmine: "Our sacraments confer grace. Those of the Old Law do but signify."[252]

Circumcision, then, was classified as a type of baptism largely because of its alleged inferiority in efficacy. But the Reformers came to the question with a new interest in meaning as well as efficacy, and with a pronounced sense of the unity of the Old and New Testaments. The result was that they soon began to ask themselves whether there was any essential difference at all. The position of Luther was somewhat

---

248. Lombard, IV, *Dist.* 1, K.
249. S., III, qu. 70.
250. C.T., II, 1, qu. 6.
251. C.D., Sess. VII, *Sacram. Can.*, 1.
252. T.B., p. 347.

equivocal. On the one hand he found it hard to abandon the view that a special grace attaches to the sacraments by virtue of the evangelical promises.[253] But on the other he claimed boldly that the Old sacraments were identical with the New in that they too had effect as well as signification.[254] The truth seems to be that although Luther did distinguish between the sacraments and the ceremonial figures of the Old Testament,[255] he included circumcision in the former class. This was why Luther could use circumcision as an argument for infant baptism.[256] It was also the explanation of Henry's charge in the *Assertio* that according to Luther "the sacraments of the Evangelical Law do not differ in any kind from those of the Mosaical Law, as touching the efficacy of grace".[257] The idea that there is a special grace of justification attaching to the Gospel sacraments was strongly repudiated by Melanchthon,[258] and Bucer, too, insisted that circumcision is a full and true parallel to baptism.[259]

This concept of the unity of the Old and New sacraments was carried to its logical extreme by the Swiss reformer Zwingli, who in face of the Anabaptists found his strongest defence in a covenantal theology in which the sacraments were primarily signs of the covenant. The argument was roughly this. In the Old Testament God had entered into covenant with the family and nation of Israel, and He had given them circumcision as the ratifying sign of covenant-membership. In the New Testament the covenant was extended by Jesus Christ to the New Israel, but the underlying principle remained the same, so that the covenant-privileges, and therefore the covenant-sign of baptism, still belonged not only to professing Christians, but also to their descendants. Now obviously the cogency of this argument demands amongst other things a substantial identity between the Old and the New Testament signs, and again and again Zwingli laboured to make this plain. The purpose of the two sacraments was the same: "For as circumcision is a sign of the covenant, so too is baptism."[260] The efficacy of the two was also equal, for neither the one nor the other could as an external sign either confer

---

253. Seeberg seems to suggest that this involves a distinction between the Old Testament sacraments and the New, *op. cit.*, p. 316.
254. W.A., VI, p. 532.
255. Stange, *op. cit.*, p. 823.
256. Cf. Seeberg, *op. cit.*, p. 322.
257. *Assertio*, p. 99.
258. F. Galle, *Versuch einer Charakteristik Melanchthons als Theologen*, p. 363.
259. G. Anrich, *Martin Bucer*, p. 41.
260. C.R., IV, p. 171.

grace or even confirm faith.[261] And the two were clearly brought together by the apostle in Colossians 2: 11-12.[262] Indeed, the only true difference was in outward character, the bloody sign of circumcision having been replaced, after the passion, by the kindlier sign of baptism (as the passover was also replaced by the Lord's supper).

The later theologians of the Reformed school were much influenced by Zwingli's teaching on this point. Calvin was perhaps more concerned to assert an identity of Johannine with Christian baptism, but he too claimed an ultimate oneness of baptism and circumcision, especially as it concerned infant baptism.[263] For Calvin, baptism marked an extension to every nation of the promises previously confined to Israel. But if the promises themselves were the same, no ultimate distinction could be seen between the signs. The Old Testament signs were real sacraments, not mere ceremonies. If the external circumcision had to be distinguished from the internal, this was also true of the external and the internal baptism. Circumcision and baptism were alike covenant-signs, the one pointing forward, the other backward, but both testifying to the one covenant of grace fulfilled in Jesus Christ.[264]

On this issue the Anglican theologians came down for the most part on the Reformed side, although not always for quite the same reasons. Tyndale, for example, found in both signs a representation of the one divine covenant, with its divine promises on the one side and its human obligations on the other.[265] He thought that the nature, power and effect of baptism ought to be explained in the light of circumcision.[266] Frequently he alluded to circumcision as the precursor of baptism,[267] a thought which Cranmer also expressed in words strongly reminiscent of Zwingli: "The same to them was circumcision that to us is baptism."[268] A rather different line was taken by Becon, who argued that in spite of the basic identity of the signs[269] there was a clear difference in function, and to that extent an inferiority of the Old Testament ceremony. But the difference was only that of the forward-looking and the backward-looking sign: "The former sacraments were figures and shadows of Christ to come, whereas the sacraments of the New Law do signify, declare and

---

261. C.R., IV, p. 227.
262. C.R., IV, p. 637.
263. *Instit.*, IV, 14, 21, IV, 16, 3-4.
264. Loc. *cit.* Also *Commentary on. Colossians* 2.
265. Tyndale, P.S., I, p. 409.
266. *Ibid.*, p. 426.
267. *Ibid.*, p. 350.
268. J. III, p. 141. Cf. C.R., IV, p. 48.
269. Becon, P.S., II, p. 201.

set forth unto us that Christ is come."[270] The inferiority was that of an intimation as compared with a clear declaration, but there still remained a fundamental oneness in office and character. The same point was made in Bullinger's *Decades*, in which the change of sign was connected with the bloodshedding of Christ, and reference was made to Colossians 2.[271]

The cogency of the argument from circumcision was felt by those writers who were exercised about Anabaptism. Philpot is a typical example, for if the apostles followed the patterns set in the Old Testament they would naturally extend the covenant-sign to infants.[272] Bradford argued in a similar way: "Sithen Christ's death" circumcision had been replaced by baptism. But since there is only one church, "parents seem to be no less bound to offer their infant babes to be baptized".[273] A new and important point which emerged in this statement was that there was an identity between the Old and New Testament churches as well as the Old and New Testament signs. And behind this twofold identity there stood firmly the belief that the election and salvation of God is only the one election and salvation in Christ. It was because of this conviction that Woodman could appeal so confidently to the example of Jacob, Iveson could describe circumcision as a sign and token of Christ,[274] and all the Reformed writers could at one time or another bring together the Old and the New Testament signs. Whitgift had this same underlying unity in mind when in his comparison of the signs he went on to argue that it would be a false deduction to say that the Levites prefigured the Christian ministry.[275] The Levitical ministry formed part of the ceremonial law fulfilled and done away in Christ (cf. Article 7). But circumcision and baptism were common signs of the one and unchanging covenant of grace, and therefore in their different forms attestations of the one Christ. For that reason their identity could not be denied.

But if circumcision had to be treated as the Old Testament counterpart of baptism, what of the baptism of John which had also been classed as a type or figure in the traditional teaching? At a first glance, it might appear strange that this question should have emerged as such

---

270. *Loc. cit.*
271. Bullinger, P.S., IV, pp. 353, 293.
272. Philpot, P.S., pp. 277 f.
273. Bradford, P.S., I, p. 82. Cf. Bullinger, P.S., IV, p. 340.
274. Foxe, VII, p. 307.
275. Whitgift, P.S., I, p. 368.

a prominent and hotly contested issue in the sixteenth century, and we are perhaps tempted to ask impatiently what difference it could possibly make either way.

Yet the Reformers felt that two vital points were here at stake. On the one hand, and negatively, they rejected the implication of the traditional distinction that Christian baptism had some greater virtue than that of John. On the other, and positively, they contended for the unity of the divine revelation and redemptive action. On the opposite view, the way seemed to open up, not only to the worst types of sacramentalism, but also to a destruction of the consistency of God's working. The baptism of John was reduced to a temporary expedient, with no vital or essential part in the divine economy.

The sacramental danger was a real one, for the traditionalist magnified the distinction in order to exalt Christian baptism. It is worth noting, however, that the Schoolmen had not dogmatized as to the exact nature of the distinction. Lombard found it in the fact that while the baptism of John availed to cleanse, it was not able to furnish with grace.[276] Thomas emphasized the preparatory nature of the Johannine rite: it was not even a profession of faith, but only a preliminary act of penitence.[277] In the sixteenth century attention came to be focused upon the presumed difference in efficacy. Eck, for example, argued that the baptism of John could not remove original sin,[278] and Trent laid it down categorically that the baptism of John did not have the same force as that of Christ.[279] The divine institution was alleged in favour of this view,[280] and Augustine was also quoted: "We rightly prefer the baptism of Christ, given even by the hand of Judas, to the baptism of John, given even by the hand of John."[281] The main points of difference were later summarized by Bellarmine: John's baptism was not divinely instituted, it lacked the invocation of the Trinity, it was reiterable, it had no power even to remit sins, and it was described even by John himself as a baptism only of water, and not of the Spirit.[282]

The first serious breach in the traditional position came from the Swiss rather than the Lutheran side. Luther himself was willing to

---

276. Lombard, IV, *Dist.* 2, B, D, and F.
277. S., III, qu. 66, 9; 70.
278. D.C.R., p. 459.
279. C.D., Sess. VII, *Bapt. Canon*, 1.
280. C.T., II, 2, qu. 16.
281. C.T., II, 1, qu. 19.
282. T.B., p. 368.

concede a difference, and he admitted that the disciples of John were rebaptized.[283] But for Luther the difference was an evangelical rather than a sacramentalist difference. It was a difference primarily in signification: the baptism of John was to repentance, that of Christ to regeneration. Or again, it was a difference in the form of witness: the baptism of John pointed to the Messiah who was yet to come, that of Christ to the Messiah who had already come.[284] It was because of this coming that Christian baptism was now a baptism of the Spirit, whereas that of John had been only of water.

Zwingli, however, was not content with this evangelical reinterpretation of the difference. He contended bluntly and firmly that there was no real difference at all. God Himself had instituted baptism, and it was only one. The true difference was between the external baptism of water and the internal baptism of the Spirit. But in respect of this difference the baptism of John and the baptism of Christ were equal. As an outward baptism, neither the one nor the other could effect anything. But both equally could be accompanied by the inward irrigation of the Spirit. To the objection that John's baptism was only a baptism of water Zwingli replied that it was also a baptism of doctrine. And the doctrine of John was the same as that of the apostles: a call to repentance, and a witness to Jesus Christ as Saviour. The identity of the two was confirmed by the fact that the only baptism received by Christ and the apostles was that of John. The Ephesian incident in Acts did not affect this view, for the twelve men were either instructed more fully in the meaning of their baptism, or more likely they had known only the baptismal doctrine of John, but not his water-baptism.[285]

The attitude of the Swiss Anabaptists is interesting, for it reveals the extent to which polemical considerations can influence doctrinal positions. Grebel, for example, agreed with Zwingli, but only to the extent that John had baptized penitent adults, and therefore Christians must do the same.[286] Hübmaier, on the other hand, thought that a differentiation ought to be made, for the baptism of John had only the negative signification of repentance, whereas that of Christ had the positive signification of faith. Both, of course, were meaningful only for adults.[287]

---

283. W.A., VI, p. 472.
284. *Loc. cit.* This point was also made by Melanchthon, C.R., XXI, pp. 207 f.
285. C.R., IV., pp. 260-271.
286. C.R., III, p. 369.
287. C.R., IV, p. 603.

Calvin contended for exactly the same position as Zwingli, and his arguments were very similar: "The ministry of John is the same as that which was afterwards delegated to the apostles. Both baptized unto repentance, both for the remission of sins, both in the name of Christ."[288] His exposition of the relevant Scriptures was more elaborate and on the whole more convincing than that of Zwingli. Of Matthew 3 he said: "John merely distinguishes between himself and other ministers of the Gospel on the one hand, and the power of Christ on the other. To men has been committed nothing more than the administration of the outward and visible sign. The reality dwelleth with Christ alone."[289] Similarly in John 1:26 he saw a contrast between the external baptism of both John and the apostles and the internal baptism which only Christ can give.[290] Again and again he emphasized that the whole power and efficacy is in Christ alone. With regard to the Ephesian episode he denied that the baptism of John could be iterated, claiming that "the words of Luke import no other thing save only that they were baptized with the Spirit".[291] The men at Ephesus were not rebaptized outwardly, but they were inwardly baptized into Christ Himself, who is the reality and substance of the sacrament. The same view was steadfastly maintained by all the later dogmaticians.[292]

The Anglican teaching has a particular interest in view of the importance attached to the issue and the divergence between the Lutheran and the Reformed schools. Tyndale did not deal with the matter, but Becon came down on the Reformed side, ascribing the institution of baptism to God the Father, who "did it through the baptism of John". This baptism was the same as that of Christ, "since there is but one baptism".[293] It was by reason of this identity that the Marian confessor Denley could reject the Romanist administration because it was "altered and changed" from that of John, who "used nothing but the preaching of the word, and the water".[294] The expositor Fulke was interested in the Ephesian incident, and he came to much the same conclusion as Calvin: that the baptism of John "was confirmed by the imposition of hands rather than disgraced by reiteration".[295] He also drew attention to

---

288. *Instit.*, IV, 15, 7.
289. *Harmony of the Evangel.*, p. 198.
290. *Comm. on John* 1:26.
291. *Comm. on Acts*, II, p. 209.
292. E.g., Q.R.C., 115, R.D. Bapt.
293. Becon, P.S., II, p. 203.
294. Foxe, VII, p. 333.
295. Fulke, P.S., I, pp. 453-454.

the case of the apostles, who were either not baptized at all, or else only with John's baptism.[296] Whitgift expounded Acts 19 along similar lines, claiming somewhat naively, although not altogether unsoundly, "that it is dangerous to understand that place of the sacrament of baptism, lest we should seem to admit rebaptization".[297] Hutchinson, too, discussed the question, concluding with Calvin and many others "that the baptism mentioned is nothing but the giving of the Holy Ghost by laying on of hands".[298] The Reformed view was summed up and popularized in Bullinger's *Decades*,[299] and it is interesting that it was maintained even in the seventeenth century, although a number of non-essential differences were then perceived.[300] The position was felt to be an important one, for not only did it safeguard the supremacy of Christ Himself, and an evangelical understanding of sacramental efficacy, but it also provided a defence against the Anabaptist clamour for rebaptization.

That baptism (or at any rate Christian baptism) should not be repeated was, of course, a cardinal principle with all parties. The question had been settled quite early with the rejection of the Cyprianic deviation, but it again became a living issue when the Anabaptists began to administer baptism to those who had already been baptized as infants. Of course, the Anabaptists themselves did not admit the charge of rebaptization, for they argued that infant baptism was not baptism at all. But the traditionalists and the Reformers joined forces in rejecting this argument, and in addition the Reformers accused the traditionalists of demanding rebaptization in the case of the disciples of John. A further complication arose when the Puritans attacked the validity of irregular administrations.

The traditionalist view had been consistently held since the fourth century, and it had been developed to meet all possible contingencies. In the words of Thomas, any baptism, so long as it was by water and in the Triune name, was true baptism, and ought not to be repeated. The argument that new sins required new cleansing, or that the disciples of John or the Paulianists were baptized again, did not affect the main point, that the proper effect and signification of Christian baptism is regeneration, which does not take place more than once. Nor did it alter the fact that baptism conveys an indelible character. The baptism of

---

296. *Loc. cit.*
297. Whitgift, P.S., III, p. 17.
298. Hutchinson, P.S., pp., 114-115.
299. Bullinger, P.S., IV, p. 354.
300. Moore and Cross, *Anglicanism*, 12.

John was not regarded as Christian baptism, and that of the Paulianists was defective and therefore no baptism.[301] This view was strongly reaffirmed at the Council of Trent,[302] and the *Catechism* quoted the decisive dictum of Augustine, that there is no returning to the womb.[303] Where there was doubt, a conditional form of baptism could be used, but only with restraint.[304]

The Reformers accepted the common principle of non-reiteration, and they proclaimed it with great vigour. But they did not agree with the traditional reasons for it, and apart from the Lutherans they denied that the disciples of John ought to be, or were in fact, rebaptized. Luther himself claimed that baptism is given only once, and that it has a signification which can never be exhausted in this life.[305] Melanchthon shared this view, for, as he put it, the sign given is a permanent mark and testimony to which nothing can be added by repetition.[306] The only exception was in the case of those who had received John's baptism, which was provisional and prophetic.[307]

On the Reformed side the main interest of Zwingli was to maintain the identity of Johannine and Christian baptism. He argued against repetition on the ground that baptism witnesses to the death of Christ, which did not take place more than once.[308] A weakness in this argument is that it did not apply to the similar eucharistic testimony. Calvin insisted upon non-repetition, even to the point of saying that the traditionalists opened up a loop-hole to the Anabaptists by allowing a rebaptization of John's disciples.[309] A knotty problem was posed when Knox asked whether those baptized under the Papacy had received true baptism or not, but even in this case it was affirmed that no rebaptism was necessary. Naturally, it was not a matter of indifference which baptism was received – "God avert us from that wilfull and foulische blindness" – but once baptism is given, it must on no account be repeated.[310] The later dogmaticians endorsed this conclusion.[311]

The English church had inherited the tradition enshrined in the Tridentine statement, as may be seen from the various medieval synods and councils.[312] In the sixteenth century the Articles of 1536 had insisted that baptism is given once only, and the *King's Book* expressly

---

301. S., III, qu. 66, 9.
302. C.D., Sess. VII, *Bapt. canon*, 11.
303. C.T., II, 2, qu. 54.
304. *Loc. cit.*
305. W.A., VI, p. 472.
306. C.R., XXI, p. 471.
307. *Loc. cit.*

308. C.R., IV, p. 284.
309. *Instit.*, IV, 15, 18. Cf. *Comm. on Acts* 19.
310. Knox, IV, pp. 119 f.
311. R.D., *Baptism*.
312. Cf. E.R., p. 191.

forbade rebaptization.[313] A manifest fear of Anabaptism underlay these statements. It was no doubt the same fear which introduced the topic into the examination of Protestants under the reign of Mary. But the Reformers themselves vehemently denounced reiteration. We may see this from the case of Becon, who described rebaptization as a violation of "the institution and word of God",[314] or of Philpot, who argued that it is contrary to Scripture, and a confusion of the true signification, which is death.[315] The same points were made by Bullinger, who referred to the decisions of the early church, and condemned rebaptization as "an horrible offence" both against the imperial law of Theodosius and Honorius, and also against the law of God.[316]

The tenacity of the Reformed view was tested when Bishop Ridley in his examination was asked concerning the validity of an administration of the sacrament in an unknown tongue. The question was a subtle one in that it involved a certain conflict of principles, but Ridley rejected decisively any suggestion of possible reiteration: "It is not only not needful, but also not lawful, for any man so christened to be christened again."[317] The same topic arose in the course of a discussion between Bradford and Harpsfield, but this time the principle of reiteration was introduced by the Reformer in order to rebut the Cyprianic argument of his opponent that "only the true church has the true sacraments". As Bradford pointed out, "If heretics have baptism, and do baptize, as they did in St. Cyprian's time, you know that baptism is baptism, and not to be reiterate". Harpsfield had no reply.[318] Fulke, too, referred to the Cyprianic controversy, although in a different connection. Refuting the contention of Martin that difference of opinion is a manifest proof of heresy, he pointed out that in the age of Cyprian "it were hard to condemn them both for heretics, least of all them that held the truth", just because there was a difference of opinion on this issue.[319] Hutchinson found a Scriptural proof of the principle in the difficult passage, Hebrews 6: "St. Paul in this place forbiddeth all iteration of baptism": but his main concern was to establish that it is only the renewal of baptism which is forbidden, and not of repentance.[320]

---

313. K.B., p. 43.
314. Becon, P.S., II, p. 226.
315. Philpot, P.S., p. 380.
316. Bullinger, P.S., IV, p. 393.
317. Foxe, VII, p. 420.
318. *Ibid.*, p. 169.
319. Fulke, P.S., I, p. 35.
320. Hutchinson, P.S., p. 114.

A fresh turn was given to the question in the long and bitter controversy between Cartwright and Whitgift. Cartwright was disputing the
validity of lay-baptism, and in support of his view he alleged a doubt
which had been expressed by Augustine. But as Whitgift pointed out,
if those who have received lay-baptism are not validly baptized, then
"numbers are not baptized that are supposed to be baptized, and it
must of necessity fall out that they ought to be rebaptized".[321] But such
questions "spring out of the school of the Anabaptists, and tend to
the rebaptization of all, or the most part, of them that this day are
living".[322] A similar argument was used by Whitgift in face of the
Puritan insistence that the preaching of the word is an essential part
of the sacrament.[323] The Separatists further complicated the issue by
refusing to recognize any Anglican baptism. They were exposed to the
damaging accusation that they denied even the Queen to be validly
baptized. But Penry seems to have felt the force of Whitgift's argument,
for he conceded that the elect and converted are truly baptized
irrespective of the external minister.[324] There could, therefore, be no
value in rebaptization.

It was Hooker who finally summed up the Anglican teaching.
Rebaptism, he pointed out, was not permissible except where the supposed
baptism was obviously defective. To repeat the sacrament was contrary
both to the clear teaching of Scripture and also to its signification as the
new birth: "Iteration of baptism once given hath been always thought
a manifest contempt of that ancient apostolic aphorism 'One Lord, one
faith, one baptism'. How should we practise iteration of baptism, and yet
teach that by baptism we are born anew?" The principle itself was so sure
that, as he pertinently observed, those who wish to repeat their baptism
must always invent some pretext for denying the baptism which they
already have.[325] It may be noted that the Prayer Book office guards against
any possible iteration by prescribing the question: "Hath this child been
already baptized, or no?" In cases of genuine doubt a conditional form
was permitted.

The Reformers did not bring anything essentially new to this question.
They differed from their traditionalist opponents in that they stressed
the argument from signification rather than effect. They also accepted

321. Whitgift, P.S., III, p. 525.

322. *Ibid.*, p. 552.

323. *Ibid.*, p. 576.

324. Penry, *Exhortation*, pp. 27-28. Cf. Pierce, *John Penry*, p. 188.

325. L.E.P., V, 62, 4.

the identity of the baptism of John with that of Christ. But, basically, they agreed with the traditional theology that baptism is a divinely appointed sign, and that it must be administered only according to its institution. Baptism was not merely an ecclesiastical rite which was to be explained in human and historical terms and could be manipulated according to human convenience. It derived both its origin and meaning from God Himself. According to that origin and meaning it ought not to be administered more than once. Reiteration was a revolt not merely against human law but against the divine will and prerogative, and therefore not to be tolerated in the church.

(4) Necessity

A crucial question in baptismal teaching is that of the necessity of the sacrament.

The teaching inherited from the medieval period was clear and consistent, and of a piece with the whole sacramentalist interpretation. It rested ultimately upon a literal exegesis of John 3:5, and Augustine's gloomy prognostication concerning the fate of unbaptized infants. It had been stated by Lombard, who claimed that water-baptism was absolutely necessary to salvation except in the case of those who receive the thing signified without the sign (i.e. by a martyr's death, or a special endowment of the Spirit).[326] Thomas was no less dogmatic. As he saw it, the text of John 3:5 constituted a universal law, to which martyrdom and the inward sanctification of the Spirit were the only possible exceptions. Hope could perhaps be held out for catechumens dying suddenly, so long as they died in good works and with a desire for baptism, but apart from these well-defined cases there was an absolute necessity of the sacrament. In the case of infants, who were of course the normal recipients in the Middle Ages, neither the faith of the church nor the desire of the parents could make good the lack of actual water-baptism.[327]

The rigorous medieval teaching was approved and codified at the Council of Trent, which taught that the sacraments of the New Law are necessary to the grace of justification, and that baptism in particular is absolutely necessary to salvation.[328] In the *Catechism* a special warning

---

326. Lombard, IV, *Dist.* 4 D, E.
327. S., III, qu. 68.
328. C.D., Sess. VII, *Sacram. Canon*, 5.

was addressed to both parents and also converted infidels, although it was conceded to the latter that "in cases of accident their intent and determination to receive baptism and their repentance for their previous ill-spent life will suffice them to grace of justification".[329] It was emphasized, however, that even for adults the way of baptism was the better way, since it provided a good test of intention, and was a safeguard against all possible risks. To cover the possibility of emergencies the *Rituale Romanum* allowed baptism in any place, at any time, and by any person, even in the case of adults undergoing baptismal instruction.[330]

The severe teaching concerning the damnation of unbaptized infants involved a special problem, for many theologians felt that children who had not committed any actual sin could hardly be classified with the rest of the damned. Even Augustine had argued in favour of a milder punishment, and there was a strong school which claimed that this consisted only in the deprivation of the vision of God without any pains of sense. Indeed, some writers even suggested that unbaptized infants could obtain a real measure of happiness in the special department of the nether regions reserved for them, although naturally this happiness could not be compared with the bliss of heaven which they had forfeited. The rigorists would usually concede that their physical torments would be proportionate to their lesser sensibility.[331]

It was almost inevitable that an ignorant and ill-instructed populace would understand the doctrine of absolute necessity superstitiously. Popular writings like those collected by Manning from the fourteenth century prove that this was the case, and they help us to see why it was that Wycliffe and his reformed successors attacked the traditional view with such vehemence. In the poem *Handlyng Synne*, for example, we read:

> "*Adam's synne was so grefe,*
> *That thyr was to God none so lefe,*
> *That he ne shulde to helle gone,*
> *But he wasse in the fonte stone.*"

Again, Hilton pointed out that the soul which is not baptized "hath no likeness of God", and he denounced as a heresy the view that

---

329. C.T., II, 2, qu. 23, 24.
330. *Rituale Romanum*: Bapt. On the attitude of the Eastern church cf. Schaff, p. 423.
331. On this whole question see *Catholic Encyclopedia*, Art. Baptism.

"Jews and Turks by keeping of their own law may be saved, though they believe not in Jesus Christ".[332] It is true, of course, that the writers of these works had some grasp of the doctrinal basis, but it may be doubted whether the ordinary people did. All that they knew was that the child was guilty and under the threat of eternal damnation until it was cleansed and renewed by baptism. And since baptism was administered in a language which was not understood, it did not carry with it any clear meaning, and could hardly be thought of except as a necessary and powerful charm. Against this view Wycliffe seems to have argued that the sacrament is not necessary to any who die in infancy,[333] but his protest merely called down episcopal and conciliar denunciations, and even at a later date "Wycliffe of damnable memory" was still condemned for his conclusion "that it is presumptuous to say, that infants dying without baptism will not be saved".[334] In defence of the established view the usual references were made to John 3:5, Augustine, and ecclesiastical custom, including the constant refusal of the church to permit the burial of the non-baptized in consecrated ground.[335]

The failure of Wycliffe's protest meant a perpetuation of the official teaching, and in the sixteenth century it could still be presented with blood-curdling eloquence. As an example we may cite the passage quoted by Pierce from the *Drych Cristian* of Gruffydd Roberts, in which the writer reminds catholics of their high calling and privilege "among the thousands that have gone and will go to hell for want of baptism. Know that there are thousands of thousands of little children in hell, without hope of mercy, who never have thought any evil, and yet are lost because they never received baptism to cleanse them from the sin they received from Adam."[336] The same doctrine was stated even in the early Reformation formularies, for the *Ten Articles* spoke of baptism as necessary for the attaining of everlasting life, and the *King's Book* repeated the phrase with the addition "according to the words of Christ" and the explanation that baptism is our incorporation into the church, outside which "neither infants nor no man can be saved".[337] The *Bishop's Book* had been even more explicit: "Insomuch that infants and children dying in their infancy shall undoubtedly be saved thereby [by

---

332. B.L. Manning, *The People's Faith in the time of Wyclif*, pp. 52 f.
333. E.R., p. 365.
334. E.R. p., 386.
335. See Woodford's *Fasciculus Rerum*.
336. Pierce, *op. cit.*, p. 140.
337. K.B., p. 42.

baptism], and else not." The sentence reappeared in the *King's Book*, but without the dogmatic "and else not", and it was in the amended form that it found its way first into the Order of Confirmation and later into that of Holy Baptism.[338] Possibly the omission of the words indicates that belief in an absolute necessity was already weakening under the pressure of the Reformation. In *Cranmer's Catechism* there was a similar silence with regard to the fate of the unbaptized children of Christians, although no hope was held out for the children of heathen parents dying without the sacrament.[339] The 1549 Prayer Book had a request that the baptized child might be received into the ark of Christ's church and so saved from perishing, but the final phrase was dropped in the 1552 revision, together with the reference to the destruction of Pharaoh and his hosts.

Throughout the Reformation period the traditionalists made every possible effort to maintain an absolute necessity of baptism. As early as 1530 Warham had condemned the article that "infants be holy and clene though they have not receyved baptysme, because their parents be holy and clene".[340] Again, in the examination of John Lambert, inquiry was made concerning the necessity of baptism and the legitimacy of lay-baptism.[341] The Men of Devon protested that insistence upon a public administration jeopardized the salvation of sick infants: they had evidently not read or not understood the new book.[342] With the accession of Mary, Bonner exhorted his clergy "diligently to move and exhort their parishioners how and in what manner their children should be baptized in time of necessity",[343] and many heretics were warned of the dangers incurred when Papist baptism was refused. Thus Harpsfield threatened Haukes: "Admit your child die unchristened, what a heavy case you stand in."

> *Haukes*: "I admit that. If it do, what then?"
> *Harpsfield*: "How is original sin washed away?"

When Haukes claimed the promise of 1 Corinthians 7 Bonner retaliated by quoting John 3:5.[344] In a similar argument between Smith on the one side and Bonner and Mordant on the other, Mordant affirmed his belief with an oath: "By our Lady, sir, I believe that if my

---

338. E Daniel, *The Prayer Book*, p. 432.
339. *Cranmer's Catechism*, p. 50.
340. Foxe, VII, p. 498.
341. *Ibid.*, V, p. 182.
342. Strype, *Cranmer*, p. 96.
343. Burnet, *op. cit.*, II, 2, p. 15.
344. Foxe, VII, pp. 103 f.

child die without baptism, he is damned."[345] It is not clear whether the personal application was hypothetical or not. Langdale in his debate with Woodman leaned upon Mark 16, although this text had the inconvenience of demanding faith as well as baptism, and of the two faith seemed to be the less dispensable, But Langdale boldly concluded that "all that be not baptized, be damned".[346]

The revolt when it came was not against the underlying presupposition that salvation is only by the grace of God. Nor was it against the principle that the sacrament itself is a means of grace. It was against the tacit assumption that baptism is the only means of the divine operation, the claim that grace is bound to this sacrament by an indissoluble bond. And the revolt gained in power in the sixteenth century because of the new clarity on these issues which came with the rediscovery of the Pauline doctrine of justification.

Yet strangely enough, Luther himself did not make any clear or definite stand against the traditional doctrine of necessity. He was more concerned, perhaps, to find a right place for the sacrament than to oust it from a wrong. He maintained a high view of baptism as he did of both the dominical sacraments. He certainly thought it of sufficient general necessity to warrant a private administration in cases of emergency. And he had no desire to open the door to the Anabaptists by a disparagement of infant baptism. If pressed, he could hardly have held the view that the mere lack of baptism will exclude Christian children from all hope of salvation. His final conception was not sacramentalist, but evangelical. Yet his emphasis was always upon the ordinary necessity rather than the extraordinary exception. So striking was this emphasis that opponents could mark off his teaching on the subject from that of Bucer and Calvin.[347]

With Zwingli the matter was otherwise. He did of course defend infant baptism, and to that extent he could urge the importance of its administration. But his very defence carried with it a denial of the absolute necessity. Christian children had a right to the sign of the covenant because by divine election they were already members of the covenant. The sign itself did not effect covenant-membership: it merely signified a covenant-membership already existing. If the sign lacked, the covenant-membership, and therefore salvation, still remained.

---

345. Foxe, VII, p. 352.
346. *Ibid.*, VIII, pp. 356 f.
347. Cf. du Val, *Les Contrarietez et Contredicts*, p. xxix (Paris, 1561).

A difficulty in this view is that it seems to make the sign futile and unnecessary, at any rate in the case of infants. But against this Zwingli could point out that the sign is ordained by God, and ought therefore to be administered to all who have the right to it. A further difficulty is that baptism is reduced to a mere sign of grace, and is not in any sense a means of grace. Zwingli himself unashamedly admitted this fact, as far as the external action is concerned, for he argued that the outward sign is not able either to cleanse from sin or even to confirm faith. On the other hand he did not preclude an inward operation of the Spirit in fulfilment of the sign or even in conjunction with it. What he denied was that the external rite is indispensable to that inward operation.[348] A final difficulty is that in his anxiety to ascribe salvation to the infants of Christians only by the covenant and election Zwingli commits himself to what is virtually a denial of original guilt.[349] The traditionalists argued that baptism is absolutely necessary for the remission of original sin. Zwingli retorted not merely that water-baptism cannot cleanse from sin, but that there is no original sin to be cleansed. In this respect he approximated closely to the teaching of the Anabaptists, for although Hübmaier retained some doctrine of original sin,[350] the majority of Anabaptists were frankly Pelagian in outlook.[351] It must be emphasized, however, that in Zwingli's case it was not so much an original defect, or disability, or even sin, which was denied, but the guilt which was supposed to attach to it. And if there was no guilt of original sin, there was no obstacle to salvation without the baptismal washing: indeed, Zwingli could hold out hope for the children of the heathen, as well as for those who had the privilege of a Christian descent.

Calvin adopted the same general position as Zwingli, but he argued it with a new perspicuity and consistency. Calvin would not deny to baptism a certain general necessity, but as he saw it it was a formal and not an absolute necessity, a necessity of precept and not of efficacy. Baptism was a sacrament demanded by Christ Himself, and certain specific promises had been annexed to it. It was, moreover, a definite means of grace. Therefore "if any one of his own accord abstains from the use of the sacrament ... he contemns Christ, spurns His grace, and

348. C.R., IV, pp. 307 f.
349. *Loc. cit.*
350. *Ibid.*, p. 624.
351. D.A., p. 172; B.R.N., IV, p. 418.

quenches His Spirit".[352] It is true, of course, that on occasion God can and does work by extraordinary means, but "it does not follow we are to cast away anything which he ordained for our salvation, as if it were superfluous".[353] The necessity of the sacrament was the necessity of not refusing the sign and means of grace which God Himself had ordained and instituted. But this did not mean "that all who have not obtained baptism must perish",[354] and Calvin attacked the traditionalist teaching with vigour. He laughed at the solemn discussion, to which it gave rise: "Whether an infant, at the point of death, if water is not at hand, ought to be plunged into a well, rather than committed to God to wait the event", or, "whether in the absence of ordinary water an infant ought to be baptized with lotion, or with artificial or distilled water".[355] He pointed out that to maintain an absolute necessity is to fail to perceive that "baptism is not added to faith as if it were the half of the cause of our salvation, but as a testimony".[356] He condemned outright all irregular administrations, arguing that it is better to omit the rite altogether than to profane it.[357] According to his view, if Christians are under the yoke of an absolute necessity, their "condition becomes worse than that of God's ancient people",[358] but this he could not allow. So long as "in omitting the sign, there is neither sloth, nor contempt, nor negligence, we are safe from all danger".[359] In relation to the much quoted verse in John 3, he flatly denied that there was any possible reference to water-baptism. What Christ really meant when He uttered these words was that "without the inward purgation which it is the office of the Holy Ghost to accomplish", and which is signified in water, "it is impossible to enter the kingdom of heaven". The word water was, in fact, simply a pointer to the Spirit. Calvin defended this interpretation on the ground that baptism with the Holy Ghost and with fire does not necessitate a literal baptism with fire, but that fire is another symbolical intimation of the Spirit.[360]

The deep impression made by Calvin's teaching is at once evident from the works of his contemporaries and successors. Knox, for example, followed Calvin in arguing for a necessity of precept while denying an absolute necessity: "Without injurie infants cannot be debarred from the common syne of God's children", "neither yet is this outwarde

---

352. *Tracts*, II, p. 85.
353. *Ibid.*, p. 236.
354. *Harmony of the Evangel.*, p. 387.
355. *Tracts*, I, p. 73.
356. *Harmony of the Evangel.*, p. 387.
357. *Tracts*, II, p. 319.
358. *Instit.*, IV, 15, 20 f.
359. *Loc. cit.*
360. *Comm. on John* 3:5.

action of such necessitie, that the lacke thereof shuld be prejudiciall to their salvation, yf that prevented by death, thei may not conveniently be presented to the church".[361] A similar balance was preserved by Beza, who on the one hand saw a "need to extol, and magnifie the dygnitie and lawfull use of the sacraments", but on the other denied that the necessity was so absolute that "those which have faith and yet have not the means to be partakers of the sacrament, shall ... be despised or excluded from the salvation".[362] Writing to Grindal, Beza pointed out the danger of making salvation dependent on the "seales annexed unto the covenaunte" and therefore "on the diligence or negligencies of ye parents".[363] The later Reformed theologians rejected private baptism largely on the ground that there is no absolute necessity. Heidegger even suggested that if there were such a necessity it would still be wrong to try to save men in defiance of the divinely appointed order.[364]

In England there had been a long tradition of protest against the belief in an absolute necessity, and Wycliffe had already made some pertinent criticisms of it. Perhaps the main reason for his rejection was his refusal to believe that God cannot and will not "save an infant unless an old woman or someone perform this ceremony of baptism". But again, his doctrine of the twofold baptism made it impossible for him to accept the external rite as the test of the internal work, for after all, could not Christ "without any such washing, spiritually baptize, and by consequence save infants?"[365] The difficulty posed by John 3:5 was obviated by referring to the water which flowed from the side of Christ.[366] The spread of Wycliffe's views had been prevented by the official persecution, but his teaching was obviously not without its influence, for at a later date Walter Brute made the same distinction between an outward and an inward baptism, deducing that without a knowledge of the inward work of the Spirit we cannot know whether an infant has the true water, faith, and is therefore saved.[367] Again, Thomas Arundel in 1409 was compelled to abjure amongst other heresies the belief "that the infant, though he die unbaptized, shall be saved",[368] and a few years later, in 1424, some

---

361. Knox, IV, p. 186.
362. B.P.S., p. 35.
363. P.M., p. 53.
364. R.D., *Bapt.*
365. *Trialogus*, p. 160.
366. *Ibid*, pp. 156 f.
367. Foxe, III, p. 168.
368. *Ibid.*, p. 249.

citizens of Norwich were charged with denying water-baptism altogether because they opposed "the opinion of such as think such children to be damned who depart before they should come to their baptism".[369]

By the early sixteenth century, of course, Lollardy had spent its force, but certain Lollard groups still remained, and it was probably under Wycliffite influence that in 1511 John Browne and "the five blessed martyrs of Kent" denied the necessity of baptism or confirmation to salvation.[370] The rise of Lutheran teaching gave a new and powerful impetus to the lingering native revolt, and in the first period of the English Reformation both Tyndale and Frith attacked the traditionalist teaching. Tyndale based his argument primarily on the covenant-relationship, from which he deduced that "the infants that die unbaptized of us Christians are in as good case as those that die baptized".[371] He could also allow that adults who believed in Christ and lived a Christian life might well be saved even without the sacrament.[372] This latter view was more loosely expressed by Bainham, who claimed that "if a Turk, a Jew or a Saracen, do trust in God, and keep his law, he is a good Christian man, though he be not baptized".[373] But stated in this more general way it seemed to carry implications which the majority of the Reformers would not be prepared to accept. For Frith, the main error in the traditionalists' doctrine was that it put too "great confidence in the outward sign".[374] The Scottish martyr Hamilton was feeling after the same view when he expressed doubts concerning that assurance which is given merely by an external administration of water.[375]

During the Edwardian phase, the English Reformers dealt with the question at some length, for they realized that a vital principle was at stake. The Reformed position was clearly stated by Hooper, who acknowledged a general necessity of baptism, but thought it "ill to condemn the children of Christians that die without baptism, of whose salvation we are assured: *Ego Deus tuus et seminis tui post te*".[376] Indeed, Hooper was ready to "judge well of the infants of infidels who have none other sin in them but original".[377] But he was none too sure about this latter point, for elsewhere he claimed that the extra-baptismal salvation

---

369. Foxe, IV, p. 589.
370. *Ibid.*, V, p. 648.
371. Tyndale, P.S., I, p. 350.
372. *Ibid.* p. 351.
373. Foxe, IV, p. 703.
374. Frith, B.R., p. 91.
375. Foxe, IV, p. 560.
376. Hooper, P.S., I, p. 129.
377. *Loc. cit.*

applies only to "the children of the faithful, unto whom the promises of God do appertain, and not to the infidels and reprobate".[378]

The emphasis of Cranmer was rather like that of Luther. He was more concerned to show the need of the sacrament than to proclaim its dispensability. He told the Men of Devon, for example, that the administration of private baptism was not "letted" where necessity compelled,[379] and he complained bitterly when the traditionalists tried to prove infant baptism only from tradition and not from Scripture.[380] But while he insisted upon the general necessity, he rejected "as impious the unscrupulous superstition of those who so entirely confine the grace of God the Holy Spirit to the elements of the sacraments as to affirm that no infant of Christians will obtain eternal salvation, who shall have died before he could be brought to baptism, which we consider to be far otherwise".[381] Obviously the necessity urged by Cranmer was a necessity of precept only, not an absolute necessity.

The conclusion of Becon was similar. On the one side he could say that those who "cast away baptism" "had no portion in the inheritance of God".[382] But on the other he perceived that it is only the inward baptism of the Spirit which is absolutely necessary.[383] He had several arguments in favour of this view. First, he pointed out that it is the divine promise which saves, not the ceremony.[384] Second, he thought that to base salvation upon the contingency of baptism is inconsistent with the divine election.[385] Third, he could cite the Old Law, under which the covenant had not been overthrown by a want of circumcision.[386] Fourth, he could refer to the case of martyrs.[387] And fifth, he argued that "the Holy Spirit is not so bound to the water that it cannot work his office where the water wanteth".[388] As far as unbaptized infidels were concerned, he thought it better to leave them to God, "to whom they either stand or fall", but he was confident that "even among the Turks, and other heathen, there are many spiritually baptized, and so are saved".[389] The text John 3:5 was applied by him only to "such as may conveniently be baptized", and he

---

378. *Ibid.*, II, Art. 62.
379. Strype, *Cranmer*, II, p. 96.
380. Cranmer, P.S., II, p. 60.
381. *Reformatio Legum, De Bapt.*
382. Becon, P.S., II, p. 215.
383. *Ibid.*, p. 203.
384. *Ibid.*, p. 216.
385. *Ibid.*, pp. 221-222.
386. *Ibid.*, p. 223.

387. *Ibid.*, p. 217.
388. *Ibid.*, III, p. 617.
389. *Ibid.*, II, pp. 214, 221.

quoted Bernard (*Epist.77*), Ambrose (De *Morte*) and Augustine (*con. Don.*, 1, 4) in favour of this view.[390]

The main concern of the later Anglicans was to defend the retention of private baptism, but against the traditionalists they still contended that there is no absolute necessity. Rogers pointed out that this denial of an absolute necessity did not involve the denial of infant baptism, which was "the runagate Hill's report".[391] The misconception was of long standing, for it had appeared in Mary's reign in the discussion between Jeffrey and Palmer:

> *Jeffrey*: "Ye have forgotten yourself, i wis; for ye write that children may be saved without it."
> *Palmer*: "So I write, and so I say."
> *Jeffrey*: "Then it is not necessary to be frequented and continued in the church."
> *Palmer*: "Your argument is not good, master doctor."[392]

And it was not good because the necessity of precept remained even where an absolute necessity was rejected. Yet while they maintained this general necessity, the Reformers could not return to the older view, which seemed to restrict and confine the freedom and sovereignty of the Holy Spirit. Even Harpsfield had been impressed by this argument, for in face of the affirmation of Bradford: "I will not tie God where he is not bound", he had had to concede that God might show mercy to infants "whose parents desire baptism for them, and may not have it".[393] It was the same consideration which decided Jewel, who cited the penitent thief as an example of the operation of the Spirit apart from the sacrament.[394] Fulke developed the same line of thought in relation to John 3:5, which referred to the working of the Holy Spirit either with or without water-baptism.[395] At the close of the Elizabethan period Hooker returned to a literal interpretation of John 3:5,[396] but there can be no doubt that the Elizabethans as a whole rejected the idea of an absolute necessity. Haddon,[397] Some,[398] Bridges,[399] Sparke,[400] Barlowe,[401] and Babington[402] may all be quoted as witnesses to this truth, for all of them distinguished

---

390. Becon, P.S., II, p. 224.

391. Rogers, P.S., p. 279.

392. Foxe, VIII, p. 216.

393. *Ibid.*, VII, p. 168.

394. Jewel, P.S., II, p. 1107.

395. Fulke, P.S., II, p. 392.

396. L.E.P., V, 61, 1.

397. E.B.I., p. 356 f.

398. *Loc. cit.*

399. Bridges, *Defence*, p. 564.

400. Sparke, *Brotherly Persuasion*, pp. 72-73.

401. Barlowe, *Defence*, pp. 141-147.

402. Babington, *Notes on Genesis*, p. 53.

between an "absolute, simple and inevitable necessity, and a necessity of consequence, of condition and of conveniency", and they agreed in rejecting the former and maintaining only the latter. Even Hooker did not argue that exclusion from baptism meant inevitable exclusion from salvation, but only that there is a greater assurance where the condition of John 3:5 has been fulfilled.[403]

The general position of the Elizabethan Anglican is, then, hardly open to question, but a certain obscurity was thrown over it by the controversy concerning private baptism. In this controversy, of course, the alleged necessity or non-necessity of the sacrament was not by any means the only or even the decisive issue. Superficially, however, this might easily appear to be the case, for the Puritans tried to exploit the supposed doctrinal implication, and the Anglicans certainly emerged from the controversy with a different ecclesiastical and theological emphasis. It is, therefore, important to consider the Puritan view, and to see in what respects it differed from the accepted teaching.

The Puritan doctrine of baptismal necessity derived directly from Reformed sources. In this regard it differed hardly at all from the Anglican. Neither party claimed an absolute necessity, and both admitted a necessity of precept. The difference arose in relation to the urgency and compass of the necessity allowed. On the one side, the Anglicans felt that the commandment of Christ ought to be carried out at all costs. Therefore, if danger threatened, it was better to obey by baptizing privately – lay-baptism was at first permitted although not enjoined – rather than to risk waiting for a public administration. On the other side, the Puritans did not think the necessity sufficiently great to justify a departure from the normal practice of congregational baptism. Behind the Puritan protest there was no doubt a real fear that the retention of private baptism would foster the belief in a necessity which was absolute rather than contingent. Indeed, it is likely enough that many of the priests and people who had accepted the Elizabethan Settlement on authority did subscribe to this view. But it must be insisted, and the evidence makes it absolutely conclusive, that the Anglican leaders themselves had no wish either to maintain or to foster the traditional teaching.

The quarrel about private baptism dated at least from the Frankfurt exile, when the extremer elements had tried to set aside the 1552 order.

---

403. L.E.P., V, 61.

However, it was not until the return under Elizabeth that the struggle intensified, and at first it was overshadowed by the vestiarian controversy. Cartwright eventually emerged as the main exponent of Precisian views, and in his defences of the *Admonition* he argued, first, that the doctrine of an absolute necessity is the true source of private baptism, and second, that this doctrine rests upon a false deduction from John 3:5.[404] Cartwright would go to the extreme that "even if infants which die without baptism should be assuredly damned (which is most false), yet ought not the order which God hath set in His church to be broken after this sort".[405] The commandment of Christ was not simply to give baptism, but to give baptism according to a certain rule and order. No necessity could legitimatize a breach of that order.

In the mass of Puritan propaganda which flooded the country many attempts were made to foist upon the official formularies the doctrine of an absolute necessity. It was claimed that the Prayer Book "makes baptisme a thing of absolute necessitie to salvation",[406] particular objection being taken against the rubric concerning the salvation of baptized infants.[407] In a conference at Lambeth, Whitgift was directly accused by Travers of doubting whether there can be any salvation without baptism. When he appealed to Calvin, his opponent claimed that the necessity taught by Calvin was not the same as that taught by the Archbishop.[408] Elsewhere Travers argued that the provision of private baptism and communion indicated a false view not only of their necessity but also of their efficacy. He would concede a necessity of precept, but he did not regard it as contempt or neglect to allow a child to die unbaptized in default of a public administration.[409] But it was over this lesser point of the interpretation of the necessity of precept that the Anglicans really differed from their accusers, and if the Puritans had not been blinded by anxiety or prejudice they must surely have seen how irrelevant were the more serious theological charges which they brought.

The situation was further complicated by the Separatist contention that the only true sacraments are those which are administered in a pure church, i.e., the Brownist or Barrowist. But this meant that the

---

404. Whitgift, P.S., I, p. 521.
405. *Ibid.*, p. 537.
406. S.P.R., I, 78.
407. *Ibid.*, I, 131.
408. *Ibid.*, I,173.
409. Travers, *Ecclesiastical Discipline*, p. 13.

bulk of the population was not really baptized at all, and since not even the Separatists could hope for a mass rebaptization, they had to conclude either that the sacrament was generally dispensable, or that only the Separatists are elect and saved. In effect, then, even the necessity of precept was dissolved by the Separatist teaching, for it was sadly admitted that in the majority of cases "baptism could by no means be had".[410]

In their defence against the various objectors the Anglicans make it clear beyond all possible doubt what the official view of baptismal necessity really was. Ridley had been an early spokesman when the controversies first arose in Frankfurt. He had rejected any absolute necessity, but had asked for Scriptural proof that no baptism is better than private baptism, and in default of such proof had commended "that which the old ancient writers do allow".[411] In other words, the precept of Christ is better observed by private baptism than by omission, this view being supported by the primitive teaching and practice of the church.

When the controversy reached its height under Elizabeth it was Whitgift who championed the official doctrine. Against its critics he claimed that the Articles show baptism not to be absolutely necessary to salvation,[412] and exerted himself to clear the Prayer Book rubric of any suggestion that grace is conferred *ex opere operate*.[413] Replying to Cartwright, Whitgift established the fact that what he contended for was only a necessity of precept: "Although the necessity of baptism is not so tied to the sacraments, that whosoever hath the external sign shall therefore be saved, yet it is so tied to them, that none can be saved that willingly and wittingly is void of them."[414] In favour of this type of necessity he could refer to such authorities as Zwingli, Bucer and Calvin,[415] and he could point out that the lack of baptism had sometimes been regarded as "a probable sign and token of reprobation".[416] Cleverly, if rather unfairly, he urged that all the arguments which could be used against the Anabaptists could be turned with equal force against those who refused private baptism.[417] But his main contention was obviously this. Baptism is not in any sense mechanically necessary, but it has

---

410. Pierce, *op. cit.*, p. 349.
411. Ridley, P.S., p. 534.
412. S.P.R., I, 173.
413. Strype, *Whitgift*, I, p. 257.
414. Whitgift, P.S., II, p. 537.
415. *Ibid.*, p. 538.
416. *Loc. cit.*
417. *Ibid.*, pp. 521-523.

been commanded by Christ and therefore it must not be neglected. In cases of emergency, a failure to administer it privately constitutes neglect, for the commandment itself is greater than the circumstances of its fulfilment. To urge that the child is saved in any case may be true, but it is an extension of allowable exceptions for which we have no definite warrant. The Puritans, of course, could not accept this, for they did not agree that a private administration is a genuine fulfilment of the commandment of Christ, and therefore they denied that there was any neglect or contempt except where public baptism was resisted. In other words, the exception extends to all cases where a public administration does not prove to be possible.

The controversy came to a head at the Hampton Court Conference, and although Bancroft went beyond the arguments of Whitgift at some points, he did not let go the main contentions, that there is no *ex opere operato* grace, and no absolute necessity. The position of Bancroft was not dissimilar to that of Hooker. The baptized have an evident assurance which the unbaptized do not have. They have the certainty of a sealed promise rather than the mere possibility of a secret mercy. Therefore, "the case put, that the state of infants dying unbaptized was uncertain, and dying baptized there was evident assurance that it was saved, who having any religion in him would not speedily by any means procure his child to be baptized, and rather ground his action upon Christ's promise than his omission thereof upon God's secret judgement ?"[418] There was nothing essentially unreformed about this position, but it is ominous that the clear covenant-membership of the child by descent was no longer recognized, and that the question of salvation or damnation had again come to the fore and that of the necessity of precept receded. On the doctrine of election which Bancroft still held, death without the sacrament might easily be construed as a definite mark of rejection, at any rate where a private administration had been refused. But the Puritan resistance to private baptism could hardly be classified as the wicked "contemning" of which the earlier Reformers had spoken. To that extent the logic of Bancroft was not uninfluenced by his prejudices. The truth was that both parties felt that an important principle was at stake and neither could avoid misunderstanding and misrepresenting the other. That was the real tragedy of the Puritan controversy.

---

418. Strype, *Whitgift*, II, pp. 494-495.

Hooker himself, of course, was prepared to go even further than Bancroft. As we have seen already, he maintained that John 3:5 must be taken at its face value, for "nothing is more dangerous than the licentious and deluding art" of giving a fanciful meaning to a verse where the plain meaning does not present any difficulties. The text did not mean anything at all unless it taught the necessity of both water and Spirit, the one as means and the other as cause. Hooker did not wish to revive the severer doctrine of an absolute necessity, and he refrained from passing judgment upon the unbaptized. But as he saw it, John 3:5 was a definite barrier to the laxity which Puritanism would inevitably encourage. God Himself had commanded us to be baptized: therefore "it is not for us to examine Him, whether unbaptized men may be saved, but seriously to do that which is required". At root, this was simply the main Anglican contention that the necessity of precept overrides all other considerations, but, with Bancroft, Hooker introduced a new uncertainty concerning the fate of the unbaptized, and his use of John 3:5 gave a higher importance to the sacrament as a means of grace which is ordinarily or generally indispensable.[419]

There can be no doubt that even in Bancroft and Hooker the Anglicans did not return to the medieval view. For that reason their defence of private baptism could never be convincing to the traditionalist, for if baptism is not the essential means to effect a primary justification, there is no real urgency in the matter. But if the Anglicans would not accept an absolute necessity, they certainly emphasized the necessity of precept even at the expense of order and regularity in administration. And it was for this that they came under criticism from the extremists. The Puritans agreed with the traditionalists that in the last resort only an absolute necessity can justify a breaking of the regular order. To allow private baptism for any other cause can serve no useful purpose and may even result in the reintroduction or confirmation of error.

On the Anglican side, however, it may be stated, first, that even if baptism is not absolutely necessary to salvation, it is still a divinely instituted sacrament which ought to be given wherever possible, and second, that the authority of the sacrament is safeguarded only when provision is made for its general administration either in public or if necessary in private. A concession was finally made to Puritan scruples when lay-baptism was forbidden, but it was still maintained that

---

419. L.E.P., V, 59-60.

regularity ought not to be secured at the cost of a plain and overriding duty: to do that which we are commanded to do. It could even be argued that to insist upon a public administration is to introduce a new and sinister legalism, indeed a superstition, into the evangelical faith. The Anglican attitude has been well summed up by Burnet: "The Reformers steered a middle course: they judged the sacraments necessary, where they could be had, as appointments instituted by Christ; and though they thought it more expedient to have all baptism done at the church in the fonts than in private houses ... yet since our Saviour had said That where two or three are gathered together, He will be in the midst of them, they thought it savoured too much of a superstition to the walls or fonts of churches to tie this action so to these, that where children, either through infirmity, or the sharpness of the weather, could not be without danger carried to the church, they should be denied baptism."[420]

---

420. Burnet, *op. cit.*, II, pp. 159-160.

2

The Participants

(1) The Minister

Baptism as the action of washing in water necessarily involves participants, and in a developed theology of baptism it is inevitable that there should be some inquiry concerning those who take part in the ceremony. The inquiry has a twofold reference; on the one hand to the minister and his commission, and on the other to the recipient and his qualification. In the sixteenth century such an inquiry was not in any way academic or ecclesiastical, for if God Himself had instituted the sacrament it was obvious that no one ought either to administer or to receive it except in accordance with the divine will. In the case of those who pleaded an absolute necessity the further problem arose of the legitimacy of irregular administrations in time of emergency. And in every case it had to be asked whether baptism could be rightly given by those who were qualified technically but deficient in moral or spiritual character. The well-being if not the salvation of thousands of people might depend upon the answers to these apparently abstruse and theoretical questions.

Now as far as the minister was concerned, at the deepest level it had always been recognized that God Himself was not merely the author but also the true minister of baptism. The exact relationship between God and the human instrument called for some discussion but the ordinary need of both a divine and a human administrator was generally conceded. In the early church, for example, Cyprian had refused to accept heretical or schismatical baptisms largely on the ground that God is not present in them: "Either the Spirit must be there, or the washing is not baptism."[1] And the very same argument was used against Cyprian, for if God is the true baptizer, why should the opinions of the human instrument affect the validity of the administration?

It was in the context of the Cyprianic controversy that the Schoolmen considered the problem. As Lombard pointed out, the power of the sacrament is with God, for only God can forgive sins. But God has chosen to work in and through the human minister, therefore we may

---

1. *Epist.* LXXIII, 10-11.

say that He does not work without the minister, just as the minister cannot work without God. God gives the invisible grace, the minister the visible sign, by which it is mediated.[2] Thomas stated the same view, but in a different way. Baptism had two distinct causes, the principal on the one hand, which is the Blessed Trinity, and the instrumental on the other, which is the appointed minister.[3] The teaching of the Schoolmen was reproduced in the formularies of Trent which ascribed both justification and the sacraments "to one and the same God in Christ".[4]

On the Protestant side Luther laid a new emphasis upon the fact that God Himself is the only author and true minister of baptism. It was upon this belief that he grounded his confidence in the efficacy of the sacrament, at least to the believer. Because of it baptism could be given a high status as a testimony to the divine work and promise. It came by the hands of man, but it did not belong to or proceed from man. Man baptized in so far as he performed the external act. But he did not baptize to the extent that he acted only in the name of God. God was the true baptizer, "pledging His own honour in baptism and putting forth His own power".[5] Luther did not attempt to distinguish between that which man does and that which God does in baptism. In the strict sense, it is God who does everything,[6] and from this he deduced his evangelical message of baptismal assurance. At this point as everywhere it was the doctrine of justification which really determined the understanding.

Calvin saw a new application of the belief that God is the true minister, for upon it he based his identification of the baptism of John with Christian baptism. Commenting on Matthew 3:11 he pointed out that "John merely distinguishes between himself and other ministers of baptism on the one hand, and the power of Christ on the other",[7] i.e., between the human and the divine minister. The phrase "laver of regeneration" was interpreted along similar lines: "When Scripture speaks of the laver of regeneration, it joins the power of Christ with the ministry of man."[8] There is a clear connection here between the belief that God is the true and inward minister and the distinction between

---

2. Lombard, IV, *Dist.* 5 A.

3. S., III, qu. 67, 5.

4. C.T., II, 1, qu. 18.

5. W.A., XXX, 1, p. 213.

6. Cf. Hirsch, *Hilfsbuch zum Studium der Dogmatik*, p. 222.

7. *Harmony of the Evangel.* On Matthew 3:11.

8. *Loc. cit.*

the two baptisms, the baptism of water and the baptism of the Spirit. As Beza put it, "the internal operation of God" is the true work of baptism.[9]

It was upon this point that Cranmer seized when he used the example of baptism to clarify his teaching concerning the divine presence and operation in the Supper. He perceived a real presence of Christ in baptism "to clothe and apparel us with His own self",[10] but it was the spiritual presence of the true author and minister, not by an incomprehensible transubstantiation of the element, but in an internal operation in the believer. The teaching is obviously similar to that of Calvin.[11]

Apart from this more or less incidental reference the Anglican writers hardly referred to this aspect, although it clearly underlay the doctrine of Article 26, and all the endless controversies concerning irregular administrations. The Reformers accepted the traditional belief that God is the true minister, but they differed from the traditionalists in their conception of the relationship between the divine and the human ministries. On the one hand the relationship had been thought of as for the most part fixed and static. Where the human minister worked, God would also work. On the other hand the relationship was living and dynamic. Both God and man worked in the full baptism, but the external administration did not of itself guarantee the inward operation. The two ministries were still related, but not in that rigid or automatic sense which would involve a spiritual working *ex opere operato*.

God was the true author and minister, but the instrumental administration had obviously been committed to men. Yet only to authorized men, for, as the older theologians saw it, God had not left the question of authorization to be settled haphazardly by ecclesiastical enactment or historical development, but had commissioned a definite body of men to act as His ministers. In special cases the commission might perhaps be extended, but normally the privilege and responsibility of administering the sacrament belonged only to a specific class.

Now in the first instance, as the early church believed, the commandment to baptize had been addressed only to the apostles, but through the apostles the commission had been transmitted to their successors, who rightly or wrongly came to be identified with the monarchical bishops. It was to the bishops, then, that the work of baptizing properly

---

9. Q.R.C., 107.
10. Cranmer, P.S., I, p. 356.
11. Cf. too the doctrine of Bucer, Anrich, *op. cit.*, p. 128.

belonged. It would be tedious to repeat here the patristic evidence for this view, which may be consulted in detail in such works as those of Bingham and Waterland. But we may note that at bottom it rested almost entirely upon the statement of Ignatius of Antioch that without the bishop it is not lawful to baptize or to celebrate the eucharist.[12]

But although the bishop was the primary minister of baptism, the presbyter also had full authority to administer the sacrament. In the early period it was often maintained that he had this authority only by delegation from the bishop: thus Tertullian ascribed the responsibility first to the bishop, the chief presbyter, and then on the bishop's authority to the presbyters and deacons. But as the public baptism of adult converts came more and more to be replaced by infant baptisms, which were often hurried and private, the importance of the priests increased and that of the bishop declined. Indeed, in Scholastic discussions the original distinction had almost been forgotten, for although the bishop had received a higher status and dignity as a feudal overlord, his spiritual functions hardly differed at all from those of the priests except in respect of ordination and confirmation.

Thomas, it is true, did consider the view that only the bishop may properly baptize, and he saw three possible reasons in its favour: first, that the commandment to baptize is addressed only to the bishop; second, that only the chief pastor ought to admit into the congregation; and third, that baptism is greater than consecration, which is reserved for the bishop. But against this he pointed out that the priest is authorized to celebrate the sacrament of Christ's body and blood, and that baptism admits only to the lowest rank in the Christian community. At one point he does accept the view that the bishop baptizes vicariously through the priest, but the main drift of his argument is that the priest is authorized to baptize not so much by delegation as by virtue of his own office.[13] Lombard was of a similar mind, for he quoted Isidorus to the effect that the bishop and the priest are the authorized ministers.[14] The earlier distinction had virtually disappeared in the sixteenth century, when the parish priest was described as the ordinary minister.[15] In strict theory, no doubt, the bishop was still the true administrator, and adult converts were to be referred always to him, but normally the

---

12. *Epist. Smyrn.*, 8.
13. S., III, qu. 67, 2.
14. Lombard, IV, *Dist.* 6, A.
15. C.T., II, 2, qu. 23; T.B., p. 363.

priest could act entirely on his own initiative, and indeed any priest could baptize in time of need.[16]

In principle the Reformers did not challenge the traditional view of the matter, although the details of its outworking gave rise to several controversies. Luther was not greatly interested in the question: his main concern was to establish the primacy of God as the true minister. The Swiss Reformers agreed that a definite commission had been given to the apostles and their successors, although they did not agree that the medieval bishops and priests were in the true line of that succession, or that it was necessarily by the episcopal laying on of hands. However, the administration was restricted to those who had a definite commission, first by inward calling, and second, by outward separation. The Anglican position was essentially the same as that of the other Reformers except that in England the traditional threefold order was retained. The Reformed school laid great emphasis upon the conjunction of baptism and preaching in the dominical commission and the rigid exclusion of non-ministers; two points which were to cause considerable trouble in Elizabethan England. The only groups which did not accept the need for a special authorization to baptize were the Anabaptist, which freely allowed the baptism of their members by each other. Theoretically, they could no doubt base this view upon the doctrine of a universal priesthood, but in practice it seems to have been largely the result of circumstances. It is interesting that in some of the later communities pastors were appointed by consent. The English Separatists did not question the need for a regularly appointed minister, although they could not agree that the Papist or Anglican clergy came into this category.

The question of deacons was one which gave rise to certain complications, for even in the early church there had been doubts whether the deacon was rightly called to the ministry of the word and sacraments. The common conclusion was that the deacon ought not to baptize except by special authorization from the bishop: "A deacon ... does not baptize without special authorization";[17] "Let not the deacon baptize except in very urgent necessity".[18] In the first centuries opinion was divided whether the necessity itself constitutes an authorization without individual episcopal sanction, but in process of time, and

---

16. E.R., p. 198.

17. *Apostolical Constitutions*, I, 8, c. 28.

18. E.R., p. 204.

largely on the authority of Chrysostom[19] and Gelasius,[20] this came to be accepted as the normal view. It was stated by Lombard, who quoted Isidorus in its favour,[21] and also by Thomas, who referred to Gelasius.[22] Thomas was even prepared to consider an ordinary authorization of deacons, for which there was an apparent precedent in the case of St. Lawrence, but it was plainly prohibited by Gelasius.[23] The Council of Trent allowed deacons to baptize only when specially authorized to do so, or in a sudden emergency when no priest was to hand.[24]

Generally speaking, the Reformers had no great interest in the problem. Indeed, in the Reformed churches the problem disappeared of itself, for deacons were again appointed only to "serve tables", and were not allowed to dispense either word or sacraments. The one controversy which arose was in the Church of England, in which the retention of the traditional ministry meant that deacons were permitted to administer baptism in the absence of the presbyter. The Puritans had natural objections to this committal of a ministerial duty to what they regarded as a non-ministerial order, and in some cases they were prepared to challenge even the validity of baptism administered by a deacon. As Cartwright put it, it was perhaps right for the Anglican deacon to baptize, for under the Anglican system the deacon was really a minister, and not a deacon, and the principal part of his work was the administration of the word and sacraments.[25] But the fact that this was so merely proved that the Church of England was perpetuating a corruption of the diaconate, and in any case, if the Anglican deacon could baptize, it was perverse not to allow him to administer the Lord's supper –" a sundering of two sacraments conjoined by divine institution".[26] Whitgift dismissed this equation of deacon and presbyter as a "stop-gap invention",[27] and in a sense he was justified, for Cartwright himself did not really regard the deacon as a minister or think that he should "meddle in ministers' matters". His main contention was that the deacons of the Anglican church "were made to other purposes than Scripture appoynteth".[28]

The matter was primarily, then, a matter of the ministry, but in favour of allowing deacons to baptize, the Anglicans could advance the

---

19. *Hom.* LXI.

20. *Epist.* IX, c. 7.

21. Lombard, IV, *Dist.* 6 A.

22. S., III, qu. 66, 5.

23. *Loc. cit.*

24. C.T., II, 2, qu. 23.

25. Whitgift, P.S., II, p. 525.

26. *Ibid.*, III, p. 59.

27. *Ibid.*, II, p. 525.

28. *A pleasaunte Dialogue*, p. 32.

precedent of the first deacons Stephen and Philip who both preached and baptized.[29] Cartwright had no very clear answer to this appeal to the New Testament. He could only take refuge in evasion: that Stephen did not preach but made an apology, and that Philip preached and baptized, not as a deacon, but as an evangelist.[30] Yet Cartwright was feeling after a genuine point, that by its nature the apostolic diaconate was not a spiritual ministry and therefore not a ministry of the word and sacraments. Against that view Whitgift and the main body of Anglicans maintained the traditional opinion that although the deacon does have practical duties (as set forth in the Ordinal), and is inferior to the bishop and presbyter, yet he is still a minister, and may therefore preach and baptize within the limits set by scriptural precedent and ecclesiastical enactment.

Another problem which arose was that of the unworthy minister. The question was of long standing in the church, for early rigorist sects like the Donatists had contended that the sacraments administered by apostate priests have no validity. The matter was again to the fore in the Middle Ages, for the standards of clerical life were in many cases very low, and thoughtful men began to ask whether the administrations of grossly licentious priests could really be owned by God. Of course, no one disputed the scandal of clerical immorality or insincerity, but as the great theologians of the early period had seen, if God is the true baptizer, we have to consider whether the divinely appointed sacrament can in fact be invalidated by the misconduct of the human instrument.[31]

It has often been asserted that Wycliffe revived the Cyprianic and Donatist teaching,[32] and in the *Articles of Ten Friars* of 1382 he was certainly accused of the view "that if a bishop or priest be in mortal sin, he doth not ordain, consecrate or baptize".[33] But his own writings do not seem to support this conclusion, for not only did he complain of the falsity of the charge: "Sickerly here is feyned thing, put on pore men, that a priest in dedly sinne cannot give the sacramentis", but he insisted that what is really required is worthiness in the recipient rather than the minister: "But Cristen men sayne, that a preyste beynge in dedly synne

---

29. Whitgift, P.S., III, pp. 58 f.
30. *Loc. cit.*
31. Cf. Chrysostom, *In Johann. Hom.*, LXXXVI; Augustine, *De Bapt. c. Donat.*
32. Cf. Daniel, *op. cit.*, p. 638.
33. Foxe, III, p. 21.

may make and gyve sacramentis to salvation of them that worthily receyven them and consenten not to the prestus synne."[34] Wycliffe agreed that there is no profit in the prayers of an unworthy minister, and that if a priest does baptize in mortal sin "it be to his dampnynge".[35] But he could not go so far as to make the grace of God dependent upon the human administrator.

There was, of course, a fairly general agreement that the administrations of simoniacal ministers are not valid,[36] and possibly some of the followers of Wycliffe went further, as Huss probably did in Bohemia. But it is not always easy to know whether their views were correctly understood or represented by their opponents. Swinderby, for example, was charged with this heresy, but if Foxe has quoted correctly, he claimed that it was a conclusion that "friars and priestes put upon me false-lie". All that he had said was that "the praiers that an euill priest praies (living in lecherie or other deadlie sinne) ouer the child when it shal be halowed, ben not acceptable to God, as ben the praiers of a good priest".[37] A similar accusation was denied by Brute, who stated that if there is a good intention on the part of the baptized or his sponsors, he is as well baptized "by a vicious or a naughty priest" as by "ever so virtuous a priest".[38]

If this represented the true Wycliffite teaching, it did not differ substantially from the official view so ably propounded by Augustine and reproduced by the Schoolmen and their successors. For after all, if Christ is the true baptizer, the baptism of Judas is of no less validity or efficacy than that of Peter.[39] In the restatement at Trent it was emphasized that as the representative of Christ the priest is always holy, even though he may be most depraved in personal character.[40] The *Catechism* accepted the fact that "to them who administer them with impure hands the sacraments bring eternal perdition and death",[41] but this did not in any way debar them from "effecting or conferring the sacraments".[42]

The Continental Reformers did not dispute the traditional doctrine. Indeed, they pressed it to the extreme, not accepting even a false intention as a ground of invalidation. Luther in particular showed a fine

---

34. Arnold, III, p. 485.
35. *Loc. cit.*
36. Cf. *Dives and the Pauper*, VII, 9.
37. Foxe, III, pp. 115-116.
38. *Ibid.*, p. 185.
39. Cf. Lombard, IV, *Dist.* 5 A.
40. C.T., II, 1 qu. 19.
41. *Loc. cit.*
42. C.D., Sess. VII, *Sacr. can.* 12.

sense of the basis of the doctrine, that God is the true administrator and the human minister only an instrument. So long as there was worthy reception, the sacrament could not be affected by any impiety on the part of the priest.[43] Calvin stated the same general view with his customary lucidity and vigour: "If the baptism administered by man is Christ's baptism, it will not cease to be Christ's baptism, whoever be the minister."[44] The Augsburg and succeeding confessions testified to the unanimity of Reformed opinion, only the Anabaptists being suspected of a contrary view.

In England the catholic doctrine reigned undisputed from the first days of Henry to the end of the period. The *King's Book* expressed it clearly: "Although he which doth minister the sacrament be of a sinful and evil conversation, yet the virtue and effect of the sacrament is not thereby diminished."[45] Becon made exactly the same point,[46] and Cranmer argued that "baptism is all one ... whether the minister be good or ill, or whether he minister it to good or ill".[47] Even Marian confessors like Woodman[48] and Mary Clements maintained the doctrine: "If a child be baptized in the name of the Father, and of the Sonne, and of the Holy Ghoste, it is trulye and sufficientlye baptized, though the minister be never so wicked ... or never so great a Papist."[49] During the Elizabethan period the Article on the subject was adopted by both convocation and parliament, and it aptly summed up the official teaching. Deriving from the Augsburg Confession, it had already appeared in the 13 Articles of Cranmer and in the 42 Articles of 1553. In its final form as Article 26 of the 39 Articles it made three points: first, that wicked ministers may in fact continue in the visible church; second, that their ministrations are not invalidated by their wickedness; but third, that appropriate ecclesiastical action ought to be taken against them. As we shall see later, the Anglicans no less than the Continentals stressed the necessity for worthy reception, but they could not suspend either the validity or indeed the efficacy of the sacrament upon the virtue or vice of the human minister.

An issue which aroused particular interest during the Reformation period was that of the minister who is unworthy by reason of theological

43. W.A., VI, 531.
44. *Instit.*, IV, 15, 6.
45. K.B., p. 44.
46. Becon, P.S., II, p. 226.
47. J., III, p. 128.
48. E.E.D., I, p. 53.
49. E.M., III, 2, p. 219.

error rather than moral weakness. The issue was a practical one, for most of the earlier Reformers had themselves been baptized by traditionalists, and in certain cases, as during the Marian reaction in England, no other baptism was available. If such baptism did not stand, then obviously rebaptization would be demanded, or some other form would have to be sought.

To this whole discussion the Reformers applied the same principles as those which had destroyed the Cyprianic and Donatist opinion. Luther hardly felt the difficulty at all. If the form of baptism was observed, and the divine commandment fulfilled, God would take charge of the rest, and neither the sin nor the error of the minister could make the slightest difference. On the Reformed side, the difficulty was felt rather more acutely, for under the Papacy there had been very little apprehension of the meaning of baptism, and therefore no great possibility of a spiritual effect. Could it then be described as true and proper baptism? The Anabaptists thought not, but of course Papist baptism was in any case inadmissible as a baptism of infants. Calvin, however, maintained his general principle that the baptism is Christ's: therefore even though "we for a long time did not hold the promise which was given us", the promise itself was not affected by the opinions of the minister.[50] Knox came to the same conclusion: "In verie deed, the malice of the divill could neither altogidder abolische Chryst's institutioun, for it was ministred unto us, In the name of the Father, etc. ... I confess ... it did not profit us ... but now the Spirit of Chryst Jesus illuminating our hartis hath purgeit the same by faith, and maketh the effect of that sacrament to work in us without any iteratioun of the externalle syne."[51] The same doctrine was maintained in the confessions, which related even the efficacy to the faith of the recipient rather than to that of the minister.[52]

In England many of the confessors under Mary refused to accept Papist baptism for their children. A casual reading would suggest either that they were Anabaptists, or at least that they denied the validity or efficacy of the official rite. But both inferences are false. In the *Martyr's Letter of Apology*, for example, we read that the traditional baptism is accepted as true baptism, in spite of the "malignancy of the minister". The position of Woodman was the same, for although he had his child

---

50. *Instit.*, IV, 15, 16-17.
51. Knox, IV, pp. 119-121.
52. Cf. *The Huguenot Confession*, Art. 28.

baptized privately by a midwife, he stated in his *Confession* "yt thoose children yt have bene or shalbe baptysed of ye papisticall mynisters, be trulye baptysed". It was simply that Woodman could not conscientiously "bringe or sende his child to the papysticall church to requyre baptysme at their handes".[53]

During the Elizabethan age the Anglicans and Puritans were of a common mind on this issue, but some of the Separatists espoused a more rigorous doctrine. Barrowe, indeed, was charged with denying that even the Queen had been lawfully baptized, largely on the ground that she had been baptized under the Papacy. Penry would not accept the argument of Dr. Some that baptism is valid so long as the Triune formula is observed, but he was possibly confusing validity with efficacy, for in his *Answer to the Slanderous Articles* he agreed that "the Anglican and Papisticall rites are true sacraments".[54] Like Barrowe, he was probably trying to emphasize the fact that it is definitely wrong to accept these official ministrations. On the other hand there could be no doubt that Separatists like Francis Johnson did consider whether Anglican and Papal baptism were true and valid.[55] At a later date John Smith the se-baptist referred to baptism in Popery as "false baptism, and in the Lord's account no better than pagan washing".[56]

The Anglicans, of course, treated scruples of this nature as absurd, for they could hardly be expected to deny the validity of their own ministrations. But even abstractly, the scruples were not legitimate. If the Separatists did not regard the Established Church as a true church, they were right to refuse Anglican baptism, as Woodman had attempted to refuse the Papist. But they were not right when they made the validity of the baptism dependent upon the instrumental ministry. At the very worst, Anglican baptism might be irregular and non-efficacious, but so long as the external form remained, its validity could not be questioned, nor the possibility of an ultimate fulfilment denied.

The Puritans, of course, accepted the validity of both Anglican and even Papist administrations, but they were not without some scruples in the case of non-preaching ministers. In theory, the Anglican Reformers agreed with Calvin that the true presbyter is a minister of both word and sacraments. But in practice they found it difficult to staff

---

53. M.S., Gonville and Caius Coll., Press Mark M. 223.

54. E.E.D., II, p. 20.

55. *Ibid.*, p. 139.

56. *Ibid.*, I, p. 48.

all the parishes with ministers sufficiently qualified to preach. The annual number of graduates had sunk to a low ebb at the beginning of Elizabeth's reign, and some of the clergy who were qualified could not be trusted because of their evident Romanist sympathies.[57] Immediate steps were taken in the *Injunctions* of 1559 to insist upon a minimal level of education and to provide exhibitions to the universities.[58] The *Homilies* were provided as preaching-matter for those who could not be given a licence to preach themselves. But although the position did improve slowly, even at a later date the choice had often to be made between a non-preaching minister and no minister at all, and it was inevitable that many not very suitable candidates should be accepted: "often ignorant artificers, who partly by their light behaviour, and partly by their trade of life were very offensive to the people".[59] The most notorious case was that of Aylmer's porter, who according to Marprelate received his cure as an easy form of retirement-pension.

Admittedly, the position was not satisfactory, but even so the Puritans were not a little unfair in their criticisms. They were applying a doctrinaire theory to a situation in which its application was at first literally impossible. Our present concern, however, is that they pursued their criticism to the point of questioning not merely the regularity but even the validity of baptism administered by a non-preacher. As they saw it, the proclamation of the word was "essential" to the work of the ministry. And proclamation of the word included the definite preaching of sermons as well as the reading of Scripture or of set exhortations. If a minister was not qualified for this work, he could not be regarded as a true minister, and therefore he had no real authority to administer the sacraments. But if this was the case, the baptism of a non-preacher was a usurped and unauthorized baptism, and therefore invalid.

Ultimately, of course, the whole question merged into that of lay-baptism, but the Anglicans at any rate considered it as a separate issue. To begin with, they could not accept the Puritan contention that preaching is "essential" to the ministry. When Travers was challenged on this point, he referred to Matthew 28, but against this the Anglicans maintained that although preaching is to be desired, the reading of Scripture and of

---

57. *Zürich Letters*, P.S., I, pp. 85, 92.

58. Gee and Hardy, *Documents*, Art. 6, 17.

59. Collier, *Ecclesiastical History*, VI, p. 334.

exhortations does constitute a proclamation of the divine word. To that extent even the "dumb" minister is still a minister of the word. Therefore the arguments against his authority fall to the ground.[60] Certainly it would be an exaggeration to describe his administration as the illegal usurpation of a layman.

Yet basically the Anglican defence was not a defence of the "dumb" minister as such. Indeed, it was freely admitted that the ordination of non-preachers was only a temporary expedient. The real defence was that the validity of the properly administered sacrament is not affected by the qualifications of the administrator. Had the Puritan charge been simply a charge of irregularity, it would have provoked only a justification of the expedient. The suggestion of invalidity constituted a direct challenge to the rule which Whitgift quoted (and no doubt misapplied) from Calvin himself: "That nothing is added or taken away from the dignity of baptism by him by whom it is administered".[61] In their zeal for a purer ministry the Puritans tended to overlook the fact that the irregularity of a sacrament does not necessarily involve its invalidity. Baptism by non-preachers might well be deplored, but it must still be accepted as valid baptism.

A final point may be mentioned. Bancroft attempted a not very successful defence of the baptism of non-preachers on the ground that even in Scripture the word and sacrament are not always conjoined, since the deacon has a precedent for baptizing but has no definite licence to preach. But even supposing that the word and sacrament ought not to be separated, he then asked concerning the Puritan "doctors", who according to Calvin "have neither to deal with the discipline, nor the administration of the sacraments".[62] For the ministry of the word certainly includes teaching as well as preaching. And if so, were not the Puritans separating the sacrament from the word as the Anglicans were alleged to be separating the word from the sacrament? Of course, Bancroft had very little interest in the status of doctors as such. His argument was controversial in both form and substance. But it may be noted that in common with all Anglicans he accepted the conjunction of the word and sacraments as a normal rule. His main purpose was to establish that there may be legitimate exceptions to that rule. And in any case the decisive issue was that of validity or

---

60. S.P.R., I, 173.

61. Whitgift, P.S., I, p. 526.

62. Bancroft, *Survey*, p. 120.

invalidity. As we shall see, the bitter controversy about lay-baptism was ultimately to narrow down to the same point.

(2) Irregular Ministers

The Anabaptists apart, all theologians agreed that the dispensing of the word and sacraments normally belongs to an orderly and regularly constituted ministry. But the further question had to be asked whether in extraordinary circumstances baptism might not be administered by heretics or laymen or even supernatural beings. Upon this issue there was a sharp division between Reformed and traditionalist opinion, with the Lutheran and to some extent the Anglican churches occupying middle ground.

In the medieval period the speculative Scholastic mind had considered the possibility of a supernatural administration of baptism by angels or the devil. If the minister were an angel the sacrament would have to be accepted as valid, since angels do not act except under divine orders. But the same could not be said in the case of the devil, for although God can and does act through wicked agents, He has nowhere commanded the devil to administer baptism, and He cannot therefore be the true author or minister of any baptism which he may give.[63]

The Reformers had no interest in abstruse and hypothetical questions of this kind, but they appreciated the relevance of the earlier controversy concerning the validity of heretical and schismatic administrations. Against this validity Cyprian had used an argument drawn from Tertullian, that the God of heretics is not the same as the God of Christ and the church, and therefore the baptism of heretics cannot be the same. But the view which finally prevailed was that heretical, including Arian, baptism is unquestionably valid so long as the correct form and matter are maintained. Augustine was willing to accept even the baptism of Marcion, for although corrupted with false and fabulous doctrine it had not lost its true form. The baptism of the Montanists and the Paulianists could not be accepted because the form had been changed.[64]

Of course, the validity of the rite did not ensure its efficacy. Heretical baptism was valid, but it was external only, and to condemnation. It had the form, but no grace. Only as heretics were confirmed into the true

---

63. For a summary of quotations, see Bingham, *Antiquities*, VIII, pp. 53 f.
64. *Loc. cit.*

church could their baptism have its proper effect. The one exception to this rule was when a catholic was forced to accept heretical baptism in default of any other, in which case the effect would not be forfeited.[65] The exception is an important one, for it indicates that under the older theology the efficacy of a sacrament was to some extent dependent upon the faith of the recipient. In all cases heretical baptism was valid, but only where it was received with a true faith could it have its effect. Again, even baptism administered in the catholic church could not be efficacious if received by a secret unbeliever or heretic.

The Schoolmen[66] and the Tridentines[67] had nothing to add to this discussion, except that a false intention was suggested as a possible ground of invalidation.[68] In all other respects they simply reaffirmed the traditional doctrine. The Reformers had a practical interest in the matter in that they regarded the Papists as heretics, but, as we have seen, they did not dispute the validity of Papist baptism, and on this particular issue they endorsed the traditional doctrine. Certainly a new emphasis was laid upon the necessity of a true faith to efficacious reception, and a distinction came to be made between baptism by a single heretic in an otherwise sound church and baptism within a wholly heretical church.[69] But the preservation of a correct form was the test of validity and even of external soundness. The Anglicans were of the same mind, and the only references which they made to the issue were controversial. Thus Whitaker pointed out that in his refutation of Cyprian Augustine had appealed to Scripture and not to tradition,[70] and Cox made use of the same illustration.[71] Cartwright rightly deduced from the earlier discussions a distinction between efficacy and legality: "For there is no man doubteth but that the baptism which is ministered by an heretical minister may be effectual [i.e. when received in faith]: and yet I think that Mr. Doctor [Whitgift] will not say that therefore an heretical minister may baptize, and that it is lawful for heretics to baptize in the church."[72] Unfortunately the Puritans did not always distinguish quite so clearly between legality and validity. Hooker, too, had a controversial interest in the matter, for he saw that the principle underlying the earlier judgment

---

65. *Loc. cit.*
66. Cf. Lombard, IV, *Dist.* 6 A.
67. C.T., II, 2, qu. 23.
68. C.D., Sess. VII, *Bapt. can.* 4.
69. Cf. R.D., *Bapt.*
70. Whitaker, P.S., pp. 506-7.
71. *Zürich Letters*, P.S., II, 73.
72. Whitgift, P.S., II, p. 532.

had an important bearing upon the disputed validity of lay-baptism. He thought that Augustine had easily the better of the argument, for on the one hand heresy "did not deprive of the power to baptize", and on the other, "even if heretics did lose the power, it followeth not that baptism by them administered without authority is no baptism".[73]

There was, of course, a difference between a heretical minister and a mere layman, for the heretical minister had perhaps been given authority, or had a pretended authority, even if he had no true faith, whereas the layman might have a true faith, but he had no ordinary authority. From a very early period, however, laymen had in fact administered baptism, although neither precept nor precedent could be found for the practice in the New Testament. Tertullian had defended the custom by what became a stock argument, that what is equally received may be equally given,[74] but this principle could be applied just as well to the Lord's supper. The underlying justification was undoubtedly the supposed overriding necessity of the sacrament.[75] The later theologians and canonists[76] all approved the practice, although in some cases there were restrictions of the right: the Council of Eliberis, for example, did not allow laymen to baptize unless they had themselves been fully baptized, and were monogamists,[77] and Basil would permit only those who had been confirmed in the catholic faith.[78] But the general opinion was against these restrictions, and the validity of lay-baptism was never questioned even if no real emergency could be proved, although the offending lay-minister was of course open to censure. The evangelical "Forbid him not" could always be invoked in these cases.

By the time of the Schoolmen the right of the laity had been firmly established, and writers like Lombard[79] and Thomas[80] simply reaffirmed the primitive teaching. Thomas did consider certain objections, but he was impressed by authorities like Isidorus and Gelasius, and also by the absolute necessity of the sacrament. At Trent care was taken to exclude the laity from ordinary ministerial functions,[81] but a specific exception was made in favour of emergency baptism.[82] As the *Catechism*

---

73. L.E.P., V, LXXII, 17.
74. *De Bapt.*, XVII.
75. *Loc. cit.*
76. Bingham, *op. cit.*, VIII, p. 32.
77. *Loc. cit.*
78. *Loc. cit.*
79. Lombard, IV, *Dist.* 6 A.
80. S., III, qu. 67, 3.
81. C.D., Sess. VII, *Sacram. can.* 10.
82. *Loc. cit.*

stated it: "In case of necessity all, even of the laity ... whatever sect they may profess ... may baptize."[83] The *Rituale* made it plain that if an ordained man was present, precedence must be given to him, and a layman ought to baptize rather than a laywoman, but in practice it was the midwife who usually undertook the task. Lay-baptism was accepted as both lawful and valid.

Of the Reformers, Luther definitely approved of lay-baptism, first, because of his high sense of the value of baptism, and second, because it favoured his view that the Christian laity are the true priesthood. Should the need arise, he argued, "laymen may elect one of their number to minister the sacraments", and he would be validly ordained. That is why in cases of necessity every man can baptize and absolve, which would not be possible if we were not all priests.[84] This view found expression in the various Lutheran service-books which authorized the laity to baptize in the absence of the minister.[85] Rather curiously, Zwingli seems to have defended at least the validity of lay-baptism. His position was not so straightforward as that of Luther, for he was not so greatly influenced either by authority on the one hand or on the other by the dignity of the sacrament and of the Christian laity. What decided his outlook on the matter was undoubtedly his determination to defend the validity of the received baptism against the Anabaptist clamour for rebaptization. To do this, he had to accept the validity even of lay-baptism as it had in fact been administered. He could do this on the ground that God Himself has the primacy in sacramental administration.[86]

The later writers, however, approached the question differently. As they saw it, extraordinary circumstances could never arise except where there was a presumed absolute necessity. But if this was the case, lay-baptism was always an unlawful usurpation, even where death threatened and no commissioned minister was available. As Calvin pointed out, "the charge to baptize was expressly given to the apostles, along with the preaching of the word".[87] If pressed, the majority of the Reformed school would have had to agree with Zwingli that lay-baptisms already given were valid even if unlawful. For if the sacrament is Christ's, the irregularity of the administration cannot

---

83. C.T., II, 2, qu. 23.
84. D.C.R., p. 64.
85. Cf. D.C.R., p. 227.
86. C.R., IV, p. 290.
87. *Harmony of the Evangel.*, p. 385.

affect its validity or possible efficacy. Only in a few cases were lay-administrations definitely pronounced "null and void".[88] But by this time the main concern of the Reformed churches was to prevent the irregularity rather than to defend the validity. In this way, with a strict insistence upon the prerogative of the minister, the question of validity tended to become a hypothetical rather than a practical one, for lay-baptisms were no longer allowed to take place.

The two divergent principles, the Lutheran and the Reformed, found a main battle-ground in Elizabethan England. The Anglicans had rejected any absolute necessity, but in their conservative litur-gical revision private baptism had been retained, and lay-baptism seemed to be implied if not categorically demanded: "and then one of them shall name the child, and dip him in the waters, etc." In point of fact, many of the Elizabethan leaders strongly disapproved of the practice, but the issue was complicated by the fact that the Puritans attacked the validity as well as the doctrinal legality of the permitted use.

In the earlier period Tyndale had apparently accepted the legality of lay-baptism on the two general grounds: first, that it is an act of charity, and second, that all Christians are priests.[89] But Tyndale had not been discussing lay-baptism as such, and both his grounds were controversial arguments rather than true reasons. Cranmer, too, had adopted a Lutheran view of the matter, accepting the century-old practice,[90] and using the simple form of lay-baptism as an argument against the elaborate and unnecessary ceremonial: "Children in danger of life are christened by the midwife, or some other woman, without any of these ceremonies."[91] In the Prayer Book revisions Cranmer did not specifically authorize lay-baptism, and he warned even against a resort to private baptism without "great cause and necessity". But he left it to be gathered that the layman ought to baptize where no priest could be had. The administration itself was more important than the order which governed it.

But even during the Edwardian period of revision, the opposition to lay-baptism had already begun. The early champion of the Reformed standpoint was Hooper, who declared roundly that lay-baptism "is

---

88. Bingham, *op. cit.*, IX, pp. 83 f.
89. Tyndale, P.S., III, p. 98; I, pp. 25-26.
90. For the medieval legislation, see E.R., p. 194.
91. Cranmer, P.S., II, p. 58.

a profanation of the sacrament, and not to be suffered".[92] Hooper did not discuss the validity of lay-baptism already given, but aimed rather to secure the prohibition of the practice. The reintroduction of the traditionalist teaching under Mary tended if anything to intensify the opposition, for on the one side lay-baptism was definitely related to an absolute necessity,[93] and on the other the exiles came increasingly under Reformed influences. The extremer element went to the point of rejecting even private baptism, but amongst the moderates, too, there was considerable dissatisfaction with private baptism as administered by the laity.[94]

The accession of Elizabeth was accompanied by a readoption of the second Edwardian service, with its indecisive rubric regarding lay-baptism. Anglican leaders like Grindal and Sandys were strong opponents of the practice, and the rubric may have been intended as a concession to unreformed elements rather than a specific authorization. Certainly, this was the view of Whitgift, who just prior to his death argued that the rubric had never been intended to permit private baptism by women.[95] Babington and Hutton, too, suggested that it had been vaguely worded in order to facilitate its passage through Parliament.[96] James, on the other hand, "urged and pressed of the wordes of the booke, that they could not but intend a permission, and suffering of women and private persons to baptize",[97] and the Bishops of Winchester and London claimed that there were letters of the Reformers which "proved that by the fore-cited rubric they did intend a permission of private persons to baptize in case of necessity".[98] Whatever the true reason for its retention, the rubric was the immediate cause of strong Puritan protests, and it gave rise to constant and bitter debates until its amendment in 1604.

The actual practice during the reign seems to have varied. Sandys made an early attempt to suppress lay-baptism on the ground that women could not be lawful ministers of the word and sacraments.[99] The rejection of his plea points to a general continuance of the

---

92. Hooper, P.S., I, p. 131.
93. Cf. the stress upon the point in Bonner's *Visitation Articles* (Burnet, *op. cit.*, II, 2, 20).
94. *Ibid.*, 79, 82.
95. S.S., p. 14.
96. Strype, *Whitgift*, II, pp., 494-495; App. III, 44.
97. S.S., p. 14.
98. Waterland, *Works*, VI, p. 129.
99. Sandys, P.S., p. 433.

abuse. Grindal made a fresh effort to end lay-baptism in 1575, asking
convocation to lay down that "private baptism, in case of necessity,
is only to be ministered by a lawful minister or deacon, called to
be present for that purpose, and by none other".[100] But the Queen
refused to sanction the article,[101] and many bishops connived at the
continued baptism by midwives. At a later date both Whitgift[102] and
the Archbishop of York[103] stated that the laity, or at any rate women,
had no authority to baptize, but it is clear that in many dioceses lay-
baptisms were still the common rule in emergency cases.

The Puritans for their part took it that the Prayer Book did permit lay-
baptism, and they pressed vociferously for amendment. They had two
main arguments against the practice: first, that it derived from the belief
in an absolute necessity, and second, that it has no authority in Scripture:
"It is not only against the word of God, but also founded upon a false
ground, and upon an imagined necessity (which is none indeed)."[104] A
third and more precarious suggestion was that the administration by a
minister belongs to the original institution and therefore to the "essence"
of the sacrament.[105] But this view carried with it the implication that lay-
baptism is not a fulfilment of the original institution and therefore invalid,
in spite of the fact that it is given with water and in the name of the Trinity.

It was upon this implication that Whitgift seized in his rejection of
the Puritan demands. He could argue that lay-baptism is not definitely
forbidden in Scripture, and that it was accepted by the Fathers and
even by Zwingli.[106] But basically, he agreed with his opponents that as
a point of ecclesiastical order lay-baptism ought not to be permitted.
What he could not agree to was that however irregularly administered,
even in defiance of established order, lay-baptism did not constitute
a valid sacrament: "Baptism administered by women is true baptism,
even though it is not lawful for women to baptize."[107] Hooker would
go further, for he revived the suggestion of Tyndale that lay-baptism is
an act of charity. But he, too, insisted that since "the grace of baptism
cometh by donation from God alone", the question of its administration
can never be more than one of order or regularity, certainly not of

---

100. Grindal, P.S., p. 188.
101. Daniel, *op. cit.*, p. 433.
102. Whitgift, P.S., III, p. 493.
103. S.P.R., II, p. 193.
104. Whitgift, P.S., II, p. 525.
105. *Loc. cit.*
106. *Ibid.*, pp. 507 f.
107. *Ibid.*, p. 532.

validity or efficacy. Even where the Anglicans did not wish to defend lay-baptism as such, they could not concede that the minister is of the very substance or essence of the sacrament, and therefore that there can be no valid or efficacious administration without him.

The position of the Separatists is interesting, for largely through the pressure of circumstances they were forced to accept even the legality of lay-baptism. The point was that in the absence of a Separatist minister the only alternatives to the abhorrent Anglican administration were either no baptism at all or lay-baptism, and of these Francis Johnson at least preferred the latter: "Seeing ther was no church to whom we might joyne with a good conscience (to have baptisme from them) therfor we might baptize ourselves."[108] Johnson himself emphasized that this was only a temporary expedient, but others like Helwys thought that "any two or three persons might baptize": a conception which perhaps found its logical conclusion in the se-baptism of John Smith.

The main controversy came to a head at the Hampton Court Conference, at which the King himself took the Puritan side on this issue, "utterly disliking, that any but a lawfull minister might baptize, and growing something earnest against the baptizing by women".[109] James would not allow that the book did not permit lay-baptism, and when the Bishop of Winchester pointed out that the minister was not of the essence of the sacrament he replied that "he was of the essence of the right and lawfull ministry of the sacrament".[110] Eventually the King gained his point, for the words: "They baptize not children", were amended to read: "They cause not children to be baptized", and the indecisive phrase: "Then they minister it" to the definite: "The curate, or lawful minister present, shall do it."[111] In defence of the continued legality of lay-baptism it is sometimes argued that there was no express repudiation of the custom, or that a layman is a lawful minister in time of necessity, but there can be no doubt that these alterations were made with the deliberate intention of putting a stop to the practice. On the other hand, the validity of lay-baptism was not questioned, and to that extent the Puritan extreme was avoided. By withdrawing ecclesiastical sanction, the conference took a definite step towards the suppression of lay-baptism, but it did so without

---

108. E.E.D., I, p. 241.
109. S.S., p. 14.
110. S.S., p. 15.
111. S.S., pp. 14 f.

prejudice to the fundamental principle that God Himself is primary in sacramental administration.

To a very large extent lay-baptism meant baptism by women, for it was usually in the first hours of life that the emergency arose and only the midwife would be present. It had not been without a good deal of debate that the practice of baptism by women had established itself, for in addition to the apparent prohibition in the New Testament Tertullian had strongly opposed it,[112] and the Fourth Council of Carthage had also forbidden it.[113] Even Augustine had had doubts about the validity of baptism by women, but his strong sense of the divine primacy had eventually overcome them.[114]

It was the argument of Augustine which led to the recognition by the Schoolmen and the medieval councils not only of the validity but even of the regularity or legality of baptism by women.[115] Indeed, it was conceded that the mother of a child had a right to baptize, in spite of the spiritual relationship supposedly contracted.[116] An important duty of the priest was to ensure that midwives knew the essential parts of the service,[117] and it was ordered that water should always be available when birth was expected.[118] The high incidence of infant mortality made this an urgent and pressing matter, as we may judge from the insistence with which the Marian bishops demanded a careful instruction of midwives.[119] The right of women was recognized at the Council of Trent,[120] and the *Rituale* laid down the circumstances under which they might properly administer the sacrament.

The practice does not appear to have been specifically challenged by earlier reformers, although Brute had asked "why women may not as well administer the Lord's supper, in like case of necessity".[121] Luther accepted the legality as well as the validity of women's baptism, and it was permitted in many of the Lutheran orders, at Hesse, for example,[122] and in the *Pious Consultation*. Zwingli did not dispute the custom.[123] In England it found a defender in Tyndale, who asked: "Do not our women now christen and administer the sacrament of baptism in

---

112. *De Bapt.*, XVII.
113. Bingham, *op. cit.*, IX, p. 49.
114. *Loc. cit.*
115. Cf. Lombard, IV, *Dist.* 3 A;
    S., III, qu. 67, 4; E.R., p. 202.
116. E.R., p. 204.
117. Cf. *Handlynng Synne*, 9613.
118. Wilkins, *Concilia*, II, p. 293.
119. Foxe, VIII, p. 298.

120. C.T., II, 2, qu. 24.
121. Foxe, III, p; 179.
122. D.C.R., p. 227.
123. C.R., IV, p. 290.

time of need?"[124] But the main concern of Tyndale was to establish the general rights of the laity. Even when he invoked the law of charity as a scriptural justification,[125] it was to counter the claim of his opponents that it rested solely on the tradition of the church. Cranmer seemed to be of much the same mind as Tyndale. His permission of a private baptism at home undoubtedly meant baptism by the midwife in the majority of cases,[126] and he could refer to baptism by women as an accepted and non-reprehensible custom.[127]

The theologian who more than any other turned the scale against the traditional practice was Calvin. He had two main objections to it: first, that it implied an absolute necessity,[128] and second, that "nothing was more at variance with the ordinance of Christ".[129] He also appealed to the early repudiation by Tertullian, the Council of Carthage, and Epiphanius, and to the evident doubts of Augustine.[130] The alleged case of Sephora he dismissed as irrelevant: "What a foolish woman did is ignorantly drawn into a precedent."[131] The views of Calvin were embodied in the *Memorandum of the Ministers* of 1537,[132] and enforced upon Geneva in the later *Ecclesiastical Constitution*.[133] The point was specifically mentioned in many of the Reformed confessions,[134] and Bullinger,[135] Beza,[136] and all the later dogmaticians[137] attacked baptism by women as "a wicked profanation" for which the Papacy was largely responsible.

In England Hooper was a pioneer of the Reformed stand-point. He describes "the action of the sage femme, or midwife, as a particular profanation of the divine ordinance".[138] During the Marian exile the Prayer Book party could not easily resist Reformed pressure on the point, and when the 1552 book came under scrutiny it was generally admitted to be a blemish.[139] Horn attempted the defence that it was permitted only when "the infant is like to die",[140] but Bullinger expressed his strong disapproval,[141] and the extremer Anglicans like Humphrey and Samson heartily endorsed his criticisms. The Anglican leaders did not need much convincing, for Sandys and Grindal were both firm

---

124. Tyndale, P.S., III, p. 18.
125. *Ibid.*, p. 29.
126. Cf. Strype, *Cranmer*, II, p. 96.
127. Cranmer, P.S., II, p. 58.
128. *Instit.*, IV, 15, 20.
129. *Harmony of the Evang.*, p. 385.
130. *Instit.*, IV, 15, 20-22.
131. *Loc. cit.*
132. D.C.R., p. 568.

133. *Ibid.*, p. 569.
134. Cf. *The Second Helvetic*, XXII.
135. Bullinger, P.S., IV, pp. 370 f.
136. Q.R.C., 139.
137. R.D. *Bapt.*
138. Hooper, P.S., I, p. 31.
139. *Zürich Letters*, P.S., I, 71.
140. *Ibid.*, II, Appendix.
141. *Ibid.*, I, Appendix.

opponents of the practice, and Rogers made a scathing reference to it: "A woman, be she young or old, sacred or wicked, every male, that hath his wits, and is neither dumb, nor so drunken but that he can utter the words, may baptize."[142] Fulke[143] and Some[144] were of the same opinion, and Some was exposed to the banter of Marprelate because of his apparent disagreement with Whitgift on the point: "But Dr. Some, one of their affinitie now, he calleth the Archbishop of Canterbury an absurde heretike, because he holds baptism administered by women to be the seale of God's covenaunte, page 5 of his booke against Master Penri."[145] Yet even Whitgift did not wish to defend the custom, and he did not think "baptizing by women to be expressed in the book".[146] All that he aimed to do was to show that the question was more open than Cartwright thought. To that end he disputed the derivation from Pope Victor, cited the authority of Zwingli, referred to the stock example of Sephora, and quoted the canon of Carthage in its extended form: "except in urgent necessity".[147] His own conclusion was that baptism by women is not regular, but that he could not allow any doubts concerning its validity: "But that Baptism ministered by women is lawful and good, howsoever they mynister yt lawfully or unlawfully, so that the institution of Christ touching the words and element be dulie used, no learned man ever doubted, untyll now of late some one or two."[148]

The Puritans were not satisfied with this apparent compromise. To their mind it meant a perpetuation of the abuse. For the most part their persistent attacks upon lay-baptism were attacks upon baptism by women, and in all their propaganda this practice was singled out for especial mention. Support was enlisted from the Reformers abroad,[149] and some Puritans gave this defect as their reason for non-subscription to the Book of Common Prayer. The arguments against the practice were stated fully in the *Admonition* and in Cartwright's defensive treatises. They may be summarized as follows. First, it was maintained that the Prayer Book did actually permit the practice. As Cartwright pointed out, the wording allowed some other than the minister; it was the midwife who would usually be present "where the child is so shortly

---

142. Rogers, P.S., p. 236.
143. Fulke, P.S., II, p. 391.
144. S.P.R., 72.
145. Cf. Marprelate, *Minerall and Metaphysical Schoolpoints.*
146. Whitgift, P.S., II, p. 495; III, p. 546.
147. *Ibid.*, II, pp. 507 f.
148. Strype, *Whitgift*, III, Appendix 16.
149. E.g., Beza in 1566.

after it is born in great danger of death", and the magistrates sanctioned "the daily practising by women in baptizing children".[150] Second, attention was drawn to the fact that Scripture does not allow women to participate in the administration of word or sacrament: "Women have no more right to baptize than they have to preach, for the two go together." This point was proved from Matthew 28 and 1 Corinthians 14:35. The precedent of Sephora was not accepted, first, because "hers was a particular case", and second, because she circumcised, "not of a mind to obey the commandment of God, or for the salvation of God, but in a choler only".[151] Third, it was argued that the practice was Papal in origin and that it had been opposed by the majority of the Reformers.[152] Fourth, it rested upon the false conclusion of Augustine that without baptism there can be no salvation.[153] And finally, it had probably "been borrowed (with a number of other profanations), from the heathen, who had recognized priestesses".[154]

As in the case of private baptism, the ultimate issue was that of validity, for there was a fairly general agreement concerning its undesirability. On the one hand, the Puritans took it "to be no more the sacrament of baptism than any other daily or ordinary washing of the child".[155] On the other, the Anglicans, while they stated the antiquity of the custom and pointed to the pressure of necessity,[156] had as their main interest, first, the separation of their plea for validity from a supposed absolute necessity, and second, the point that the validity itself is not affected by an irregularity in administration. Hooker summed up the whole Anglican case with two characteristic judgments: that "it stand with no reason ... that baptism by women should cease to be baptism, as oft as any man ... will gather that children which die unbaptized are damned"; and that "the administration of this sacrament by private persons, be it lawful or unlawful, appeareth not as yet to be merely void".[157]

A final question which had agitated the traditional theology, that of the validity of baptism administered by a pagan, had no practical interest for the Reformers, although the point was briefly mentioned in Rogers's exposition of the Articles. Thomas had discussed the matter with great fullness. He had eventually decided in favour of the baptism,

---

150. Whitgift, P.S., II, p. 496.
151. *Ibid.*, p. 497; p. 524.
152. *Ibid.*, pp. 497 f.
153. *Ibid.*, p. 539.
154. *Ibid.*, p. 521.
155. *Ibid.*, p. 325.
156. L.E.P., V, LXII, 3.
157. *Loc. cit.*

on the three grounds that it was approved by Isidorus and Nicholas, that Christ Himself is the true baptizer, and that in baptizing, the pagan belongs in intention to the church.[158] A similar view was adopted at Trent, which allowed Jews and Turks to administer baptism in exceptional cases of extreme urgency.[159] But as Rogers perceived, the true basis of this judgment was the alleged absolute indispensability of baptism rather than the divine primacy in its administration.[160] The legitimacy of pagan baptism was in fact the *reductio ad absurdum* of the sacramentalist system. Technically, no doubt, Protestants would have to grant that the baptism is valid enough once it has been given. But the point is that this is a situation which not only need not but ought not to arise. Certainly, baptism may from time to time be given by ministers who themselves are secretly infidels. But externally these men have made a profession of faith and received the divine commission. It is only the doctrine of an absolute necessity which can give rise to the wholly anomalous situation of a Christian being baptized in the Triune name by one who does not even make an external profession of the Christian faith.

Surveying the whole question of the validity of irregular administration, we find that there were many contradictory principles at work. On the traditionalist side, the two determining factors were the divine primacy in administration, and the indispensability of the sacrament to salvation. These combined to make any baptism valid and even lawful so long as the correct form and matter were observed. The Reformers retained the doctrine of the divine primacy without that of indispensability, and the result was a contradiction. On the one hand, it could be argued that if God is the true minister, it is a matter only of ecclesiastical order who is the human instrument; the more so as all Christians are priests according to the New Testament. This was the Lutheran view. But on the other, it could be argued that if God is the true minister, the only baptism which is His baptism, and therefore valid, is that which He Himself has commissioned, the more so as there is no absolute necessity which justifies a transgression of the divinely appointed order. This was the Reformed view.

It was in England, where private baptism was retained but within the context of a theology which was for the most part Reformed, that

---

158. S., III, qu. 66, 5.
159. C.T., II, 2, qu. 23.
160. Rogers, P.S., p. 236.

the principles and their application came to be thoroughly weighed and tested. The doctrine of indispensability was not maintained, and that of the priesthood of believers definitely slipped into the background. It was a clear struggle between those who believed that the divine primacy guarantees validity and those who believed that it forbids irregularity. Theologically, the Anglicans seem to have had the better case, for to tie God to a single form of administration is to introduce a new and oppressive legalism, and in fact the Puritans themselves were not prepared to press for rebaptization in particular instances. Ecclesiastically, however, the Puritans had good reason on their side, for many of the bishops winked at irregularities, of which good order demanded the prompt and efficient suppression. The tragedy of the dispute is that for mainly controversial reasons extreme positions were adopted which clouded the true issues and emphasized the points of difference rather than the substantial agreement. The amendments of 1604 did something to solve the practical problems, but they were too late and too small to bridge the ecclesiastical and doctrinal gulf which had now revealed itself.

(3) The Subjects

The divine institution of baptism carried with it an obligation to ensure that it was administered not only by the right minister but also to the right subject. In a real sense this question of the subject was of greater importance than that of the minister. At best, the minister was merely an instrument, and necessary only as such. But the subject was clearly essential to the whole being of the sacrament. There could be no washing with water in the Triune name unless there was a proper person to be washed. And the efficacy of the sacrament depended upon its administration to those who were qualified to receive it according to the divine mandate. Administered otherwise, it could only be rendered useless and brought into disrepute. The fact that ultimately only God can know the inward fitness of the recipient did not affect the clear duty of the church to see that baptism is not administered except to those classes appointed to receive it, and to individuals within those classes who externally at least fulfil the basic requirements.

Generally speaking, there has always been agreement concerning the proper recipients in lands where the Gospel is preached for the first time. But in lands already evangelized some serious controversies have arisen. There were two such controversies in the sixteenth century: the Anabaptist denial of infant baptism, and the Puritan objection to indiscriminate baptism. Both these issues, however, must be considered against the more general teaching of the Reformers if their attitude towards them is to be properly understood.

The baptism of adult converts was of course the first and commonly accepted duty of the church. From the very earliest times baptism had been administered to those who made a confession of faith in Jesus Christ. There were no limitations of age, sex or class. It was simply asked that the recipient should have understood the message and turned to Jesus Christ with at least an external profession of repentance and faith.

As long as the church remained a minority, it was inevitable that the baptism of adult converts should still be a normal rule. Indeed, the first baptismal orders were clearly framed for adults. It was natural, too, that the church should draw up some very general tests of the sincerity of the candidate. One of these was the exclusion of any whose avocation was obviously at variance with Christian faith or discipleship. Thus a heathen priest, a gladiator, or an idol-maker could not be baptized unless he was ready to renounce his profession.[161] Again, the church insisted upon a long catechumenate in which there would be opportunities for thorough instruction and testing. But these conditions grew naturally out of the basic spiritual requirements, and the church resisted strongly all attempts to impose "natural" limitations, like those of the Marcionites, who would administer baptism to "none but persons single, virgins, widows, and women divorced from their husbands".[162]

With the passage of the years the baptism of adult converts became progressively rarer in the established areas. But missionary work did not altogether cease even with the conversion of the successive barbarian invaders, and the Schoolmen could still insist that the first subjects of baptism are adult converts.[163] A new era of overseas expansion opened up in the sixteenth century, so that the Tridentine statement to the same effect had something more than an antiquarian or hypothetical interest.[164]

But the outbreak of sectarian Anabaptism in the sixteenth century also carried with it a fresh attempt to impose more rigorous conditions

---

161. Cf. *Liturgy and Worship*, pp. 410 f.
162. Rogers, P.S., p. 274.
163. Lombard, IV, *Dist.* 4 A; S., III, qu. 68.
164. C.T., II, 2, qu. 30.

even upon the adult recipient. Certain of the Anabaptists seem to have claimed that only those who knew that they could live without sin were fit subjects for baptism.[165] The Family of Love were responsible for the curious view that since Christ was baptized at 30, no one ought to be baptized before attaining that age.[166] The Socinians went further and pointed out that only the first generation of converts should receive the sacrament, the children being baptized already in their forefathers.

Against these heretical limitations, traditionalists and Reformers alike maintained the scriptural and catholic teaching. For the Protestant churches the question was very largely theoretical, for they had neither the opportunity nor perhaps the zeal for much evangelistic work. But they had no doubts that where Jews or Turks did accept the Gospel, the mere profession of faith made them fit subjects for baptism. In the words of Calvin, the sacrament belonged primarily to those of adult age who, previously alien to the covenant, made a profession which satisfied the church.[167] As he saw it, the command in Mark 16 applied properly only to missionary preaching, "to which baptism was added as a kind of appendage".[168] The insistence upon sinless perfection, and the circumstance that Christ was baptized at the age of 30, he dismissed as absurd and irrelevant.[169] The other Reformers were of a similar mind.[170]

Adult baptism does not seem to have had much place in sixteenth-century England, for the service-books did not even provide for it: the present office was added only in 1662. However, the successive formularies had references to the baptism of adult converts. The 1536 Articles spoke of the promise of remission to those "who, having the use of reason, come thereunto perfectly and truly repentant".[171] There was a similar mention in the *Bishops' Book* and the *King's Book*.[172] The *Catechism* under Edward stated that baptism ought first to be given "to him that believeth in Christ, professeth the articles of the Christian religion, and mindeth to be baptized (to speak now of them that be grown to years of discretion)".[173] Of the individual writers Becon stressed the fact that there are no distinctions or restrictions: baptism is a "holy sacrament ...

---

165. C.R., IV, p. 229.
166. Rogers, P.S., p. 280.
167. *Instit.*, IV, 16, 24.
168. *Instit.*, IV, 27.
169. *Ibid.*, 28.
170. e.g., Q.R.C., 118.
171. Strype, *Cranmer*, I, p. 85.
172. K.B., p. 41.
173. *Catechism*, P.S., p. 516.

reverently to be received of all degrees and estates".[174] Philpot construed the "all" of Matthew 28 in the same way, for when a "morrow-mass priest" refuted individual baptism from this text, he pointed out that it meant "all sorts of men", He clinched his argument with the example of the eunuch.[175] In spite of these references, however, it is evident that adult baptism was hardly known in England. Whitgift could defend the omission of sermons on the ground that they could not profit the infants to whom it was now given. Cartwright took him to task for this parochialism: "Is there no cause, or may there not be, when they that be of age may be baptized, Jews and Moors in noblemen's and gentlemen's houses?"[176] But Cartwright himself envisaged only a very modest and exceptional expansion of the church.

The Reformers had, therefore, only a limited practical interest in the topic. All the same they had a considerable theoretical interest, for the requirement of faith in the adult recipient provided an excellent parallel by which to combat the doctrines of *ex opere operate* efficacy and a literal feeding upon Christ in the case of the Lord's supper. If faith was demanded in the one sacrament, and an insincere faith constituted an obstacle to its grace or benefits, so too it must be in the case of the other sacrament. Into the intricacies of this quite separate controversy, however, it is not necessary to go.

Of course, even in relation to adults there were special cases which demanded special consideration. The first and most obvious was that of those adults who were not in possession of their rational faculties. The baptism of idiots had been allowed by some of the earlier councils,[177] and Thomas was of the opinion that the imbecile had at least a right to baptism, although imbeciles ought not to be baptized unless they had previously desired the sacrament, or made a profession of faith during a lucid interval. The permanently afflicted could be treated as infants so long as they belonged to a Christian household, or proper sponsors could be found.[178] These judgments were largely repeated at the Council of Trent.[179]

On the Protestant side this question did not arouse any great interest, for, after all, where infant baptism prevailed, it was largely hypothetical. In the Anglican works there are only two references, and both of them

---

174. Becon, P.S., II, p. 215.
175. Foxe, VII, p. 63.
176. Whitgift, P.S., III, p. 134.
177. e.g. E.R., p. 192.
178. S., III, qu. 68, 12.
179. C.T., II, qu. 38.

controversial. The first is in Jewel, who was arguing against Harding that penitence and faith are necessary to true absolution. He foresaw the objection that this would exclude the insane, which was contrary to traditional practice and also to the parallel of baptism. But while he was ready to concede (on the authority of Augustine) that "men might be baptized in madness and in sleep", he denied that a general rule could be deduced from the exceptional case, or that a correct procedure could be laid down for all such cases.[180] Hooker did not follow the wise ruling of his former patron, for he attempted to use the "baptizing of deaf and dumb men and furious persons" as a proof that baptism may lawfully be administered without the exacting of a personal confession, but on the vicarious profession of others.[181] The conclusion of Jewel perhaps sums up best the Anglican, and indeed the whole Reformed, attitude to the question.

A rather different matter was that of the baptism of the dead, as suggested by the curious phrase of Paul in 1 Corinthians 15. It is, of course, a disputed point whether the apostle is referring to an actual practice of baptizing the dead, either vicariously or otherwise, but the Marcionites and Novationists were thought to have practised a vicarious baptism of the dead, and the Cata-phryges a literal baptizing of corpses.[182] It was, therefore, necessary, first, to consider whether the dead might properly be baptized, and, if not, to discover an alternative explanation of the Pauline saying.

The traditional theology had consistently opposed any idea of an actual baptizing of the dead, either vicarious or literal, but there was a division concerning the true meaning of the words of Paul. Some took it that he was referring to a corrupt practice of vicarious baptism of the dead, of which he himself did not approve. Others argued that he was speaking of the baptism of the dying, or simply bringing out the significance of baptism as a baptism to death and resurrection.[183]

The Reformers were greatly interested in the question, partly because of their exegetical concern, but partly, too, because of its bearing upon vicarious masses. Calvin discussed the text with great care. He rejected out of hand the idea of vicarious baptism or the suggestion that Paul

180. Jewel, P.S., III, p. 358.
181. L.E.P., V, LXIV, 4.
182. On this point see the *Catholic Encyclopedia*, Art. Baptism.
183. See *Catholic Encyclopedia*, Art. Baptism.

was arguing from "a horrible sacrilege, by which baptism was polluted, and converted into a mere magical abuse". He concluded that Paul was either alluding to the wider meaning of the sacrament, or more likely referring to the fact that in baptism we are reckoned dead to this world and pointed to our true life in heaven.[184]

Of the Anglicans it was Rogers who dealt most fully with the question, but in accordance with his usual method his energies were for the most part devoted to the refutation of false interpretations.[185] Hutchinson made a brief suggestion that in the early church baptisms often took place "over dead men's graves, in token that the dead should rise again".[186] He did not bring any evidence to support this view, and in any case his main point is that the supposed practice is linked with the basic significance of the sacrament.

It was quickly realized in England that the rejection of vicarious baptism is a good reason for the rejection of the vicarious mass. The question of the vicarious efficacy of the mass was raised even under Henry, and conservatives like the Bishop of Salisbury had to concede that "the sacrament of the altar was not instituted to be received of one man for another, any more than one man to be christened for another". But he could still defend the private mass on the ground that the grace received by one communicant can be of profit to the whole mystical body of Christ.[187] Less conservative divines like Tyler pressed the parallel with baptism much more closely: the vicarious mass could profit others only "so much as the christening of one man profiteth another, which after my opinion profiteth nothing".[188] Although the prohibition of vicarious baptism was not mentioned, it obviously underlay this whole discussion.

Philpot gave a different turn to the question by claiming that without a genuine recipient there is no baptism: "Though ye speak the words of baptism over water never so many times, yet there is no baptism, unless there be a christian man to be baptized."[189] But Philpot also made use of the earlier argument that "baptism is only baptism to such as be baptized, and to none other".[190] In the reign of Elizabeth Cooper made the same

---

184. *Comm. on i Corinth.* 15.
185. Rogers, P.S., p. 266.
186. Hutchinson, P.S., p. 138.
187. Burnet, *op. cit.*, II, 2 Collection, XXV.
188. *Loc. cit.*
189. Foxe, VII, pp. 637-638.
190. *Loc. cit.*

point, that if a private mass may benefit those who do not communicate, baptism may benefit those who are not baptized.[191] Against this line of reasoning, the traditionalists could, of course, argue that those who are not baptized do not belong to the church, whereas non-communicants do; but the main point of Cooper was that the sacraments can be of profit only as they are used or received.

It was Jewel who made a definite link with the earlier and rejected practice of vicarious baptism, for in his controversy with Harding he suggested that the private mass probably derived from vicarious baptism as practised by the Marcionites.[192] He did not mean, perhaps, that there was a literal historical connection, but he certainly did mean that there was a theological affinity which had influenced the development of the private mass. It was also of advantage to be able to add to his other objections to the mass this identification with a particularly obnoxious heresy.

(4) Infant Baptism

In the first instance, baptism was to be administered to adult converts. But this fact gave rise to an important question concerning the status and rights of the children of such converts. In the ancient world generally, and not least among the Hebrews, religion was very much a matter of family and even race, and from a fairly early period the infants of Christians came to be thought of as themselves Christian, at any rate by external profession and environment. Ought they then to be baptized?

Unfortunately there cannot be any absolute certainty with regard to the New Testament period, but by the end of the second century, and probably much earlier, it was regarded as right and proper to administer the sacrament to the children of Christians.[193] Fear of the post-baptismal lapse formed a restraining influence in some cases.[194] It has also been argued that the administration was frequently delayed to the more responsible age of 6 or 7.[195] But the custom of infant baptism was reasonably well established by the beginning of the third century, and in the fifth it could be utilized by Augustine and Jerome in their

---

191. Cooper, *Private Mass*, p. 115.
192. Jewel, P.S., II, p. 774.
193. H.D., pp. 142 f.
194. Cf. Tertullian, *De Bapt.*
195. Cf. *Liturgy and Worship*, pp. 410 f.

defence against the Pelagian heresy. The Pelagians did not dispute the practice, for they regarded baptism as an entry into that kingdom of heaven to which the natural man has no inherent right, however innocent.[196]

In the Middle Ages the question was largely a theoretical one. The Petrobusians and other medieval sects have been claimed as early Anabaptists, and were definitely accused of the error. But it is not clear that they did more than renounce the official baptism offered by the church.[197] On the traditional side, Lombard regarded infant baptism as securely grounded upon Scripture, tradition and spiritual necessity.[198] Thomas could see some possible objections. He was convinced, however, by the three arguments: first, that the apostles had practised it; second, that infants are under original sin and therefore in need of the baptismal washing; and third, that infants are not as such debarred from divine grace.[199]

The revolt against the practice did not break out openly until the early period of the Reformation, but then a powerful attack was launched upon it, first by the Zwickau prophets and then by the extremists at Zürich. Storch and his followers caused momentary confusion at Wittenberg,[200] and Bucer in Strassburg[201] and Zwingli in Zürich[202] were at first greatly influenced by the Anabaptists. It is noteworthy that Müntzer on the radical side was also not too clear on the matter, for although in his correspondence with the Anabaptists he condemned infant baptism,[203] in a letter to Œcolampadius of Basel he supported the traditional practice.[204]

The main objection brought by the Anabaptists was that they could not find any definite mandate or precedent for infant baptism in the text of the New Testament. There were a few extremists, like the fanatical Zwickau men and the free-thinking Denck, who had no very high estimate of the letter of Scripture, but as presented by the more thoughtful and ultimately the more influential groups like the Swiss and the Dutch, the Anabaptist case rested upon a direct appeal to the

---

196. See Wall, *The History of Infant Baptism*, I, pp. 265 f.
197. *Ibid.*, II, c. 7.
198. Lombard, IV, *Dist.* 4 A.
199. S., II, qu. 68, 9.
200. G. Ellinger, *Philipp Melanchthon*, p. 165.
201. Anrich, *op. cit.*, pp. 38 f.
202. D.C.R., p. 451.
203. See Muralt, *op. cit.*
204. D.C.R., p. 452.

apostolic records.[205] Evidence from the Old Testament was not accepted as relevant, for the New Testament alone was regarded as the distinctively Christian revelation.

In their appeal to the New Testament the Anabaptists had a twofold task. The first and destructive part of their work was to show that Christ Himself did not command, and the apostles did not practise, the baptizing of infants. As far as the traditionalists were concerned John 3:5 was the main point at issue, for this text seemed to exclude infants from all hope of salvation if they were deprived of baptism. But the Anabaptists would not allow that the text implied an absolute necessity of the sacrament. If it referred to water-baptism at all, it was only in respect of those who were of age to hear and respond to the Christian message.[206] The records of household baptisms, especially in the book of Acts, also gave rise to some discussion. In opposition to both the traditionalist and the Protestant view, that these passages do suggest at least a probable baptization of infants, the Anabaptists argued that there is no express mention of infants, that the circumstances did not permit of the presence of children, and that the members of the households are said to believe as well as to receive baptism.[207]

In controversy with the Reformers some reply had to be made to the favourite argument from circumcision. A first objection was that the new covenant of the New Testament was an individual covenant in contradistinction to the family covenant of the Old. Second, it was argued that even if infants do belong to the covenant, it does not follow that baptism has to be administered to them. Third, circumcision under the old covenant applied only to boys, from which it may be seen, first, that it is not indispensable, and second, that the sign ought to be given only as God had commanded and not according to our own fancy.[208]

These, then, were the serious negative arguments of the Anabaptists, supported popularly by such wild assertions as that infant baptism was an invention of Pope Nicholas II, or the Devil, which was much the same thing.[209] But obviously, it was not enough to argue negatively, although this was the easier and happier part of the task. It was also necessary to show positively that the New Testament does restrict baptism to adult

205. C.R., III, p. 369 (Grebel).
206. B.R.N., II, p. 191.
207. Cf. C.R., VI, pp. 48 f.
208. Loc. *cit.*
209. D.A., p. 176.

believers. In their attempt to do this the Anabaptists turned first to the divine mandate in Mark 16:16, in which the disciples were ordered to go, to teach, and to baptize. Great stress was laid upon the order: the disciples were to baptize only those who had already learned and believed. But this meant that they had no instructions to baptize uninstructed and unbelieving infants.[210] The records of baptism in the New Testament make it clear that they followed these instructions to the letter, for just as John had baptized only those who repented, so the apostles exacted a profession of faith before administering the sacrament.[211] A final point made by the Anabaptists was that the exposition of the meaning of baptism in Romans 6 demanded a definite movement of faith and repentance on the part of the recipients.[212]

In addition to the purely exegetical argumentation, the Anabaptists did attempt a more general theological defence, although in this respect their strict literalism, and their unfortunate isolation of the New Testament from the Old, placed them at something of a disadvantage. It must be remembered, too, that for the most part the Anabaptists were not trained theologians. They were ordinary lovers of the Bible, with the plain man's understanding of the text, but with no very profound grasp of the implications of that which they deduced from it. Their denial that Christ took flesh from the virgin is hard to explain except on the assumption not only that they had little knowledge of the Christological controversies, but also that they did not perceive even the basic requirements of a satisfactory understanding of the incarnation.

The first theological deduction made by the Anabaptists was that faith is an indispensable qualification for baptism, and that it cannot be conferred by the sacrament itself. They rejected as absurd Luther's contention that infants do in fact believe. Against the traditional notion of an infused faith they objected that baptism might just as well be administered to the children of Jews or Turks if it confers this gift.[213] Of course, on the medieval view, the unbelief or unwillingness of the parents constituted a sufficient obstacle to any such possibility; but, as the Anabaptists saw it, faith is plainly required in all those who receive the sacrament.

But this requirement of faith gave rise to an apparent difficulty. If

---

210. C.R., IV, pp. 576 f.; B.R.N., V, p. 155.
211. C.R., III, p. 369.
212. *Loc. cit.*
213. B.R.N., II, p. 130.

infants have no faith, and are without that grace of remission of which baptism is the sign, are they not doomed to perdition by virtue of their original guilt? On the other hand, if that guilt is remitted, why refuse them the sign and seal of that remission? In their attempts to avoid this dilemma, the Anabaptists made a second theological deduction, which in a true sense underlay their whole rejection of infant baptism, that there is no original guilt, and that each child has a definite freedom of the will in respect both of sin and also of salvation. On this view, the infant did not need remission. Even if it had inherited a predisposition to sin, it was not guilty of any definite sin either original or actual. Not having the grace of baptism, it had, therefore, no right or title to the sign, but it was not on that account excluded from the hope of salvation. A final and smaller point was that if infants are admitted into the church by baptism, it is illogical to debar them from joining in the church's meal of fellowship. A reception of the one sacrament necessarily carries with it the right to receive the other.[214]

The obvious theological weakness of Anabaptism was perhaps the secret of its undoubted strength, not only quantitatively, but also in the quality of Christian life. The Anabaptists came to a generation which was just learning to read and to know the Bible, and they advanced the attractive view that all thought and practice must have the sanction of plain Scriptures. Theological principles could only introduce confusion. The simple were better qualified to understand and follow the Bible than those whose minds were clouded by theological teaching and exegetical discussion.[215] Not unnaturally, a doctrine of this kind was both convincing and intoxicating. Jack was even better than his master. But because of that very superiority, and the obstinacy which it engendered,[216] he did not always see that when subjected to scrutiny the plain Scriptures were not always quite so plain as at first appeared, and that the theological deductions from them were usually most precarious, to say the least. He was in fact blind to the answer which could be and was made, not only on ecclesiastical but also on exegetical and doctrinal grounds.

---

214. This argument is stated and answered by Calvin, *Instit.* IV, 16, 30: mainly by an appeal to the rule of 1 Corinthians 11:28 (cf. Jewel, P.S., I, p. 230). The Reformers overlooked the defence that in baptism the recipient is wholly passive, whereas in communion action is required.
215. Cf. D.C.R., p. 103.
216. Zwingli gives some illuminating examples of this: C.R., IV, pp. 215 f.

On the traditionalist side there was a strong temptation to defend infant baptism almost exclusively on the basis of tradition and the Fathers.[217] It could then be conceded that there was no clear example of infant baptism in the New Testament, but the practice could be maintained as one which had been handed down from the apostles by an unwritten tradition. The patristic evidence seemed to confirm this view, for first Origen and later Augustine claimed that infant baptism had an apostolic basis. But the emphasis upon tradition was largely for polemical purposes, to demonstrate the authority of tradition side by side with that of Scripture. In fact, the Tridentine confessions no less than the writings of the Schoolmen did find a scriptural basis for baptism in the text John 3:5.[218] This text was thought to impose a law of baptism upon infants as well as adults. The implied necessity of baptism, together with the existence of original sin,[219] and the promise of a sacramental infusion of faith,[220] made it an obligatory act of charity to administer baptism to them.

The Reformers, of course; could not allow that the authority of tradition and the Fathers was of itself a sufficient ground for combating the Anabaptist teaching. Indeed, they resisted strongly the polemical use made of this argument. As Cranmer put it, to argue that baptism is absolutely necessary to salvation and yet to admit that it is not directly enjoined by Scripture is not only self-contradictory, but it "opens a gap both to the Donatists and the Anabaptists!"[221] Again Whitaker insisted that when Origen and Augustine referred to an apostolic derivation they had in mind the written tradition of Scripture rather than that of word of mouth or unbroken practice.[222] Even if no plain texts could be adduced in favour of the custom, he argued that "it could be inferred by the strictest reading".[223] But just as the traditionalists did in fact appeal to Scripture in spite of their emphasis upon tradition, so the Reformers could appeal to tradition in spite of their primary emphasis upon Scripture. This was true not only of Lutherans like Melanchthon, who found support for infant baptism in all the ancient writings,[224] but also of Zwingli, who quoted the stock passage from Origen.[225] And although Calvin preferred the sole

217. e.g. Harding, Jewel, P.S., I, pp. 223-224.
218. C.T., II, 2, qu. 31.
219. Cf. D.R.C., p. 459.
220. C.T., II, 2, qu. 32.
221. Cranmer, P.S., II, pp. 59-60.
222. Whitaker, P.S., p. 506.
223. *Loc. cit.*
224. C.R., XXI, p. 295.
225. C.R., VI, pp. 184 f.

arbitrament of Scripture he too could refute as a "shameful falsehood" the Anabaptist ascription of the practice to the later papacy.[226] Bullinger and Beza both accepted the unbroken continuance of infant baptism from the apostolic period, and they could cite Jerome and Augustine as witnesses from the earliest days.[227] The Anglicans were of a similar mind, for not only in conservative statements like the *King's Book*,[228] but also in the individual Reformers there was an appeal to tradition and the Fathers. Becon supported his other arguments with quotations from Jerome, Ambrose, Austin and Hyginus.[229] Philpot alluded to "the more antiquity" of the custom, and he claimed that he could "declare out of the ancient writers [Origen, Jerome, Austin and Cyril] that the baptism of infants hath been continued from the apostles' time unto ours".[230] When Rogers came to discuss the question, he branded the Anabaptists as innovators and revolutionaries, who oppugned a truth known and held by all Christians from the very earliest days.[231]

Both abroad and at home, therefore, the Reformers were quite ready to use the historical testimony as at least a subsidiary argument. But for two reasons they were unable to exploit the appeal: first, because controversialists claimed that infant baptism was a test-case for the alleged sole-sufficiency of Scripture; and second, because the Anabaptists themselves demanded proof from the New Testament rather than from tradition or the Fathers. In these circumstances even a patristic scholar like Jewel could make no reference at all to tradition, and the Reformed reply had to be made primarily in the exegetical and doctrinal field.

The first instinct of the Reformers was to turn to the Old Testament analogy of circumcision. Tactically, it was a sound instinct, for the linking of the two Testaments disclosed both the traditionalist differentiation between the sacraments of the old and new Law and also the Anabaptist depreciation of the Old Testament at the expense of the New. In addition, it opened up to them that whole covenantal theology by which the children of believers have a definite and well-defined status in the church.

Rather strangely, the Lutherans did not develop the argument to any great extent, although Luther obviously appreciated its

---

226. *Instit.*, IV, 16.
227. Bullinger, P.S., IV, p. 392.
228. K.B., p. 43.
229. Becon, P.S., II, p. 210.
230. Philpot, P.S., p. 274.
231. Rogers, P.S., p. 279.

force.[232] Zwingli, however, made it his main starting-point, and he worked it out in considerable detail. As he saw it, the children of Christians belong to the people of God no less than those of the Israelites. The latter received circumcision as the token of their covenant relationship with God. The former have a right to baptism as a sign of the same relationship.[233] The fact that circumcision applied only to boys was a detail of administration, perhaps to emphasize that the call of the "old people" of God was through the male seed. But in Christ the distinction between the sexes has been done away. In any case, girls were called as well as boys, for all the people of God had received the figure of baptism when they passed into and through the Red Sea.[234] Much the same points were made by Calvin, who showed from Scripture that the favour of God is not only to the parents but also to the children, so that the covenant sign applies both to the faithful and also to their posterity.[235] This did not mean that all the infants of believers were necessarily elect, but it did mean that they could be externally reckoned as heirs of the promises of grace, and therefore "presumed justly to be the children of God."[236]

Of, the Anglicans, Cranmer and Philpot made the greatest use of the argument. In the *Reformatio Legum* Cranmer stated it in a form which is purely Zwinglian. Producing his "plain scriptures" in defence of infant baptism, he referred first to "the figure of the old law, which was circumcision", and to the promise which had accompanied it: "I will be thy God, and the God of thy seed after thee."[237] Perhaps it was due to Cranmer's influence that the same reasoning had appeared in the *King's Book*: "The infancy of the Hebrews in the Old Testament did not let, but that they were made participant of the grace and benefit given by circumcision",[238] although it will be noted that in this case the sacrament is linked with conferred benefits rather than with an accompanying promise, as in the later work. Philpot based his argument upon the principle to which we have already referred, that the apostles consciously fulfilled the shadows and figures of the Old Testament, from which it followed that "they did attemperate baptism according to circumcision, and baptized children".[239] Like Zwingli, he pointed out that in the Old Testament type "the people

---

232. Seeberg, *op. cit.*, p. 322.
233. C.R., II, p. 207.
234. C.R., VI, p. 71.
235. *Instit.*, IV, 16, 3-6.
236. B.P.S., p. 48.Cf. Bullinger, P.S..IV, p. 390.
237. Cranmer, P.S., II, p. 60.
238. K.B., p. 43.
239. Philpot, P.S., p. 278.

of Israel passed through the Red Sea, and the bottom of Jordan, with their children".[240] Of others who made reference to the Old Testament example we may mention Becon,[241] Nowell,[242] Jewel[243] and Rogers.[244]

The Reformed case did not end, of course, with the Old Testament precedent. Passages could also be adduced from the New Testament which seemed to favour infant baptism. Of these the blessing of the children was the most commonly used. Melanchthon derived from the incident, first, an assurance that infants are heirs of the divine promises; and second that they belong to the church, and have therefore a right to the initiatory sign.[245] Zwingli laid greater emphasis upon the command: "Suffer little children", and he did not see any other way of fulfilling it than by granting to children the sign of membership of Christ.[246] Calvin brought the pronouncement and the command into a clear relationship, dismissing as quibbles the two Anabaptist objections, first, that the children must have been of an age to respond, and second, that it is those who are like children who are said to pertain to the kingdom.[247] In England, Cranmer linked up the incident with the warning: "See that ye despise not one of these little ones"; which the Anabaptists seemed to him to ignore.[248] The fuller Marcan version was substituted for the Sarum Matthean in the revised service-books, probably in imitation of the Lutheran orders.[249] Nowell had a reference to the incident, and Philpot bluntly asked: "What do they nowadays else, that bring their children to baptism, than they did in time past, which brought their children to the Lord?"[250] Like Cranmer, Philpot related the incident to the other sayings about children. He concluded that God "receiveth them freely unto His grace, although as yet they confess not this faith", challenging his opponents to say "why the sign of the promise, which is baptism in water, should then be withdrawn from children".[251] The argument was later popularized in Bullinger's *Decades*, in which the text "Of such is the kingdom of heaven" was used to prove infant discipleship: "He manifestly calleth the littler ones, not yet able to confess, believers."[252]

---

240. *Loc. cit.*
241. Becon, P.S., II, p. 207.
242. Nowell, P.S., p. 87.
243. Jewel, P.S., II, p. 1104.
244. Rogers, P.S., p. 279.
245. C.R., XXI, p. 295.
246. C.R., III, p. 298.
247. *Instit.*, IV, 16, 7.
248. Cranmer, P.S., II, p. 60.
249. Daniel, *op. cit.*, p. 419.

250. Philpot, P.S., p. 227.
251. *Ibid.*, p. 275.
252. Bullinger, P.S., IV, p. 385.

A second text to which the Reformers turned was that at the end of Matthew in which Christ instituted the sacrament. Two points were at issue here: first, the Anabaptist contention that teaching is to precede baptism; and second, the objection that the disciples were not clearly commanded to baptize infants. Against the latter objection Melanchthon claimed that in the absence of an express prohibition the general phrase "all nations" necessarily included children.[253] In this he was supported by Zwingli.[254] The argument was attractive, because it threw the onus of proof upon the Anabaptists. Against the former argument Zwingli drew attention to the fact that in the Matthean version baptism precedes the fuller instruction, just as water precedes Spirit in the famous text John 3:5, which some of the Swiss Anabaptists wished to take literally.[255] Zwingli did not press the point, but simply used it to show that too great an importance must not be attached to the grammatical order. Calvin drew a similar lesson. He thought that most of the difficulties would disappear if sound rules of exegesis were followed and the text related to the first and missionary preaching to which it obviously applied.[256] The Anglicans had nothing new to say on the point. Becon thought that the universality of the mandate favoured an extension to infants,[257] and Philpot made a similar deduction: "The Lord commanded His apostles to baptize all nations, therefore also children ought to be baptized."[258] Like Calvin, Philpot thought that preaching ought to precede baptism where the Gospel was first preached. But this was not a permanent rule to exclude children: "Gentiles must first be taught and confess: but not the children of believers. It is a general rule, He that doth not labour must not eat; but who is so barbarous that might think thereby, that children should be famished?"[259] In other words, even plain texts must be correctly interpreted and applied.

Two further proofs from the New Testament both concerned John the Baptist. In general, the Anabaptists did not emphasize the identity of John's baptism with that of Christ, but for controversial reasons Grebel contended that we ought to follow the example of John, who baptized only those who repented and brought forth the fruits of repentance.[260] But against this,

---

253. C.R., XXI, p. 295.
254. C.R., III, p. 211.
255. C.R., IV, pp. 215 f.
256. *Instil.*, IV, 16, 9.
257. Becon, P.S., II, p. 209.
258. Philpot, P.S., p. 276. Cf. Bullinger, P.S., IV, p. 389.
259. *Ibid.*, p. 282.
260. C.R., III, p. 369.

Zwingli pointed out that all Judea, etc., went out to him and were baptized. This did not mean that every single individual went, but all types or classes, which necessarily included children.[261] Whitgift dealt with much the same difficulty when Cartwright argued that John preached at his baptism. His answer was quite different, however, for he maintained that the details of administration might vary. If we were to do only as John had done, we should be committed to "baptizing only in the river Jordan, and none but those that be of age".[262]

The person of John was of interest as well as his baptism, for according to the New Testament John was filled with the Holy Ghost from his mother's womb. But if the infant John could enjoy the inward baptism of the Spirit, this destroyed the Anabaptist contention that infants cannot have the thing signified by baptism, and therefore have no right to the sign. Indeed, as Zwingli pointed out, a mere profession of faith is no more guarantee of spiritual baptism than a Christian descent. Only God can know the secrets of the heart. All that man can do is to administer the sacrament to those who are externally qualified.[263] Calvin would even deduce from this example that elect infants who die before they come to an adult faith may enjoy an interior illumination of the Spirit.[264] He did not think, as Luther did, that all children have faith, nor did he agree with Melanchthon that the Holy Ghost is given to them in and through the sacrament to incline them to faith. But he did accept the probability of a special and direct work of the Spirit as in the case of John. In the words of Beza: "It is not likely that ye have faythe except God work in them extraordinary",[265] but this extraordinary working could be presumed in the case of the elect dying in infancy.[266]

A similar argument was used by the Anglican Becon, although Becon gave to it a decided Lutheran twist. As he saw it, children do have faith: indeed, if they are to be saved at all, they must, for without faith it is impossible to please God. They do not have it in the ordinary way, however, but by a special operation of the Holy Spirit whose gift and fruit it is.[267] And the fact that they do have it in this way is proved by the examples of Jeremy, John and Jacob.[268] The gift which they enjoyed

261. C.R., IV, p. 239.
262. Whitgift, P.S., II, p. 508.
263. C.R., IV, p. 632.
264. *Instil.*, IV, 16, 19.
265. B.P.S., 48.
266. Q.R.C., 124.
267. Becon, P.S., II, 211-212.
268. *Loc. cit.*

Becon seemed to ascribe to all infants born within the covenant, for he referred to the children of believers as "endued with the Holy Ghost even from their cradles".[269] In the case of those who grew to adult life there was a lapse from this primitive faith, with the need for a subsequent conversion, but the many who died in infancy were accepted by God in the faith which they had by this special operation. The later decline in Lutheran influence led to a definite abandonment of this view of the matter, so that Cartwright could state categorically that "children have not, nor cannot have any faith, having no. understanding of the word of God".[270] But this did not preclude a special illumination of the Holy Spirit after the manner taught by Calvin. At the end of the century, Hooker revived a conception not unlike that of Melanchthon, that in baptism "the Holy Ghost might truly be said to work, giving that grace which is the first and most effectual cause out of which our belief groweth".[271] This interpretation clearly differed from that of the Calvinists, but in their different ways all the Reformers agreed that infants may have the Holy Spirit as John did, and that they cannot therefore be excluded from water-baptism.

In addition to the direct texts of Scripture the Reformers considered certain passages which seemed to reflect the apostolic practice. Of these the records of household baptisms in Acts were the most outstanding, and they were examined with great care and considerable dialectical skill, especially by Zwingli. Zwingli allowed, of course, that there is no express mention of children. But he contended that a household may justly be held to include children unless there is any information to the contrary. The reference to an acceptance of the message would obviously apply only to those capable of making such acceptance, who were after all the most important part of the household.[272] Calvin did not consider these passages in any way vital to the argument, but he, too, thought that a household normally includes children even if it did not do so in any of the cases mentioned.[273] Thus the burden of proof rested upon the innovators. Bullinger and Beza both thought the baptism of infants a reasonable and almost necessary inference from these accounts.[274] There were not many Anglican references to the records, but Becon asked: "Do we not read that

---

269. *Ibid.*, p. 207.
270. Whitgift, P.S., III, p. 115.
271. L.E.P., V, LXIV.
272. C.R., VI, pp. 48 f.
273. *Instit.*, IV, 16, 8.
274. Bullinger, P.S., IV, p. 391; B.P.S., 48.

the apostles baptized whole households ?"[275] and Philpot boldly claimed: "Also the scripture evidently telleth us, that the apostles baptized whole families of households, but the children are comprehended in the family or household, as the chiefest and dearest part thereof"[276] – a delightful touch of sentiment all too rare in sixteenth-century disputation. Cartwright attached considerable importance to the argument, ranking it with the circumcision of the Old Testament to which it corresponded: "What stronger hold have we, to prove the baptism of children and young infants, than circumcision in the Old Testament, and the example thereof in the New Testament, for that the apostles baptized whole families, where by all likelihood there were children ?"[277]

Another passage which seemed to have a bearing on the question was the much disputed verse, 1 Corinthians 7:14. Calvin discussed this text at considerable length. He thought that it could not refer to civil sanctity, or legitimacy, but only to a sanctity peculiar to the children of believers. In other words, the children of Christians belong by descent to the people of God, and they have therefore a right to the covenant sign.[278] Knox expounded the verse in much the same way.[279] Amongst the many Anglicans who used it we may number Cranmer, who included it in his "plain scriptures",[280] and the martyr Haukes who based upon it his idea of a vicarious faith of the parents.[281] A final passage which had to be noted was the baptismal section of Romans 6, from which the Anabaptists had argued that only those who can know the inward experience of baptism ought to receive the sign. But to this deduction Calvin made the forcible rejoinder: "By this the apostle means not that he who is to be initiated by baptism must have previously been buried with Christ; he simply declares the doctrine which is taught by baptism, and that to those already baptized: so that the most senseless cannot maintain from this passage that it ought to precede baptism."[282]

From the purely historical standpoint the Reformers had not been able to prove that infants were in fact baptized in apostolic times, although it must be remembered too that the Anabaptists could not prove that they were not. But in their perception of the whole coherence and meaning

---

275. Becon, P.S., II, p. 209.
276. Philpot, P.S., p. 278.
277. Whitgift, P.S., II, p. 363.
278. *Commentary on 1 Corinth.* 7: 10.
279. Knox, IV, pp. 186-7.
280. J., IV, p. 232.
281. Foxe, VII, p. 103.
282. *Instit.*, IV, 16, 21.

of Scripture, there can be little doubt that the Reformers had the better of the argument, and that they had established a strong probability of the scriptural nature of the practice. This superiority became even more pronounced when they turned to their theological justification of infant baptism, in which they penetrated to many basic and crucial doctrinal issues. It is not always appreciated, perhaps, that when the Reformers defended infant baptism they were not merely justifying a convenient ecclesiastical practice. They were contending for fundamental theological positions, which not unjustly they thought to be threatened by the Anabaptist aberration.

Ultimately, the true basis of the Reformed retention of infant baptism was their doctrine of the election. This is, perhaps, only another way of saying that infants have a right to the sacrament because they belong to the covenant people, or are heirs of the divine promise. But it could be stated more plainly and bluntly than that. For instance, when Zwingli considered the Anabaptist argument that faith must precede baptism, he retorted that it is not faith but the election which is the ground of our adoption into the family of God. The elect man is the son of God even before he comes to faith. It is nonsense to say: "Infants do not believe and therefore they are damned. For Jacob was elect even when he did not believe; it does not follow then to say, he does not believe, therefore he is not elect."[283] It is true, of course, that we cannot say of any infant, or professing adult, that he is inwardly elect, but where there are the outward marks of election, profession or a Christian descent, there the outward sign of election may also be given. Much the same points were made by Calvin. He too claimed that the gift of adoption is prior to baptism, and he presumed a special operation of the Spirit in elect infants dying in infancy.[284] Calvin held with Zwingli that the election is ultimately the secret of God, but he accepted profession and descent as the external marks which qualified for at least the external sign. Bullinger popularized the argument in England when, in reply to the "babbling objection" that infants cannot believe, he pointed out that the baptism of infants is not based upon their belief, but "upon the free mercy and grace of God".[285]

As we have seen, the covenantal idea had been widely accepted

---

283. C.R., IV, p. 177.
284. *Instit.*, IV, 16, 19.
285. Bullinger, P.S., IV, p. 343.

in England, but only a few of the writers made explicit the implicit connection between baptism and the election. Perhaps the clearest statement was that of Philpot, who did not hesitate to include infants "in the number or scroll of God's elect", which were to be judged, not only by "the confession of faith", but also by "the free and liberal promise of God".[286] Bradford thought that the divine election had determined even our descent from Christian parents,[287] and Coverdale argued briefly that whereas the baptism of adults is grounded in faith, that of infants is grounded in the election.[288] There is perhaps a hint of the same doctrine in the baptismal prayer that the child "may ever remain in the number of thy faithful and elect children". Several commentators think that this implies a general but defectible grace after the Lutheran manner, but the verb "remain" need not imply more than that all infants (and confessing adults) are reckoned in the elect people of God, but only those who are inwardly and truly elect will have the grace of final perseverance.[289]

The interrelating of baptism and the divine election points to a fundamental difference between the Reformed conception and the Anabaptist. For the Anabaptist the sacrament was primarily a sign of faith, with a subjective reference. The approach was anthropocentric. But for the Reformers it was primarily a declaration of the divine grace, with an objective reference. The approach was theocentric. This was the basic cleavage between the Reformers and their Anabaptist opponents. It is exposed with no less clarity in the second of the theological arguments, the argument from original sin.

By scriptural definition, baptism is the sacrament of remission. If it is denied to infants, then logically that means, either that infants have no sin which needs to be remitted, or that their sin is not remitted. The Anabaptists could not avoid this dilemma, and the majority quickly revealed themselves to be frankly Pelagian in their conceptions of original sin and the freedom of the will. Infants are saved without the remission of sin (and therefore without baptism) because they have no sin which needs to be remitted.

But to the Reformers this was a repudiation of the very heart of the Gospel, that all men are sinners and guilty by nature, and that there is no salvation for any man except in and through the redemptive

---

286. Philpot, P.S., p. 275.
287. Bradford, P.S., II, Letter 43.
288. Coverdale, P.S., II, p, 268.
289. Cf. B.P.S., 48.

work of Jesus Christ. Melanchthon emphasized this point: the death of Jesus Christ was for infants as well as adults, and by it infants have the remission of original sin, and therefore the inward work of baptism.[290] The *Defence of the Augsburg Confession* contained a similar statement: Infants are included in the divine promise, and baptism is to them a sign of the remission of sin by non-imputation. Zwingli was perhaps feeling after this idea when he claimed that in the case of Christian children there is an inherited defect of nature, but no original guilt, although his statement was not very cautiously worded.[291] Calvin, however, put the matter very clearly: "We are born sinners and we stand in need of forgiveness and pardon from the very womb."[292] But the forgiveness and pardon of original sin is assured to the elect in Jesus Christ. Therefore Christian children have a right to the sign of forgiveness. Bullinger followed the same line of argument. He went too far when he accused Pelagius of denying infant baptism, but he was right in so far as logically, and theologically, Pelagius ought to have done so.[293]

The close relationship between baptism and original sin appears plainly in the various Anglican formularies, especially of the early period. In the words of the *King's Book*, "Infants, because they be born in original sin, have need and ought to be christened"[294] – but of course the *King's Book* made the necessity absolute as in the teaching of tradition. The opening exhortation in the Baptismal Office claimed original sin as the underlying reason for baptism. Although the reference to John 3:5 might seem to imply an absolute necessity, the Reformers hardly meant it in that way. In their view, infants are under wrath by nature, but they have remission and spiritual renewal by virtue of the covenant-mercies signed and sealed in baptism. The individual writers did not elaborate the argument, but it was plainly stated in Turner,[295] Jewel,[296] and Rogers.[297] Whitaker, too, saw the interconnection.[298] The statement of Jewel clearly reflects the language of the Prayer Book: "For this cause are infants baptized, because they are born in sin, and cannot become spiritual but by this new birth of water and of the Spirit." Jewel cannot have meant this in the traditionalist

---

290. C.R., XXI, pp. 295, 466.
291. C.R., IV, pp. 307-310.
292. *Instil.*, IV, 16, 21.
293. Bullinger, P.S., IV, p. 376.
294. K.B., p. 43.
295. Turner, *Preservative, passim.*
296. Jewel, P.S., II, p. 1104.
297. Rogers, P.S., p. 279.
298. Whitaker, P.S., p. 515.

sense, for elsewhere he rejected an absolute necessity, and distinguished carefully between the sign and the thing signified.

Against the Reformers' pressure the main bulwark of the Anabaptists was that infants cannot have faith, and therefore lack the essential qualification for the sacrament. The Reformers felt the force of this argument. On the one hand they could not accept the solution of the traditionalists, that infants are baptized in the faith of their sponsors or the church, and that they receive in baptism the gift of habitual faith. On the other, they were concerned to stress the indispensability of faith to a true and effectual reception of both the sacraments.

In the attempt to deal with the problem, a division arose between the Lutherans on the one side and the Reformed school on the other. The teaching of Luther was not altogether consistent. In places he seemed to accept the notion of a vicarious faith of the sponsors.[299] Elsewhere, however, he asserted boldly that infants do have an actual faith.[300] For after all, he argued, adults do not lose their faith when they are asleep or unconscious. If it is objected that infants cannot believe, the answer is that without God adults cannot believe either: indeed, it is easier for God to work in the unresisting hearts of infants than to soften the hard hearts of adults.[301] He was not satisfied with the suggestion that infants are baptized in respect of a future faith, for he saw an urgent and pressing need of present remission.[302]

Many of the English Reformers were obviously influenced by Luther's solution. Becon, for example, thought that infants believe, "not by preaching, but by the Holy Ghost". He also referred to the continuance of faith in the sleeping adult. The lack of tokens or fruits of faith he explained by the lack of time or age, and he admitted the possibility of a fall from this early faith and the loss of the Holy Spirit.[303] The martyr Woodman seemed to hold a similar view.[304] In spite of its traditionalist ring the teaching was not inconsistent with a generally Protestant interpretation. Even Bullinger could speak of a defection from baptismal grace, and "a receiving of it again by faithful repentance".[305]

During the Henrician and Edwardian period, however, many

---

299. Hamel, *op. cit.*, p. 156.
300. Cristiani, *Du Luthéranisme au Protestantisme*, p. 290.
301. W.A., VI, p. 538.
302. W.A., XVII, 2, p. 81.
303. Becon, P.S., II, pp. 210 f.
304. Foxe, VIII, pp. 538 f.
305. Bullinger, P.S., IV, p. 323.

writers still clung to the notion of a vicarious faith of the sponsors or the church. The 1549 interrogatories suggested this teaching, for the questions were addressed direct to the child but answered by the sponsors. Becon and his school could argue, no doubt, that it is the profession which is vicarious, not the faith; but either way the form was severely criticized by Bucer and the Reformed party. On the other hand, it is not easy to make a clear distinction between a vicarious faith, a vicarious profession, and a guarantee of faith, and the various statements are seldom free from ambiguity. Discussing the question, Jewel could not dismiss entirely the possibility that "children are in some way holpen by the faith of their parents", as the Fathers seemed to believe, and yet he had to confess that "the just man shall live, not by the faith of his parents, but by his own faith".[306]

The two Lutheran answers, that children do have faith, or that they believe in the sponsors, were both rejected out of hand by the Reformed school, which asserted plainly that infants are baptized by virtue of the election, and in respect of a future repentance and faith, which will be evoked by effectual calling.[307] Knox made this clear when he addressed the baptismal questions direct to the sponsors, who simply made a personal profession as a guarantee of Christian descent and upbringing.[308] But there were still qualifications; for apart from the special illumination of those who died in infancy, Calvin could regard baptism as a seed, "which when thrown into the ground, though it may not take root and germinate at the moment, is not without its use".[309]

It was the Reformed view which finally prevailed in England, for in the 1552 revision the baptismal questions were addressed to the sponsors, and they did not offer a vicarious faith or profession, but a guarantee of future fulfilment on the part of the child. Cranmer himself made it plain that in baptism infants do not believe either vicariously or actually, but sacramentally; i.e. they have the sign of faith.[310] Philpot, too, did not think that infants may make any profession of present faith.[311] The Elizabethans were if anything even more definite, for Whitaker disowned the Lutheran view in his controversy with Bellarmine, although he stressed the fact that his opponent was

---

306. Jewel, P.S., III, p. 460.
307. *Instit.*, IV, 16, 19-20.
308. Knox, IV, p. 190.
309. *Tracts*, II, p. 341.
310. Cranmer, P.S., I, p. 124.
311. Philpot, P.S., pp. 274 f.

misrepresenting it.[312] Rogers flatly denounced it as an error: "Others are of the opinion that none are to be baptized which believe not first. Hence the Anabaptists: Infants believe not, therefore they are not to be baptized. Hence the Lutherans: Infants do believe, therefore they are to be baptized."[313] The Puritans, of course, took up the Reformed view with vigour, and they objected that even in their amended form the interrogatories were still administered to the infant.[314] The more thorough revision which they demanded was not regarded as necessary by the Anglicans, however, for as they read it the book no longer implied either an actual or a vicarious faith on the part of the child.

Normally, then, the Reformers felt that they had good theological as well as scriptural grounds for the continuance of the received practice. But with infants as with adults there were certain special cases which demanded special consideration. In some of these the Reformers had no particular interest, but they may be mentioned briefly for the sake of completeness.

A first problem was that of monstrosities, in which there was doubt concerning the true humanity of the creature. The traditional solution had been to administer a conditional form of baptism *"Si tu es homo"*[315] but the issue was not a live one in the Reformation period. A more common difficulty was that of prenatal baptism, which involved the whole question of the commencement of independent life. The consensus of medieval opinion was against pre-natal baptism, largely on the ground that regeneration cannot precede generation, but the baptism of any member which had emerged, especially the head, was normally sanctioned.[316] Luther considered the possibility,[317] but the Reformed school regarded the whole discussion as foolish and futile, since baptism is not in any case necessary. In England pre-natal baptism was neither envisaged by the rubrics nor in any way recommended in the doctrinal formulations.

A problem of rather a different type was that of the foundling about whose prior baptism there was a genuine doubt. The earlier solution had been to administer the sacrament on the assumption of non-baptism, and this was enjoined even by some of the medieval councils.[318] But a plain administration in this way seemed to involve

---

312. Whitaker, P.S., p. 540.
313. Rogers, P.S., p. 281.
314. Whitgift, P.S., III, p. 115.
315. Cf. *Rituale Romanum*.
316. S., III, qu. 68, 11. Also *Catholic Encyclopedia*, Art. Baptism.
317. W.A., VI, pp. 526 f.
318. E.R., p. 203.

the risk of reiteration, and to meet the difficulty a conditional form was evolved at least as early as the time of Boniface of Mainz (*c.* A.D. 730).[319] The conditional baptism gradually became the normal practice. The Swiss Reformers provided a more radical although incidental solution by never permitting any but a public administration by the ordained minister, which abolished all possibility of doubtful cases except in the most extraordinary circumstances. In fact they attributed the confusions and uncertainties of the medieval theologians and canonists entirely to the Papal corruption of the pure institution of Christ. The retention of private baptism in England made necessary the provision of a conditional form in cases of doubt, but with the prohibition of lay-administration in 1604 this became largely redundant.

A more serious problem was that of the forcible baptism of the children of unbelievers, either by kidnapping or by legal enactment. This possibility was inspired by the presumed indispensability of the sacrament, and it applied to Jews living in Christian states and to Turks encountered on the Crusades. The matter was thoroughly discussed by Thomas. In spite of the many plausible reasons in its favour he decided against action of this kind, mainly on the ground that parents have the chief responsibility for their children.[320] But in defiance of this opinion forcible baptisms continued throughout the Middle Ages, as we may see from the protest in the time of Wycliffe: "It is an abuse if Criste men stele yong childre of Jewes and of hethen peple and baptise them agen the wyl of ther fader and moder."[321] Indeed, in the fifteenth century Spain and Portugal decreed the enforced baptism of all Jews both adult and infant, with expulsion as the only alternative to non-compliance. The Council of Trent laid it down that faith is only to be proposed to persons born of infidel parents,[322] but there are records of kidnapping until well on in the eighteenth century.

Of the Protestants it was Calvin who took the lead in opposing enforced baptism. He could not allow that children ought to be baptized unless their parents were Christians, and he condemned strongly "the wicked and insane superstition of Popery to steal and carry off children from Jews and Turks, and immediately hurry them to baptism",[323] a practice which he attributed to their false belief in

---

319. Daniel, *op. cit.*, p. 434.
320. S., III, qu., 68, 10.
321. Manning, *op. cit.*, p. 53.
322. C.T., II, 2, qu. 34.
323. In Knox, VI, pp. 95-96.

the absolute necessity of the sacrament. Baptism belonged only to those who were within the covenant either by profession or descent. Since the children of infidels do not belong to the covenant, "and there is for their baptizing neither command, promise nor example in any part of the New Testament", they must be left to the judgment of Almighty God.[324] The English writers had no occasion to discuss the question, but clearly they did not envisage the baptism of heathen children, accepting the broad principles upon which Calvin based his judgment.

A rather different issue was that of the children of Papists, and of the wicked and apostate generally. The traditionalists themselves were faced with a similar problem in relation to the children of Protestants. Normally they would permit baptism if there was the guarantee of Roman Catholic instruction.[325] On the Protestant side the question arose first amongst the followers of Calvin, and contradictory answers were given. Hooker quotes a letter from Calvin to Farel which forbade the practice,[326] but in his later reply to Knox, Calvin recommended a different course. He pointed out that God's covenant is with believers and their descendants even to a thousand generations. Therefore a wicked, apostate or heretical generation cannot of itself "abstract the virtue and efficacy" of baptism. "The progeny of holy and pious ancestors, although their grandfathers and parents may have been apostates, belong notwithstanding to the body of the church." So long as the Christian faith did not perish altogether, even the children of papists, idolaters and excommunicate persons "were defrauded of their right if they were kept from the common symbol", This did not mean, of course, that baptism was to be absolutely indiscriminate. Calvin insisted that there must be proper sponsors to give the pledge of faith and to undertake the work of instruction. Again, wicked or idolatrous parents were to be sharply reproved. What it did mean was that if the necessary guarantees were forthcoming, no discrimination was to be exercised against the children because of the shortcomings of the parents.[327]

This problem of the children of the Papists and ungodly became a central issue in the Anglican controversy, first with the Puritans,

---

324. Valäus, in R.D. *Bapt.*

325. See *Catholic Encyclopedia*, Art. Baptism.

326. L.E.P., III, I, 12.

327. Knox VI, p. 96. It may be noted that in the case discussed in the letter to Farel the conditions were not fulfilled.

and later with the Separatists. Cartwright stated the objection to indiscriminate baptism, and he showed rather a greater strictness than that of Calvin. His ultimate aim, of course, was the introduction of the Genevan discipline into the admittedly lax and undisciplined Elizabethan church. For Cartwright, baptism belonged only to adult converts and to the children of the faithful. To apply it indiscriminately was "to make of the church an inn for passers by rather than an household". He would concede that if one parent would make a profession, or if the two parents were not obstinate sinners, the child ought to be baptized. Similarly, the child of unknown parents should not be debarred from the sacrament if sponsors could be found. But the children of Papists, heretics and the obstinately wicked ought to be reckoned with those of the Jews and Turks, and not baptized "unless their faith doth first appear by profession".[328] The Separatists, with their dream of a pure church, were if anything even more severe, for according to Rogers the Brownists denied baptism to all the children of open sinners, and the Barrowists specifically to "the seed of whores and witches".[329]

The case against this type of discrimination was stated by Rogers, Whitgift and Hooker. Rogers simply condemned the contrary opinions in his usual fashion.[330] Whitgift used several cogent arguments. He denied that the sin of the parent disqualifies or harms the infant. He challenged the ability of his opponents to judge the fitness of the infant recipient. He pointed out that even "the excommunicate kept still their baptism", And he appealed both to Beza and also to a dictum of Zwingli, that "when we add only external signs, and minister only external doctrine, we must also be content with external confession".[331] Hooker argued out the matter very much along the lines of the Genevan reply to Knox. He concluded that "we may not deny unto infants their right by withholding from them the public sign of holy baptism, if they be born where the outward acknowledgement of holy baptism is not clean gone and extinguished".[332]

Two different issues were involved in the controversy: first, a theological, concerning the nature of the church, and second, an ecclesiastical,

---

328. Whitgift, P.S., III, p. 137.
329. Rogers, P.S., pp. 265 f.
330. *Ibid.*, pp. 265 f.
331. Whitgift, P.S., III, p. 137.
332. L.E.P., III, I, 12.

concerning its discipline. Behind much of the agitation for discriminate baptism, especially on the Separatist side, there lay undoubtedly the rigorist ideal of a pure church of believers completely separate from the world at large. It was against this conception that the arguments of Calvin no less than Whitgift and Hooker were ultimately directed. The Reformed view was that in the administration of the external sign we must rest content with an external qualification. The secret of the heart belongs only to God.

But also behind the agitation, especially on the Puritan side, there lay the desire for a far stricter discipline within the church: the punishing of notorious evildoers, the provision of properly qualified sponsors, the firmer guarantee of a Christian upbringing. With much of the Puritans' programme few would be prepared to quarrel. Their mistake was that they went too far, condemning not merely indiscriminate sponsorship, but indiscriminate baptism as well. Even in the case of sponsors it was evident that only external tests applied, and these could not well be more than baptism, perhaps the ratification of the baptismal vows in confirmation, and a minimal fulfilment of the religious and ethical demands of the faith. But in the Prayer Book and the various injunctions a machinery of discipline had already been set up. The primary problem was simply that of setting it and keeping it in motion. The Puritans were not satisfied either that the tests were exacting enough or the machinery sufficient. Perhaps they were right, although the imposition of too high a standard may easily lead to the creation of particularist, and often hypocritical, churches. But by calling for baptismal discrimination rather than for disciplinary reform they entered on a dangerous road. Their successors in every age would do well to consider the wise and pertinent question with which Hooker summed up the controversy: "Were it not against both equity and duty to refuse the mother of believers herself, and not to take her in this case [i.e. the children of the wicked or apostate] for a faithful parent ?"[333] While that final possibility remains, the case for discrimination has still to be proven.

There was one final matter which engaged the attention of the Reformers, and that was the extension of baptism to inanimate objects, especially bells, and sometimes flags and ships. At least as early as Charlemagne baptisms of this kind had had to be forbidden. From the time of John XIII they became extremely common. The most

---

333. L.E.P., v, LXIV, 5.

elaborate services were staged, with the bishop as celebrant, a definite christening, sponsors, the sign of the cross, the Triune formula, and the usual baptismal ceremonies. The theologians, of course, understood well enough that the term baptism was used only figuratively and by extension in these cases, but superstitious notions were encouraged among the common people, as we may see from the prayer "that the dew of the Holy Spirit might be infused into the bell", and "that the devil might always flee before the sound thereof".[334] In addition, extortionate fees were usually demanded by the episcopal officiants.

It was the financial aspect which underlay the early protest at the Council of Nuremberg, for apparently rich sponsors were usually appointed, and there was a "sumptuous banquet" as well as a large reward for the officiant. But it was noted, too, that superstition was encouraged, and that in a sense true baptism was caricatured by the ceremony.[335] Luther bluntly condemned the practice as ridiculous. However, he found in it a useful argument against the private mass, for the correct observance of the external form could never make a true sacrament in default of the living recipient.[336] The Reformed theologians naturally attacked the custom, and the Anabaptists, too, condemned it as unscriptural and unapostolic.[337]

It was the scriptural test which decided the matter for the English writer Hooper, for, as he pointed out: "The word sheweth ... that only men, reasonable creatures, should be baptized. So it condemneth the gentility and superstition that hath been used in the christening of bells."[338] Becon went further, for he saw in the corruption "a plain mocking of God's ordinance and a very profanation of this sacrament".[339] To say that no true baptism was intended was only to make it more obviously a caricature. That was why Calfhill regarded the practice as devilish, in spite of the solemnities observed.[340] Rogers combined the arguments of Hooper and Becon when he condemned those who abused baptism by baptizing "things without reason, yea sometimes without life or sense. So have the Papists baptized both bells and babels."[341]

---

334. E.R., p. 246.
335. Foxe, IV, p. 311.
336. Audin, *Luther*, p. 145.
337. B.R.N., IV, p. 191.
338. Hooper, P.S., I, p. 533. By "gentility" he perhaps means "gentilism."
339. Becon, P.S., I, p. 11.
340. Calfhill, P.S., p. 15.
341. Rogers, P.S., p. 266.

The controversy was not important, but it illustrates the totally different outlook of the traditionalist and reforming parties. The traditionalists, with all their stress upon the sacraments, would not hesitate to alter or augment that which God had appointed. Their very emphasis upon the external sign caused them to ascribe a spiritual value even to the consecrating of bells. The want of scriptural authority could always be supplied by that of the church and its ordinances. The Reformers, on the other hand, brought to their theology and ecclesiastical practice a high sense of the divine transcendence. In consequence, they stressed the need always to observe strictly that which God Himself had ordained. The sacrament did not have its efficacy merely by the correct performance of certain acts, irrespective of the divinely appointed conditions. The power of the rite depended upon the doing only of that which had been commanded. To turn the ordinance of God to other uses than those ordained by God, in the hope perhaps of spiritual profit, constituted a direct breach of the divine prerogative and could only expose the sacrament itself to ridicule, the perpetrators of the abuse to the just judgment of God, and the church at large to confusion and error.

3

The Rite

(1) Prerequisites

The ordained minister was the proper administrator of baptism, but from the Middle Ages onwards it had been maintained that even in the minister a correct intention was required. For this contention there was very little patristic support: indeed, in a famous case it had been argued by some writers that baptism in jest is still a valid baptism if correctly administered. Similarly, the Schoolmen had not tried to press the doctrine of intention too far. Lombard taught that the observance of the true form was in itself a guarantee of intention.[1] Thomas agreed, except in those obvious cases where the minister confessed to some quite different intention.[2] By the sixteenth century, however, a personal intention was regarded as necessary in each case, and in spite of a minority party, which alleged the authority of Catharinus, the Council of Trent adopted this stricter view,[3] and apologists like Bellarmine defended it. According to Bellarmine, the minister had not merely to do what the church did, but he had also to intend to do what the church did. This did not exclude altogether the baptism of heretics and schismatics, for in this respect the heretical minister could still intend to do what the church universal did.[4] The mischief of the view was not the mere demand for intention, for it is reasonable that there should be an evident desire to do as Christ commanded if baptism is to be regarded as valid, but the demand for a personal intention, which means that the validity of the sacrament is suspended upon what are ultimately unknowable or unverifiable factors.

Calvin went quickly to the main point when in his *Antidote to Trent* he brought two objections against the traditionalist teaching: first, that it "did utterly overthrow whatever solid comfort believers have in the sacrament", and second, that it "suspended the truth of God on the will of man", thus destroying the divine objectivity of the sacrament.[5] The phrase "doing what the church does" Calvin dismissed as meaningless

---

1. Lombard, IV, *Dist*. 6 E.
2. S., III, qu., 64, 8.
3. C.D., Sess. VII, *Sacr. can*. 11.
4. T.B., p. 342.
5. *Tracts*, III, *Antidote to Trent*, VII, *can*. 11.

and silly, but his main fear was that the doctrine would enhance the status of the priest at the expense of the divine sovereignty on the one hand and the faith of the recipient on the other. The very same points were made by Jewel when the topic arose in his controversy with Harding. To suspend the validity of our baptism on the intention of the minister is to destroy its objectivity and certainty: "The heart of man is unsearchable. If we stay upon the intention of a mortal man, we may stand in doubt of our own baptism."[6] Hooker, too, rejected out of hand the insistence upon an individual intention: "What a man's private mind is, as we cannot know, so neither are we bound to examine."[7] Even if the minister later confessed that he had been a hypocrite or an infidel, Hooker did not think that this affected the administration, "for in these cases the known intent of the church doth suffice".[8] But this kind of intention was, of course, only an obvious and superfluous generality.

From the Reformed standpoint the intention of the minister could never be regarded as in any way a decisive question. But the case was far otherwise in respect of the intention of the recipient, at any rate so far as it concerned the efficacy of the sacrament. In the one case, it was the Reformers' task to safeguard the objectivity of the ordinance against an undue exaltation of the human minister. In the other, it was their task to prevent that objectivity from degenerating into a guaranteed and automatic efficacy. They admitted that in the last resort only God can know the inward disposition of the recipient, but they also emphasized that some demonstration of fitness may legitimately be required at least in the case of adults.

A first and essential prerequisite was that the candidate for baptism should have at least an elementary understanding of what it was that he proposed. In other words, there must be instruction. In New Testament days, this instruction seems often to have been of the briefest, but of course those to whom the message came usually had a knowledge of the Old Testament background, and it was sufficient if they understood that the life and death and resurrection of Christ, to which they committed themselves in baptism, were the fulfilment of the Messianic prophecies. But with the widening of the field of evangelism the Gospel came more and more to those who had no basic knowledge, and the need for instruction grew. The answer to the

---

6. Jewel, P.S., I, p. 139.

7. L.E.P., V, LVIII.

8. L.E.P., V, LVIII.

problem was the fully developed catechumenate, with its ceremonies as well as the intellectual instruction, and with a careful progression from the initiatory to the more advanced stage.

The conversion of Western Europe meant that baptismal instruction ceased to be a major activity of the church except in missionary districts, but it was still recognized to be a necessary prerequisite to normal adult baptism. Thomas considered the objection that life ought to precede teaching, but he answered that the faith which is demanded in an adult can come only by hearing.[9] He divided the instruction into four types: the elementary given by any Christian, the more detailed by the priest, the moral by the sponsors, and the most profound by the bishop.[10] The question acquired a new point in the sixteenth century with the great expansion overseas, and the Council of Trent insisted that in all normal cases, i.e. except where there was extreme sickness or other peril, there must be a long period of instruction and testing before the adult can be admitted to baptism.[11]

The Reformers had no great opportunity for missionary work, and therefore no very practical interest in the subject, except in the case of the Anabaptists. But a few adults were evangelized, mainly Jews and Lapps, and the need for prior instruction was strongly emphasized. Apart from an incidental reference to the catechumenate in Jewel,[12] the Anglicans did not even mention the subject, although when the confusion of the Civil War and the needs of the plantations made necessary a service of adult baptism, the usual preparation by instruction and fasting was clearly enjoined. The insistence upon thorough instruction was wholly in line with the Protestant call for a proper understanding of the sacrament, and indeed of the Christian faith as a whole.

A second and no less essential prerequisite was the renunciation of the former life and the public avowal of faith in Jesus Christ, often accompanied by the expression of a desire for baptism. This profession served as the external guarantee of the sincerity of the candidate. It probably developed out of New Testament examples like that of the eunuch, although in apostolic days the public manifestation of the Spirit often rendered it superfluous. The simple confession of faith was gradually expanded, especially with the conversion of pagans

---

9. S., III, qu. 71, 1.

10. *Ibid.*, 71, 2.

11. C.T., II, 2, qu. 35, 64.

12. Jewel, P.S., I, p. 119.

and the development of heresies. The early liturgies make it plain that great importance was attached to the confession, for in some rites there was a threefold renunciation and profession in addition to the interrogatories.[13] The Lutheran, Reformed and Anglican offices all preserve something of this primitive feature.

The need for an expressed intention on the part of the adult recipient was keenly felt by the Schoolmen, in spite of the possible objections that the recipient is passive, that reiteration might be necessitated, and that baptism has primary reference to original sin for which there is no personal responsibility. For as Thomas pointed out, in answer to these criticisms, intention is equivalent to desire, which is self-evidently necessary, and in any case there can be no true penitence unless there is the will to repent. Even the passiveness of the recipient is a voluntary passiveness.[14] Intention and determination to receive the sacrament were still demanded in the *Catechism* of Trent,[15] and adults were required to answer the usual interrogatories and make the traditional profession:[16] something which had to be done in person.[17]

Of the Protestants, the Anabaptists laid the greatest emphasis upon the confession of individual faith, for of course their baptisms were exclusively adult baptisms. Calvin did not agree with the Anabaptists that repentance and faith must always precede the sacrament, but naturally he called for a public profession in all those whose age made them capable of it.[18] Beza taught that those adults who could not render a clear account ought to be excluded.[19] The same point was made by the English formularies and theologians. The Article of 1536, for example, laid down that the benefits of adult baptism depend upon "their coming thereunto perfectly and truly repentant, confessing and believing all the articles of the faith, and having firm trust and credence in the promises of God adjoined to the said sacrament".[20] The *King's Book*, too, described belief, service, and the forsaking of sin as the human side of the baptismal covenant.[21] Amongst individual writers Frith,[22] Nowell,[23] and Hooper[24] all mentioned the need for an expressed repentance and

---

13. Cf. *Liturgy and Worship*,
    pp. 410 f.
14. S., III, qu. 68, 8.
15. C.T., II, 2, qu. 35.
16. C.T., II, 2, qu., 42.
17. C.T., II, 2, qu. 43.
18. *Tracts*, II, p. 87.
19. Q.R.C., 119.
20. Strype, *Cranmer*, I, p. 85.

21. K.B., p. 44.
22. B.R., p. 92.
23. Nowell, P.S., p. 87.
24. Hooper, P.S., I, p. 74.

faith, and Becon made it plain that "ungodly and wicked hypocrites, which feign repentance and faith, only receive outward baptism".[25] Jewel thought it only reasonable and right to demand of adult converts an "acknowledgement of the error in which they lived, and the seeking forgiveness of their former sins".[26] Hooker quoted some words of Isidorus on the twofold covenant of the Christian, demanding "an express confession of faith ... on the receipt of the first sacrament of faith".[27] It was everywhere agreed that the external confession could never be a perfect guarantee of internal disposition, but it was also agreed that it was the necessary prerequisite for an external administration, and that it could be charitably accepted as the evidence of true conversion, and therefore of a true intention.

But if instruction and profession were necessary in the case of adults, it is obvious that neither could be demanded where the recipient was still an infant. The Anabaptists deduced from this fact the conclusion that infants ought not to be baptized, but the deduction was not accepted either by the traditionalists or by the Reformers, who agreed that in the case of infants the requirements may in some sense or form be met by the sponsors.

The representing of infants by sponsors could hardly claim to be scriptural, but it was certainly of great antiquity, and it possibly derived from the Old Testament demand for two or three witnesses (as at the Jewish proselyte baptisms).[28] Where adults were baptized, the function of sponsors was more purely one of witness: to guarantee the sincerity of the candidate, to witness his profession, and to assist him in the new life. But when infants were baptized, their task became rather more onerous, for in a sense they had to represent the child as well as to undertake its future instruction. In the first centuries the parents themselves were usually the sponsors,[29] for, as Augustine said, the child believed in the parent. But others could also act on occasion: e.g. the master for infant-slaves, or a virgin for foundlings.[30] The hazards of death or apostasy during the great persecutions probably helped to popularize the practice of having at least one sponsor who was not the parent.[31] The number of sponsors was not fixed, but there would usually be two, or at the most three.

---

25. Becon, P.S., II, pp. 224-225.

26. Jewel, P.S., II, p. 1105.

27. L.E.P., V, LXIII, 1; LXIV. 4,

28. Daniel, *op. cit.*, p. 412.

29. E.R., p. 202.

30. Wall, *op. cit.*, I, p. 137.

31. Daniel, *op. cit.*, p. 412.

During the Dark and Middle Ages many regulations were passed in relation to sponsors. The most revolutionary was that of the Council of Mentz in 815, which in defiance of all antiquity forbade parents to be sponsors for their own children.[32] The Penitential of Ecgbert laid it down that a man should receive a girl from the font, and a woman a boy.[33] The Council of York restricted the number of sponsors to two men and a woman for a boy, two women and a man for a girl,[34] but the Sarum Liturgy specified only two sponsors, and the Greek and Latin churches both regarded one as sufficient.[35] Perhaps the most curious development was the postulating of a spiritual relationship between godparents and godchild and between the godparents themselves,[36] a relationship which brought them within the prohibited degrees.[37] It is difficult to see what solid foundation there was for this theory, although it had no doubt the advantage of widening the field of ecclesiastical discipline and dispensation. Yet it was endorsed in the *Catechism* of Trent,[38] in which the rules concerning sponsors and their qualifications and duties were carefully set out.[39]

The office of godparent survived in all the Protestant churches in spite of Anabaptist objections and certain scruples on the part of the Reformed school. The Lutherans took over the traditional teaching very much as it stood, except that they demanded a real understanding on the part of the sponsors, and made a more definite effort to instruct them in their duties. The use of the vernacular was a great help in this connection.[40] The Anglicans approached the matter in much the same way. In the early period Frith and Tyndale drew attention to the need for properly qualified sponsors who "should know their office and do it".[41] Tyndale in particular complained bitterly of the laxity in instruction and the evasion by all parties of their responsibility: "And when the bishops no longer opposed the children one by one, the priests no longer taught them, but committed the charge to their godfathers and godmothers, and they to the father and mother, discharging themselves by their own authority within half an hour. And the father and mother taught them

---

32. E.R., p. 202.
33. E.R., p. 194.
34. E.R., p. 202.
35. Daniel, *op. cit.*, p. 412.
36. And also the baptizer, as foreshadowed perhaps in the earlier prohibition of the kiss, E.R., p. 194.
37. E.R., p. 202.
38. C.T., II, 2, qu. 26.
39. C.T., II, 2, qu. 25-28.
40. Jacobs, *op. cit.*, Baptism.
41. Frith, B.R., p. 95.

a monstrous Latin paternoster. And in process, as the ignorance grew, they brought them to confirmation straight from baptism, so that now ofttimes they be volowed and bishopped both in one day; that is, we be confirmed in blindness to be kept in ignorance for ever."[42] Rather strangely this demand for capable and conscientious sponsors was resisted by the Warham régime,[43] which no doubt feared a Lutheran infiltration, but the demand grew steadily, and Becon claimed that parents ought at least "to be suffered to be present at the baptism of their own children".[44] A good deal of ground was gained in the Prayer Book revisions, in which three sponsors were permitted, their duties were clearly and forcibly defined, and an instruction was appended. Parents were still not allowed to act as sponsors, but they were no longer forbidden to attend the service.

The Reformed group was not at all satisfied with the Lutheran and Anglican revision. The exclusion of parents from the office of sponsor was one of the most fiercely contested issues. Calvin and Knox both thought that the parent ought to be the chief sponsor,[45] and the Elizabethan Puritans pressed strongly for this reform.[46] In the words of the *Admonition*, parents themselves ought normally "to make rehearsal of their faith", deputies being permitted "only if upon necessary occasions and business they be absent".[47] Some Puritans apparently took the law into their own hands, for in 1584 the "Person" of Eastwell was cited for admitting a father as godparent.[48] The Separatists pressed for a complete abolition of the office, although what they probably had in mind was the replacement of the traditional godparents by parent-sponsors.[49]

The Anglicans could not accept the full Puritan demand, but they were ready to make concessions. In the *Advertisements* parents were given clear permission to attend, although not as sponsors.[50] To prohibit child-sponsorship, communicant-membership was made a necessary qualification for the office.[51] The apologists of the church maintained this position, complaining that the Puritans "betrayed a useless and over-busy fondness for innovation",[52] although in this case they were

---

42. Tyndale, P.S., III, p. 72.
43. Foxe, V, p. 592.
44. Becon, P.S., II, p. 228.
45. Knox, VI, p. 97, IV, p. 190.
46. *Zürich Letters*, P.S., I, 106.
47. P.M., p. 14.
48. Strype, *Whitgift*, I, p. 277.
49. E.E.D., I, p. 143; S.P.R., II, 70.

50. Gee and Hardy, *Documents,
    Advertisements, Articles for
    Administration*, 9.
51. *Ibid.*, 10.
52. *Zürich Letters*, P.S., II, 94.

obviously appealing to antiquity as well as to the best Reformed churches and the evident fitness of the arrangement. The real reason for the rejection of the demand was probably because it formed part of that wider programme of readjustment which the church, and especially the Queen, was not prepared to accept. In addition, the vociferousness of the Puritans no doubt helped to stiffen the opposition. The judgment of the *Advertisements* was finally ratified and enforced in the canons of 1604.

A primary duty of the godparents or sponsors was to make some guarantee of faith on behalf of the infant. All parties agreed concerning the demand for this guarantee, but the exact nature of it was the cause of considerable debate and even controversy. The whole issue narrowed down ultimately to the meaning and significance of interrogatories as administered in the case of infants, and of the – in some sense – representative or vicarious replies which were made by the sponsors.

Even in the early church, in which the adult service had first been applied to infants in this way, there was no great clarity or unanimity on the point. Augustine seems to have inclined to the view that the sponsor was professing his own faith and that of the church, in which the child itself participated.[53] In this he was followed by Thomas, who argued that lack of personal faith does not constitute an obstacle to baptism or baptismal grace so long as there is no positive unbelief.[54] Other possible views which emerged were that the child has a genuine faith, to which the sponsor gives expression, that the sponsor guarantees the future faith of the child, or that the faith confessed by the sponsor establishes its covenant-right to the sacrament. In practice, the latter view cannot easily be distinguished from that of Augustine and the Schoolmen, although there is a real difference in implication.

By the sixteenth century two points at any rate were clear: first, that in the traditional service the interrogatories were definitely administered to the infants themselves; and second that the infants were regarded as pledged to the faith of their sponsors. On the latter ground the Protestants were frequently accused of treachery to their baptismal sponsors",[55] although Woodman raised an interesting point when he asked to what faith infants are engaged if their sponsors are at heart

---

53. Wall, *op. cit.*, I, p. 137.
54. S., III, qu. 71, 1.
55. Foxe, VIII, pp. m, 142, 450.

unbelievers. The answer would presumably be to the faith of the church as externally acknowledged by the sponsors.

Luther did not quarrel with the directing of the interrogatories to the infants, for as we have seen he believed that the infants do have a real faith of which the sponsors are simply the mouthpiece. In this view he was followed by quite a few of the earlier Anglicans, Becon, for example, and probably L. Ridley; but it was strongly opposed in Reformed circles, for Calvin did not think it proper to speak of faith in infants, or to exact a vicarious profession of that which by its very nature cannot be known. The Edwardian Anglicans were obviously influenced by this criticism. In place of the Lutheran teaching they inclined to the idea that godparents give a pledge of future repentance and faith of which mouthpiece. their own faith is as it were the surety. On this view, the questions ought properly to be addressed to the sponsors, but they undertake repentance and faith in the name of the child. In the words of Hooper, "the testimonies of the infant to be christened are examined in the behalf of the child",[56] and it is on the answer and pledge given that the child is declared to be an inheritor of the covenanted blessings.

The issue came to a head in England with the publication of the 1549 Prayer Book, in which the interrogatories were still addressed to the infant. To the more radical group this seemed to imply either the traditional or the Lutheran teaching. In any case, if the godparents were guarantors of the future faith of the child, as the Catechism seemed to suggest, it was to them that the questions ought properly to be directed. The malcontents were supported by Bucer, and they gained their point, for in the 1552 revision the questions were addressed to the sponsors, who answered in the name of the child. Taken in conjunction with the Catechism and the Confirmation service, the new form obviously suggests that the sponsors are engaging the child to a future individual faith, rather after the manner of Hooper's teaching. But of course the profession of the sponsors was still evidence of the child's title to the sacrament, and Lutherans could easily interpret the answers as the vicarious profession of a faith already present in the infant.

The Puritans of the Exile quickly became dissatisfied even with the revised order. Under the tutelage of the Swiss they had learned to regard all forms of infant interrogatories as "needless and trifling", and the

---

56. Hooper, P.S., I, pp. 129-130.

result of the negligent application to infants of the form "which in the beginning was used in the baptism of adult catechumens".[57] According to the Swiss view, all that was necessary was a confession made by the parent in his own name, in order to ensure a discriminate use of the sacrament. The Anglican form was unsatisfactory because the profession was still made in the name of the child. The sponsors were asked to make vicarious promises which even they themselves found it too hard to perform.[58]

The opposition gathered strength during the reign of Elizabeth, and with the support of Beza[59] the Puritans pressed for the complete abolition of the interrogatories, or at any rate for the replacement of the words "Dost thou believe" by "Do you believe", in order to make it clear that the question is addressed only to the sponsors.[60] Grindal himself favoured the alteration, for he confessed that he tolerated the interrogatories to infants only "until the Lord shall give us better times".[61] The point was mentioned in all the Puritan tracts and protests. Marprelate scoffed at the bishops' English which construed "My desire is that I may be baptized in this faith" to mean "My desire is, not that I myself, but that this child, whereunto I am a witness, may be baptized in this faith".[62] Some Puritans altered the service simply on their own authority, for Hall of Bury St. Edmunds was "indited" on this charge,[63] and Settles imprisoned.[64] The matter was finally raised both in the Millenary Petition and also at the Hampton Court Conference.

The main objections to the interrogatories were stated by Cartwright in his *Defence of the Admonition*. Historically, he could not agree that "these interrogatories and demands ministered to infants have so many grey hairs as Mr. Doctor would have us believe", for his Dionysius was "a counterfeit and start-up", and Augustine did not favour the Anglican view.[65] Theologically, he regarded it as a profanation and "foolish toying" to "ask questions of an infant which cannot answer".[66] He accepted the possibility of a special work of the Holy Spirit, but not of our knowledge of that work: "It can no more be precisely said that it hath faith, than it may be said precisely elected."[67] But even if we did know that the child

---

57. Strype, *Grindal*, I, Appendix 41.

58. Grindal, P.S., p. 349.

59. P.M., p. 48.

60. Strype, *Whitgift*, I, pp. 386 f.

61. *Zürich Letters*, P.S., I, 75.

62. *Marprelate Tracts*, p. 373.

63. S.P.R., I, 111.

64. S.P.R., I, 138.

65. Whitgift, P.S., III, p. 110.

66. *Ibid.*, p. 114.

67. *Loc. cit.*

has faith, there is no point in pretending that it answers to that faith: all that may be done is to "ask those that presented the child, and not the infant, whether it were faithful", as Augustine seems to envisage.[68] He could not agree that the sponsors ought to make pledges which it was not in their power to fulfil. All that Cartwright himself recommended was a simple confession of faith on the part of the sponsors themselves.[69]

The Anglican defence was first conducted by Whitgift, who condemned the Puritan demand as "unsound, smelling of divers errors, contrary to the use of the primitive church, impious also and inconvenient ... the direct way to that heresie of the Anabaptistes".[70] Apart from abuse, his main weapon was the appeal to antiquity; although he did make one useful point, that we ought not to seal the evangelical promises without a corresponding obligation on the part of the child.[71] As he saw it, the sponsors accepted on behalf of the child that repentance and faith which it would later take up for itself. He did not exploit the argument, but it was adopted by Hooker. As Hooker saw it, the church cannot waive its usual conditions in the case of infants, but the conditions ought to be accepted for the time being by the sponsors as their spiritual guardians.[72] At the Hampton Court Conference the Bishop of Winchester returned to the older notion of a vicarious faith: "Just as infants have sinned vicariously, so they can believe vicariously."[73] At bottom, this did not differ greatly from the Reformed view, that the child has a right to baptism by virtue of its Christian descent. The main difference was that the Reformed party would not speak of any faith of the child, either actual or vicarious.

An impartial consideration suggests that the area of agreement between Anglicans and Puritans was far greater than that of disagreement. It was agreed that there is no actual faith in the child (apart from a special and secret operation of the Spirit). It was agreed that in some sense it is the faith of the parent which establishes the title to baptism. It was agreed that some profession of faith ought to be made by the sponsors. It was also agreed that the child was baptized to a future repentance and faith. The only disputed point was the propriety of allowing the sponsors to guarantee that future repentance and

---

68. *Ibid.*, p. 118.
69. *Ibid.*, p. 138.
70. Strype, *Whitgift*, III, Appendix 16.
71. *Loc. cit.*
72. L.E.P., V, LXIV, 4.
73. S.S., p. 65.

faith. The Puritans did not think this right or necessary: as an infant the child enjoys the privileges of the covenant simply by descent, and without any vicarious undertakings. But the Anglicans took the opposite view. The sponsors are the spiritual guardians of the child, and as such they have a duty to act for the child, and as it grows to years of discretion to recall to it both the promises sealed and also the pledges given. In short, the Anglicans retained the interrogatories, not merely because they were ancient, but because they set out the baptismal conditions, tightened the bond between sponsor and sponsored, and provided a starting-point for subsequent catechetical instruction. It is to be regretted that for polemical reasons this small difference of emphasis was magnified into a dominant and malignant issue, with all the misrepresentation and bitterness which that inevitably involved.

(2) Matter and Form

Baptism necessarily demands a liquid, and from the earliest times it had been recognized that water is the proper and fitting element to use, as was the obvious custom in the New Testament period. Various possible alternatives were considered by the Schoolmen: fire, for example, and oil: but, as Thomas pointed out, water corresponds most closely to the effects of the sacrament.[74] Its almost universal accessibility was emphasized in the *Catechism* of Trent.[75] The Reformers were impressed both by the correspondence between water and that which is "figured and represented", "the bloud of Christ",[76] and also by its simplicity and ubiquity. "What is so common as water?" asked Latimer in his homely way. "Every foul ditch is full of it. There we begin."[77]

In face of this unanimity it might seem unnecessary that there should be any discussion of the element, but various small points had cropped up from time to time. The first concerned the type of water used. In the first, period running water was usually preferred, probably in imitation of the baptism in Jordan. But it was understood that any form of water was sufficient. As Tertullian pointed out, it does not make any difference whether we are baptized in a sea or a pool, a stream or a fount,

---

74. S., III, qu. 66, 3.
75. C.T., II, 2, qu. 7.
76. B.P.S., 47.
77. Latimer, P.S., II, p. 127.

a lake or a trough.[78] Baptism in streams persisted, but in the larger centres it was gradually replaced by baptism in baptisteries and later in fonts. The Reformers had no difficulties on this matter, although Penry was falsely accused of the opinion that only rain-water ought to be used for baptism.[79]

The definition of water provided the medieval theologians with a nice exercise in theological subtlety. On the one hand, it might be asked whether water is still water when some other liquid is added to it; the wine, for example, which had traditionally been admixed with the baptismal water and which had been clearly prohibited in some of the earlier legislation.[80] Thomas defended the admixture on the ground that the water remained water, just as sea-water is still water in spite of the presence of salt. In fact, he thought that any water might be used in any form, so long as it had the actual constitution of water. But on the other hand, the nature and limits of water had to be defined. This involved a careful discrimination between that which was regarded as permissible, such as rainwater, and that which could not be accepted, as, for example, rose-water.[81] The Reformers had no great interest in this trifling, but they naturally accepted water as the divinely appointed element. They protested strongly against additions like oil and salt, which were "not instituted by Christ", but were rather "the inventions of men."[82]

The question of substitutes in the unavoidable absence of water also gave rise to discussion. There was a much disputed case from early times when a Jew was baptized in the desert by the cleansing sand.[83] But the Schoolmen held to the doctrine that without water there can be no sacramental baptism,[84] and a strange and no doubt whimsical Irish custom, that of baptizing in milk, was sternly forbidden at the Council of Cashel.[85] Luther gave a new turn to the debate when in his opposition to medieval legalism he made the rhetorical suggestion that beer would meet the case just as well as water:[86] no doubt it would be equally available in his country. The real point which Luther wished to make was that so long as the symbolism remained, a drowning and a resurrection, the details of administration were not of decisive importance. A failure to

---

78. Tertullian, *De Bapt.*, 4.
79. Pierce, *op. cit.*, p. 370.
80. E.R., p. 192.
81. S., III, qu. 66, 4.
82. Hooper, P.S., I, p. 533.
83. Whitgift, P.S., III, p. 528.
84. Lombard, IV, *Dist.* 3 H.
85. E.R., p. 192.
86. Cf. T.B., p. 356.

grasp this point betrayed the traditionalists into solemn discussion of the legitimacy of beer, and a definitive judgment had to be given by Gregory IX in a letter to the Archbishop of Trondhjem.[87] In practice, of course, the Reformers all insisted upon baptism in pure and undiluted water.[88]

A more important issue was that of the necessity of consecration. The custom of hallowing the water had great antiquity on its side, for Tertullian had spoken of an invoking or inviting of the Holy Spirit,[89] and the early orders all had forms of consecration. But of course this consecrating did not imply that there was any actual change in the water. The Schoolmen were obviously not very clear on the point. The doctrine of an absolute necessity of baptism made it impossible to insist doctrinally upon a consecration of the water, and perhaps prevented the development of a baptismal equivalent to transubstantiation. But it was still felt that baptism in unconsecrated water was at any rate inferior (cf. the earlier scruples in respect of clinical baptism), and it was sometimes ordained that the water used in this way should be burned or taken to the font, and that the vessel which had held it should be destroyed or donated to the church.[90] In all regular baptism the hallowing was regarded as essential to the service. The only reason advanced for it by Thomas was that it added solemnity to the occasion.[91] It naturally came to be associated with the grace supposedly given in or through the water. Normally the font would be filled and blessed on the Saturdays before Easter and Pentecost and other special occasions, and it would remain there until replaced or unfit for further use. Great emphasis was laid upon consecration in the sixteenth century, and the impious Lutheran suggestions, that "the water runnyng in the channell or common rywer (the Rhine or the Thames) is of as grete vertue as the halow water",[92] were indignantly resisted. Even under Mary, Pole could order that holy water ought always to be at hand for children to be christened.[93]

The Protestants were not necessarily averse to a ceremony of consecration, but they saw that at least in the popular mind the traditional hallowing signified the impartation of spiritual efficacy to the water, and therefore they denied its necessity. Luther regarded the

---

87. *Catholic Encyclopedia*, Art. Baptism.
88. Hooper, P.S., I, p. 533.
89. Tertullian, *De Bapt.*, 4.
90. E.R., p. 192.
91. S., III, qu. 66, 3.
92. E.M., I, 2, Appendix 73.
93. Foxe, VIII, p. 298.

consecration as indifferent in itself. For that reason he was willing to retain it. But he did not regard it as necessary, and he opposed the common notion that it added something to the water. The Reformed groups went further. They could not find any precedent for baptismal consecration in the New Testament, and therefore they dismissed it as a human invention and an addition to the original institution.

From the very first the Anglican Reformers appreciated the two points for which Luther was contending. Indeed, as early as 1511 Agnes Grebil of Kent had "believed, taught and defended that baptism was no better in the font than out of the font".[94] The book, the *Summe of the Holye Scripture*, repeated the Lutheran teaching,[95] and in the persecution which followed the Act of the Six Articles Bostock was charged with the view "that the water of Thames had as much virtue as water hallowed".[96] During the Marian persecution the confessors consistently condemned the consecration of the baptismal water. Cranmer was of the same mind. Although he retained a definite form of consecration in 1549, he did not think it in any way essential, and allowed it to be omitted in 1552. Becon, too, saw no reason to discredit a baptism "if the water were not first of all hallowed with their papish benedictions and other trifling additions."[97] The precisian Cartwright found fault even with the 1552 book because he saw an approach to consecration in "such childish and superstitious toys" as "the sanctifying of the flood Jordan and other waters by the blood of Christ".[98]

The Anglicans were in no doubt that consecration was unnecessary, but like Luther they tended to favour a retention of some kind of hallowing. As Cranmer saw it, the baptismal water is indeed holy by reason of the holy use to which it is put.[99] It does not undergo a change in substance, but it does undergo a change "into the proper nature and kind of a sacrament".[100] In accordance with this view he retained even in 1552 phrases reminiscent of the earlier benediction. Under Elizabeth these phrases were defended by Jewel and Whitgift. Whitgift claimed that it is the office only of the water used in baptism and not of water in general to point to "the mystical washing away of sin, which

---

94. Foxe, V, p. 650.
95. *Ibid.*, p. 49.
96. *Ibid.*, p. 448.
97. Becon, P.S., I, p. m.
98. Whitgift, P.S., III, p. 381.
99. J., III, p. 38.
100. Cranmer, P.S., I, p. 180.

is proper to the work of God in the blood of Christ".[101] Even Bullinger could allow that the water is holy in this sense.[102] Once that is admitted there is no reason why the setting apart of the water should not at least be indicated.

But the Anglicans no less than Zwingli and Calvin opposed wholeheartedly the quasi-magical consecration of the medieval church. According to Cranmer, the Holy Ghost was not given in the water or the font, but in the ministration.[103] The true baptismal transformation was not the transformation of the water, but "that wonderful change which God Almighty by his omnipotence worketh really in them that be baptized therewith"[104] And Cranmer pressed home the point in his attack upon the eucharistic transubstantiation. It was a clever argument, for his opponent Gardiner could not deny the efficacy of baptism even in unconsecrated water. All that he could plead for was a spiritual presence of Christ in the waters of baptism quite apart from consecration, and this was just what Cranmer desired in support of his contention that the eucharistic presence is spiritual rather than substantial. Nowell made the same point: the consecration of the water does not produce a substantial or indeed any change in the element, and so too with the consecration of the bread and wine.[105] Many of the later Anglicans developed the same theme, attacking both the popular notion that the consecration confers spiritual properties upon the water and also the theological view that a substantial change takes place in the eucharistic consecration. Calfhill concluded that the medieval consecration was a Satanic perversion of sacramental truth.[106] Jewel could allow that there may be a proper setting apart, or sanctification, but he could not allow that there takes place a miraculous change by which the element itself becomes both Lord and God, as might be deduced from the strange properties which the water displayed when "the Arian Demetrius would have baptized a man after his blasphemous sort".[107] Grindal, too, argued that the water had no power or grace or virtue to accomplish what it signifies, either by consecration or in any other way.[108] In a word, the Holy Spirit could not be localized in the baptismal water, and although the absolute necessity and the lack of a true corresponding substance prevented the development of a baptismal

101. Whitgift, P.S., III, p. 382.
102. Bullinger, P.S., IV, pp. 363-364.
103. Cranmer, P.S., I, p. 148.
104. *Ibid.*, II, p. 180.
105. Nowell, P.S., p. 91.
106. Calfhill, P.S., p. 16.
107. Jewel, P.S., II, pp. 450, 761.
108. Strype, *Cheke*, pp. 101 f.

transubstantiation it was to a localization of this kind that the insistence on consecration tended, especially amongst the ill-instructed masses. As the Reformers complained, the priest came indeed to be looked upon as a kind of magician and the hallowing as a conjuring.[109]

Like all the Reformation protests, the rejection of the traditional form of consecration rested ultimately upon New Testament precept and practice. Already in the *Summe of the Holye Scripture* it was pointed out that "Philip baptized not the eunuch in hallowed water, but in the first water they came to upon the way".[110] For the simpler confessors like Denley this argument was decisive.[111] When questioned on the point, the Marian martyrs always returned to the example of the eunuch, which proved at least the dispensability of the ceremony. It was largely upon this clear scriptural precedent that the Reformed school based their demand for a complete abolition. The Lutherans and Anglicans did not go quite so far as that. They allowed an area of things indifferent in which the church may order godly and profitable ceremonies not contrary to Scripture. But they too appealed to the scriptural example in rejection of the superstitious consecration of tradition. In the words of Becon, "there was no hallowed font when the eunuch was baptized".[112] Consecration had no theological significance. If it was to be retained at all, it could be retained only as an indifferent ceremony, or better still as a simple prayer. On the Reformed side, of course, it could be argued that a ceremony is not indifferent if it is not scriptural, but all Protestants agreed that there is no actual mandate for consecration, that it is not therefore necessary, and that it cannot in any way affect or add to the baptismal water.

Water is the primary element in baptism, but baptism is more than water. It is water applied to a specific use: not drinking, but washing. There could be no baptism where there was no water, but there could also be no baptism where there was no washing in water. The matter of the sacrament included not only the element but also the action.

Once again, this was an obvious and universally accepted truth. Yet in this field, too, considerable differences arose in points of detail. The most important of these concerned the mode of washing, and even before the rise of the Baptists this problem had attracted a certain

---

109. Cf. *Tracts*, I, p. 138.
110. Foxe, V, p. 592.
111. Foxe, VII, p. 333.
112. Becon, P.S., II, p. 207.

amount of notice. In the early church it is probable that immersion was a fairly common rule, as suggested by the New Testament symbolism. As against this, the mass-baptisms in Jerusalem might have created difficulties, and there are evidences of affusion even in early writings and inscriptions.[113] Immersion was certainly prescribed in the first liturgies, and the construction of baptistries made its fulfilment possible. But again, there was always the recognized exception of clinical baptism.[114] At least as early as Tertullian trine immersion was practised, and this became the rule in great liturgies like those of Hippolytus and Cyril. The replacement of baptistries by fonts did not mean an abandonment of immersion, for the first fonts were large enough for immersion.[115] It was still enjoined at Caelchythe in 816, when there was a strange reference to the threefold immersion of Christ in the River Jordan.[116] Even in 1172 immersion was still the rule in Ireland, for the Council of Cashel condemned the custom of excluding the right arm of boys in order not to prejudice their future valour as warriors.[117]

The Schoolmen, however, were not quite so definite on the point as the liturgies and councils. Lombard could not see any theological necessity for trine immersion,[118] and although Thomas agreed that immersion is most agreeable to the signification, he argued that washing can include sprinkling and pouring as well as bathing.[119] What was really necessary was that the water should be applied to the head as the chief member.[120] Like Lombard, Thomas could not insist upon trine immersion, for although it had been practised in the early church, Gregory had described it as indifferent.[121] The hesitancy of the Schoolmen perhaps reflected, and no doubt fostered, an increasing tendency at this period to abandon immersion in favour of other modes. By the sixteenth century, dipping had been largely abandoned in the Mediterranean countries, although it was still the rule in England and some Northern lands. The Tridentines accepted the view that so long as water was applied to the head, the seat of the internal and external senses, baptism was sufficient and complete.[122] A threefold pouring was still enjoined.[123]

---

113. Cf. C.F. Rogers, *Baptism and Christian Archaeology*.
114. *Liturgy and Worship*, Baptism.
115. E.R., p. 345.
116. E.R., p. 192.
117. *Loc. cit.*
118. Lombard, IV, *Dist*. 3 I.
119. S., III, qu. 66, 7.
120. *Loc. cit.*
121. *Loc. cit.*
122. C.T., II, 2, qu. 17, 19.
123. Cf. *Rituals Romanum*.

The Protestant theologians approached the matter from a common standpoint, but they did not come to the same conclusions. On the one side, Luther was swayed by the symbolism and the very meaning of the term baptism, and theoretically at least he favoured a full immersion.[124] On the other side, the Reformed group did not think that the external details were of great importance: the thing signified was of far greater account than the mode of signification. Even the Anabaptists did not demand more than affusion, although it was meritorious that Wolfgang Oolimann "would not simply have water poured over him from a dish, but, entirely naked, was thrust down and covered over in the Rhine".[125] Calvin could concede that the "term baptize evidently meant to immerse", and he did not dispute that immersion was the primitive mode, but the alternatives immersion or sprinkling and once or thrice he could not regard as of great moment.[126] In point of fact, Calvin did reject trine immersion, no doubt because it was unscriptural, but the matter had no theological importance.[127]

The issue was to some extent complicated in England by the fact that dipping was still practised in the Reformation period. This is proved not merely by the Sarum rubric, which might have been ignored, but by a contemporary reference of Erasmus.[128] Lutheran influences made for a continuance of the custom, for the *Summe of the Holye Scripture* advocated a full immersion.[129] Tyndale, too, described dipping or plunging as the true sign,[130] but he could also see the danger of a legalistic approach: "If ought be left out, or if the child be not altogether dipt in the water … how tremble they, how quake they."[131] Dipping was retained in the 1549 revision and again in 1552, but discretion and wariness were enjoined. If the child was weak, it was regarded as sufficient to pour water upon it. Trine immersion was retained in the first order, but in spite of its recognized antiquity Cranmer could cite against it the Toledo canon and its theological unimportance,[132] and it was abandoned in 1552.

During the late Edwardian and post-Edwardian period there was the usual movement from traditionalist or Lutheran views to the Reformed position. This combined with social influences to bring about a complete

---

124. W.A., II, p. 727, VI, p. 531.
125. D.C.R., p. 435.
126. *Instit.*, IV, 15, 19.
127. Cf. Toplady, *Historic Proof*, I, p. 350.
128. In *Tert, disput.*, 145, 2.
129. E.E.D., I, p. 59.
130. Tyndale, P.S., III, p. 247.
131. *Ibid.*, I, p. 277.
132. Cranmer, P.S., II, p. 56.

abandonment of immersion or dipping in defiance of the 1552 and 1559 rubric. Becon had stated the issue clearly. Trine immersion had good support in the Fathers, and immersion expressed the signification better. But "Christ left the manner of baptizing free in the church", and "it is all one matter whether the whole body, or some part thereof, as the head, be washed".[133] In a word, the mode of administration was quite indifferent. Nowell adopted the same line in his *Catechism*, for he defended sprinkling as well as immersion.[134] With the return of the exiles there was a definite hardening of Reformed opinion, especially against trine immersion. Whitaker insisted that sprinkling was quite sufficient in the case of infants. Against trine immersion he set the Toledo judgment.[135] Calf hill dismissed trine immersion altogether as "a strange invention of the age of Tertullian".[136] But the Puritans went further, for they attempted to replace baptism in fonts by baptism in basins. Cartwright had two arguments against the font: first, that it is not mentioned in Scripture, and second, that it has Papal associations.[137] With regard to the second of these, Cooper pointed out that a thing is not necessarily wrong because it is old and papish.[138] With regard to the first, Whitgift demanded scriptural evidence of the use of basins, to which Cartwright could make only the weak reply that there must have been basins in the houses of Cornelius and the Philippian jailer, since there could not be "any river or common water there".[139] Again, Whitgift pointed out that the font is not in any way a more reprehensible or unscriptural article of church furniture than the pulpit.[140] But his main argument was the argument of Article 34, that the church has a right to take order in indifferent details of this kind, and that so long as what is ordained is not forbidden by Scripture, it ought to be obeyed by all.[141] It is of interest that neither Parker nor Whitgift attempted to enforce dipping. Within a very short space of time the authority of Geneva and the "distaste of the refined ladies and gentlewomen" combined to render the rubrical direction almost completely obsolete.[142]

Water, and washing in water, together constitute the matter of baptism, but the sacrament is not complete without the divinely appointed

---

133. Becon, P.S., II, p. 227.
134. Nowell, P.S., p. 228.
135. Whitaker, P.S., p. 592.
136. Calfhill, P.S., p. 213.
137. Whitgift, P.S., III, p. 109.
138. Cooper: *Admonition*, p. 80.
139. Whitgift, P.S., III, p. 126.
140. *Loc. cit.*
141. *Loc. cit.*
142. Cf. Wall, *op. cit.*

"form", or word. Baptism in the strict sense is a washing in water accompanied by the evangelical formula: "Baptizing in the name of the Father, and of the Son, and of the Holy Ghost." Even in medieval theology great importance had been attached to the baptismal word. The Schoolmen narrowed down the word to a bare formula which was usually recited in a language which the people did not understand, but they still insisted that without the word there is no sacrament. As Lombard put it, baptism is a corporal washing accompanied by the prescribed form of words.[143] Thomas made the same point: "The element becomes a sacrament only when the word is added."[144] To that extent the power of the sacrament may be said to lie in the word rather than in the water.[145]

The word to which the Schoolmen referred was of course the formula of administration, and it was upon this that their more detailed discussions centred. A first problem arose out of the apostolic baptisms in the name of Christ. Lombard argued that the one Person necessarily included the whole Trinity.[146] To this Thomas agreed, although he claimed that we have no right to depart from the dominical institution except by divine revelation.[147] A second problem was that of the suitability of the formula. Thomas could see three possible objections: first, that the phrase "I baptize thee" is unnecessary; second, that there is no mention of the passion; and third, that since a name signifies a property, the three names signify three different properties. But he could not accept these criticisms. He agreed that the Eastern form "Be thou baptized" was valid, but he defended the Western on the ground that it indicated the cause of baptism: the Trinity as principal, and the minister as instrumental. And although three names were mentioned, the power operative in baptism belonged to the one essence of the Godhead, so that the names were not plural but singular.[148] A final problem was that of the alteration or corruption of the formula. The usual judgment was that of Lombard. If the error was due to ignorance, it did not invalidate the sacrament.[149] For instance, when a priest in the time of Pope Zachary baptized a child by these words, "*In nomine patria, et filia, et spirita sancta*", the baptism

---

143. Lombard, IV, *Dist.* 3 A.
144. S., III., qu. 66, 1.
145. *Loc. cit.*
146. Lombard, IV, *Dist.* 3 A.
147. S., III, qu., 66, 6.
148. *Ibid.*, 5.
149. Lombard, IV, *Dist.* 6 C.

was valid.[150] On the other hand, no priest had the right wilfully to add to, subtract from or in any way alter the given formula. As Bellarmine later pointed out, although the word signifies what is being done, it is not strictly an explanation, but a formula. The validity and efficacy of the sacrament depend upon its strict observance.[151]

The Reformers accepted the medieval emphasis upon the word, but from the very outset they insisted that it is not the form but the meaning of the word which is important. It is through the sense, not the sound of the word that the Holy Spirit operates. Luther could endorse heartily the Scholastic dictum that baptism is not water alone, but water enclosed in the word and commandment of God.[152] It was not the water that saved, but the word.[153] Indeed, in a true sense the word was even more important than faith, for, while both were necessary to true efficacy, the word was powerful to work whereas faith could only receive.[154] But to do its work the word had to be intelligible. There was no virtue in the mere pronouncement of a formula, especially in a language which the people did not understand. "He cares not much for the form of words" was Henry's charge against Luther.[155] But he did care for something which was far more important, the meaning of the words. It was of greater urgency that the people should understand than that a particular formula should be scrupulously employed.

Zwingli took up the same points, but if anything he went further. He identified the baptismal word not merely with the formula, but with the whole baptismal teaching.[156] In practice, of course, the older services had always included at least a Gospel passage in the administration, and Luther had added lengthy exhortations in the vernacular. But Zwingli thought that the word consisted necessarily in reading and even preaching as well as in the actual form. The function of the word was to illuminate and explain: otherwise the sacrament was magic, and the words of the formula were "mutterings of a magical character made by some exorcist between his teeth."[157] As Calvin said, the word is "an explanation of the advantages of baptism, the sounding of the voice of heavenly doctrine".[158] In Mark 16 it had been connected with

---

150. This reference is given by Jewel, P.S., I, p. 316.
151. T.B., pp. 335 f.
152. W.A., XXX, 1, p. 213.
153. *Loc cit.*
154. *Ibid., p. 218.*
155. *Assertio*, p. 99.
156. C.R., IV, p. 219.
157. *Comm, on Luke* 3; 3.
158. *Tracts*, II, p. 201.

the sacrament by "a sacred bond".[159] Without an actual preaching of the word baptism was not complete, and it was laid down in the Genevan orders that it must always be preceded by a public proclamation of the word.[160] In the words of Knox, "the wourd and declaratioun of the promises aucht to preceid".[161] The traditional formula was, of course, retained, but it was ordered that the words should be pronounced clearly and intelligibly.[162]

The first Anglican statements had a distinct Lutheran ring. It was maintained that English ought to be used,[163] and the whole power of baptism was ascribed to the word, which is "the promise that God hath made."[164] Alesius represented this view when he stated that the word of God is the principal thing.[165] It found official sanction in the *King's Book*,[166] in the Lutheran *Cranmer's Catechism*,[167] and in the 1549 Prayer Book, which placed the Baptismal Office within the context of Morning Prayer and immediately after the reading of Scripture. The Reformers all agreed that the mother-tongue ought to be used, and when Ridley conceded, as he had to, that baptism in Latin is valid, Latimer could break in: "Surely I would wish that you had spoken more vehemently, and to have said, 'It is of necessity [i.e. the use of English] ... for the edifying and comfort of them that are present'."[168] In the early days of Elizabeth the reintroduction of English was defended on two grounds; first, that the apostles themselves had used the language of the people, and second, that "since the sacraments are sermons of the death and resurrection of Christ, they must be had in such language as the people may perceive, otherwise they should be had in vain".[169] The Elizabethan Homily cited many patristic authorities to the same effect, including the Justinian order "that all bishops and priests do celebrate the holy oblation, or the prayers used in baptism, not speaking low, but with a loud and clear voice, that thereby the minds of the hearers may be stirred up with great devotion".[170]

The translation into the vernacular and the setting of the office within Morning Prayer had combined to give the word a new prominence in the Lutheran way, but the first Anglican Reformers did not identify the baptismal word with preaching in its narrower

159. *Loc. cit.*

160. D.C.R., p. 581.

161. Knox, II, p. 187.

162. D.C.R., p. 620.

163. Tyndale, P.S., I, p. 253.

164. *Ibid.*, p. 143.

165. Foxe, V, p. 383.

166. K.B., p. 44.

167. *Cranmer's Catechism*, p. 186.

168. Ridley, P.S., p. 140.

169. Burnet, *op. cit.*, III, 3, Collection.

170. *Homilies*, pp. 245 f.

sense. It was enough if the formula was uttered intelligibly, and the meaning of the service brought out by understandable reading and exhortation. In this respect the early Reformers were followed by the Elizabethan Anglicans. Grindal, for example, was more concerned about a right use of the formula than he was about preaching: "Neither doth baptism consist in the word *'Ego'* or in *'baptizare'*, or in the word *'te'* but in all these words spoken in order".[171] Jewel, too, exerted himself to maintain a Protestant understanding of the formula against the corrosive literalism of tradition, which would allow that the baptism was valid even if the words *et diaboli* were added to the correct form.[172] Against the contention of Harding that the example of the apostles proved the authority of the church to vary the formula, Jewel argued that the phrase "in the name of Christ" did not mean more than "according to the order, institution and commandment of Christ".[173] All the thinking of Jewel concerning the baptismal word centred ultimately upon the formula.

But the growing influence of Reformed theology carried with it an inevitable demand not merely for an intelligible formula and accompanying reading and exhortation, but also for definite preaching. Here again Hooper was a pioneer,[174] but it was left to the Elizabethan Puritans to take up the point. Strictly, of course, the Prayer Book order did provide for a sermon, at any rate after the sacrament, but in practice there was the exception of private baptism, many ministers were* not qualified to preach, and the order may not always have been followed. For the Puritans, however, the word was of the very *esse* of the sacrament, and the word meant not merely a reading of Scripture or of set exhortations, but the living proclamation of the Gospel. As Travers maintained, "preaching ought to bee joyned always with the ministrie of the sacramentes",[175] according to the best Reformed patterns. On the whole, the Anglicans sympathized with the Puritan request, but they could not agree that the baptismal word necessarily means preaching. Challenged to produce scriptural evidence, the Puritans could adduce only the preaching of John and the conjunction of teaching and baptism in Mark 16.[176] But as Whitgift pointed out, both these passages

171. Grindal, P.S., p. 197.
172. Jewel, P.S., III, p. 444.
173. *Ibid.*, I, pp. 223-225.
174. Hooper, P.S., I, p. 533.
175. Travers, *Defence of the Ecclesiastical Discipline*.
176. Whitgift, P.S., HI, p. 19.

concerned primarily the baptism of adults. Where infants are baptized it is not so important that preaching should precede the sacrament, or even that the preaching and baptism should be at the same time and on the same occasion.[177] In any case, and this was the main point made by the Anglicans, it is dangerous to make "the life of the sacrament depend on the preaching of the word".[178] According to the Puritan view, the sacrament could not exist without preaching, for preaching was the essential part of the sacramental word. But for the Anglicans, although preaching was a commendable adjunct, and baptism and preaching ought to go together, as the Prayer Book itself envisaged, it was wrong to say that preaching Was absolutely indispensable to the administration of the sacrament. Just as there could be preaching without the sacrament, so there could be the sacrament without preaching, for the sacrament had and was its own word. Even if there was no preaching the word itself remained, in the formula and in reading and exhortation. The sacrament was therefore complete.

Closely connected with the baptismal word was the giving of the baptismal name, for the name was included in the formula. The origin of the name-giving is obscure, but it probably derives from Jewish custom, and is certainly of great antiquity in the church. The giving of the name helps to underline two vital aspects of Christian baptism: first, the personal address, "Be *thou* baptized", or "I baptize *thee*"; and second, the entry into a new life and a new family by virtue of that address and the accompanying new name. No theological issues were raised by the custom, but one or two lesser points do call for brief comment.

The first concerns the character of the names given. In early days these had usually had some spiritual significance or had been taken from the Bible. Even in the sixteenth century the *Catechism* of Trent could still ask that "the name should be taken from someone who, through his eminent piety and religion, has obtained a place in the catalogue of the saints".[179] The Reformers all approved of the principle which underlay this ruling, for, as Jewel pointed out, "our names should teach us, that whether we write them or utter them, or hear them spoken, they should put us in mind of Christian duty and godliness".[180] But the Puritans, in their excess of zeal, applied the principle in an obviously absurd

---

177. Whitgift, P.S., III, pp. 15-16.
178. *Ibid.*, p. 533.
179. C.T., II, 2, qu. 75.
180. Jewel, P.S., II, p. 1109.

and extravagant way. A certain Snape of Northampton, for example, refused to baptize the child of one Hodgkinson, "because it was to be called Richard, not a godly name",[181] and there were others who adopted the same rigorist attitude.[182] Individual Puritans attempted to revive names which were descriptive of Christian virtues, emotions or experiences, typical examples being the pious appellations which Dudley Fenner gave to his unfortunate children: Joy Again, From Above, and More Fruit. This type of name was to enjoy a considerable vogue in the seventeenth century, and is still occasionally met with, especially in New England.[183]

A more serious question is that of the true significance of the name-giving in relation to the whole baptismal action. In this connection the young Luther had an interesting and suggestive thought when he related the giving of new life not so much to the emergence from the water as to the giving of the new name. The sinner was restored and adopted when he was personally addressed by God with the new name of divine sonship. In this way Luther was able to lay a striking emphasis both upon the power of the life-giving word and also upon the personal nature of the divine work. He did not follow up the suggestion, and it was not developed by the later Reformers, but it is one which can still open up wide and exciting vistas, testifying like so much else to that magnificent theological vitality of Luther which has laid the whole Protestant world under so great and lasting a debt.

(3) Ceremonies

In New Testament days the act of baptism seems to have consisted quite simply in the application of water either in the name of the Trinity or in that of Christ and perhaps upon a rudimentary profession of faith. But it was not long before additions were made to this primitive and simple rite. The *Didache* mentions fasting preparation and trine immersion,[184] and in Tertullian there are references to unction, the laying-on of hands, the partaking of milk and honey, and the prohibition of ordinary washing for a set period.[185] These ceremonies were not additional

---

181. Strype, *Whitgift*, II, pp. 9-10.
182. S.P.R., I, p. 166, etc.
183. See C.W. Bardsley, *Curiosities of Puritan Nomenclature*, London, 1880.
184. *Didache*, 7.
185. Tertullian, *De Bapt.*, 7-8.

sacraments, for they had no meaning or promise in themselves. They were imposed in order to make the ceremony more solemn and impressive, and as Tertullian explained they were all figures or symbols of Christian experiences or Christian virtues.[186] It may be that, in spite of the scriptural nature of the early imagery, the pagan background contributed to the growth and popularity of this new ceremonial. Certainly it tended to increase as the years passed, for in the more developed liturgies we find exorcism, breathings, the baptismal robe, salt, marking with the cross, the effeta, and the anointing of the back and breast. The wax taper was added at a later date, and at various times the newly baptized were given such various articles as shoes, a garland, ten siliquae and a wax image of the Agnus Dei.[187]

It was always admitted, of course, that these ceremonies were not essential to the sacrament, so that the omission of them in emergency cases did not in any way affect its validity or efficacy. But where the ceremonies could be had, the Schoolmen defended them on the ground that they belonged to the solemnity of the occasion, that they had value for purposes of edification, and that in some cases they helped to remove obstacles to grace (e.g. exorcism and spittle), or contributed to the virtue and power of the sacrament (e.g. oil).[188] The Tridentines anathematized those who said that "the received and approved rites of the catholic church may be contemned ... and omitted",[189] and in the *Catechism* the symbolism of the different ceremonies was described in detail.[190] Those which were retained were all modelled either upon the actions of Christ or upon the familiar images and symbols of the New Testament. It was no doubt felt that they had a real instructional value for ignorant congregations which could see much better than they could read. But in any case, the Tridentines would argue that the church had a clear mandate to ordain such rites and ceremonies as were thought to be necessary for the promotion of true religion.

Yet there had been protests against the continued use of the ceremonies all through the Middle Ages, usually on the ground that they had no sanction in Scripture and were plainly unnecessary. The Piedmontese, for example, "would not receive oiling and salting except

---

186. H.D., p. 141.
187. E.R., p. 175.
188. S., III, qu. 66, 10, 71, 2.
189. C.D., Sess. VII, *Bapt. can.*, 13.
190. C.T., II, 2, qu., 64-74.

the same might be proved by the Holy Scripture".[191] Again in 1429 some men of Norwich condemned the "superfluous additions" of "salt, oil, spittle, taper, light, chrisms, exorcising of water, with such other like, accounting them as no material thing in the holy institution of baptism".[192] Such protests were for the most part only sporadic and quite ineffective. Those who made them were contained or suppressed, and in any case thought to be merely odd or perverse. But the complaints were symptomatic of an underlying dissatisfaction which was to come to more open and forceful expression in the Reformation period.

Luther himself was not greatly concerned about these details of ceremonial. His primary aim was to reform the church by the word itself. He put the services in the vernacular, and gave them a decided evangelical emphasis, but he was content to move only slowly and cautiously on the liturgical side. Exorcism and the sign of the cross were retained in almost all the Lutheran orders,[193] and Luther could see the value of many of the rites for the imparting of spiritual lessons.[194] Indeed, the main test applied by the Lutherans was that of edification. In the Brandenburg-Nuremberg order, for example, the blessing of the font, oil and spittle were all rejected as trifling and superstitious, but the cross, exorcism and the chrisom were retained because they were useful and profitable.[195] Even Bucer approved of a form of exorcism in the projected order for the Archbishop of Cologne. The importance of the distinction may be seen from the dissatisfaction with the terms of the Augsburg Interim, which attempted to reinforce the whole of the traditional ceremonial.[196]

The approach of Zwingli was at first very similar to that of Luther. In the first revision at Zürich oil, spittle, exorcism, crossing, anointing and the chrisom were all retained, although with a new emphasis upon their symbolical meaning.[197] But the retention was perhaps more a matter of tactics than of general policy. Once his position was secure Zwingli took steps to purge the office of all its non-scriptural elements. In this matter he was in full agreement with the Anabaptists, who were clamouring that all ceremonies which had no sanction in the New Testament ought ruthlessly to be discarded.[198] The more radical policy of Zwingli was

191. Foxe, IV, p. 511.
192. *Ibid.*, III, p. 589.
193. Cf. Jacobs, *op. cit.*, pp. 252 f.
194. W.A., LXVI, p. 175.
195. E.B.I., Appendix II.
196. D.C.R., p. 359.
197. C.R., IV, p. 707.
198. C.R., IV, p. 245.

taken up and applied by Calvin, who saw that if the work of reformation was to be done at all it must be done decisively and thoroughly, no matter how great the initial cost. Calvin had many arguments against the traditional ceremonies. Even on the admission of their exponents they were superfluous.[199] As a human addition to a divine ordinance they were also presumptuous.[200] Their supposed symbolism merely distracted from the signification of the sacrament itself, and being pompous and foolish they destroyed the true solemnity of the divinely appointed action. In a scathing passage Calvin called for the complete destruction of this "adventitious farrago of added ceremonies, oil, spittle, and other follies",[201] and he did not retain a single one of them in the Genevan liturgies. His disciples vied with one another in their attempts to heap scorn and ridicule upon the ancient customs.[202]

It is to be noted that at bottom the difference between the Lutheran and Reformed groups was one of policy rather than of principle. Both aimed at the replacement of a legal and ceremonial religion by an evangelical and spiritual, but the one group aimed to accomplish it by means which were purely evangelical, the other by legal and ceremonial reforms according to the Gospel. Yet in this as in all kindred matter there was a point of principle as well: the nature and extent of the authority of the church in relation to the overriding authority of Holy Scripture. It was over this point of principle that the two groups came into headlong collision in Elizabethan England.

In the first period of the Reformation the English Protestants approached the question of ceremonial mainly from the Lutheran angle. Frith, for example, condemned the superstitious notion that "if a dronken priest forget to put spittel or salt in y childes mouth y child is not christened".[203] But he also thought that in relation to these rites "we must behave ourselves wisely, as charity alloweth", It is true that when the Ethiopian eunuch was baptized "there was neither fonte, nor holy water … candle, creame, oyle, salt On the other hand some of these rites had a profitable signification and could therefore be kept.[204] Cranmer seems to have been of the same mind. Against the ceremonies he could argue that in spite of their patristic authority

---

199. *Tracis*, I, p. 137.
200. *Ibid.*, II, p. 118.
201. *Instit.*, IV, 15, 19.
202. Cf. Knox, II, p. 186.
203. Frith, B.R., p. 91.
204. *Ibid.*, p. 95.

they were contrary to "so plain scriptures" and were ultimately dispensable.[205] But Cranmer did not conclude that they ought to be abolished altogether. His conclusion was rather that of the Lutherans, that those rites should be excluded "whereof some be untrue, some uncertain, some vain and superstitious", but that others which had an obvious value should still be retained and used.[206] In accordance with this policy the 1549 revision still found a place for exorcism, the sign of the cross, the chrisom, and, of course, the hallowing of the water.

But by 1549 opinion had already begun to harden against the baptismal ceremonies, and it was not long before the new order came under severe attack. Bucer had now turned against exorcism, the consecration of the water, and the baptismal robe, which he condemned as too "scenical",[207] but the main argument used by the critics was that there was no scriptural warrant for any of the ceremonies.[208] Cranmer must have felt the force of this attack, for in the fresh revision of 1552 only the sign of the cross was demanded. In the meantime the majority of Anglicans had abandoned the principle of a discriminatory use. Becon was particularly savage on this point: "They added moreover of their own brain, without any authority of God's word, certain exorcisms and conjurations, to drive the devil out of the silly simple poor infant", "neither was it counted a perfect baptism if any of these beggarly ceremonies wanted".[209] Becon returned to the old example of the Ethiopian eunuch in proof of the original simplicity of baptism,[210] and he condemned the attempted improvement as a pollution: "For Baal's priest bewitcheth the child, shutteth the church door, conjureth the devil out of the poor young infant, bespueth the child with his vile spittle and stinking slavering, putteth salt in the child's mouth, smeareth it with greasy and unsavoury oil. ... Do these papists, by adding beggarly ceremonies, any other thing than set the Son Christ to school, and advance their own fleshly imaginations above the wisdom of the Lord Christ ?"[211] By the time of Mary even the humbler confessors seemed to have adopted the same view, for they could refer to the "baptism of the chamberlain" in Acts 8,[212] the blaspheming of

---

205. Cranmer, P.S., II, p. 56.
206. Cf. Cranmer's *Preface*.
207. Burnet, *op. cit.*, II, p. 320.
208. Cf. Becon, P.S., II, p. 207.
209. *Ibid.*, I, p. 11.
210. *Ibid.*, II, p. 207.
211. *Ibid.*, III, p. 234.
212. Foxe, VII, p. 354.

Christ by "such mingle-mangle",[213] and the ineffectiveness of the ceremonies.[214] As Haukes defiantly put it: "I deny all things invented and devised by men: your oil, cream, salt, spitting, candle."

> *Harpsfield*: "But Christ used ceremonies. Did he not take clay from the ground, and spittle?"
> *Haukes*: "But Christ did never use it in baptism. If ye will needs have it, put it to the use that Christ put it unto."[215]

The Elizabethan leaders all shared the same outlook. Grindal took active steps to prohibit the old ceremonial revived under Mary.[216] When a rumour went round in 1566 that oil, spittle, clay and tapers were to be reintroduced, he and Hom assured their friends in Zürich that "the Church of England had entirely given up these practices".[217] Similarly, Jewel and Whitgift defended the plain administration practised in their church, and censured "the corrupt and superstitious ceremonies used of the Papists in baptism".[218] Calfhill regarded the added rites as devilish perversions.[219] He pointed out that the traditionalists were not even consistent enough to use all the rites for which patristic authority could be adduced.[220] Hooker Emphasized the fact that all the ceremonies are "accessory" so that "baptism may tolerably be given without them".[221]

In view of this unanimity of opinion, it is perhaps a matter for surprise that one ceremony had remained in the 1552 book: the signing with the cross. It was the retention of this isolated rite which gave rise to the Puritan protest and the consequent battle of theological principle. The protest had already been made in the reign of Edward, for Hooper had expressly included the cross in his condemnation of the older ceremonial: "Whatsoever is added, oil, salt, cross, lights, and such other, be the inventions of men."[222] Hooper had stood almost alone at first, but at Frankfurt and later at Geneva a strong group developed which regarded the 1552 book as only a stage to full reformation. Amongst the more obvious blemishes they singled out the retention of the sign of the cross, which the ministers of Geneva condemned severely when the book was submitted to them for criticism: "As for the crossing of babes, whatsoever practice there hath been in time of old, yet it is most certain that it is truly, in these days, through so late

---

213. Foxe, VII, p. 351.
214. *Loc. cit.*
215. *Ibid.*, p. 99.
216. Grindal, P.S., p. 160.
217. *Zürich Letters*, P.S., I, Appendix 106.
218. Whitgift, P.S., III, p. 87; cf. Jewel, P.S., III, p. 445.
219. Calfhill, P.S., p. 16.
220. *Ibid.*, p. 270.
221. L.E.P., V, LVIII, 4.
222. Hooper, P.S., I, p. 533.

greenness of the superstition, so most abominable, as that we judge those men to have done assuredly well, that have once driven this rite out of the congregation: whereof also we see not what the profit is."[223] With the return of the exiles there were high hopes that the reform would be accepted. When the 1552 book was re-enforced a persistent campaign was initiated to secure the removal of this defect:

Every possible weapon was tried. In the constitutional sphere, demands were made in the convocations, petitions laid before parliament, and direct suit made to the Queen herself. In the literary, polemical writings were issued, ranging from Cartwright's *Defence of the Admonition* and Udall's *State of the Church of England laid open* to the *Pleasaunte Dialogue* and *A Dossen Points of Controversy*. In the academic, disputations were held, notably the one at Lambeth in which Travers was the Puritan spokesman, and later, of course, the Hampton Court Conference. In the ecumenical, the support of foreign Reformers was enlisted. Bullinger was approached by Humphrey and Samson,[224] and Beza intervened to condemn the sign of the cross as an "execrable and novel superstition, quite without profit".[225] In the ecclesiastical, there was sheer nonconformity. Nicoll the "Person" of Eastwell,[226] Johnson of St. Clement's, London,[227] Hill of Bury St. Edmunds,[228] Settles[229] and Wilson[230] were all prosecuted for refusing to use this ceremony. When everything else failed, the weapon of abuse remained. The pamphleteers vied with each other for the strongest term by which to describe "the manifest impiety"[231] or "childish and superstitious toy."[232] Marprelate carried his hostility even to the point of attempted blackmail, for he threatened to expose all the personal iniquities of the bishops if they would not accept his conditions of peace, which included the abolition of the cross in baptism.[233]

What, then, were the arguments used in this bitter and aggressive campaign? The first was a new form of the argument from authority: an appeal to the example of the best reformed churches. Whitgift could refer to Bucer, but Cartwright opposed to Bucer "men of as great authority, yea,

---

223. Whittingham, *Troubles at Frankfurt*, p. 245.
224. *Zürich Letters*, P.S., I, 71.
225. Strype, *Grindal* Appendix 40.
226. *Ibid.*, *Whitgift*, I, p. 277.
227. S.P.R., I. 70.
228. S.P.R., I, in.
229. S.P.R., II, 194.
230. S.P.R., I, 236.
231. S.P.R., II, 93.
232. P.M., 8.
233. *Marprelate Tracts*, p. 80.

the authority of all the reformed churches".[234] The second was a refutation
of the attempted defence from antiquity, for as Calfhill admitted, if the
cross was used in the early church, so too were milk and honey, which
the Anglicans had abandoned.[235] To defend the cross was to defend "oyle
and chrisme and many other toyes".[236] The third was the superstitious
association. "When men lived amongst nations which cast them in the
teeth and reproached them with the cross of Christ, then the sign had its
value as a testimony." But the abuse of the cross under the Papacy had
brought about a new situation in which it was necessary "to do clean
contrariwise to the old Christians, and abolish all use of these crosses:
for contrary diseases must have contrary remedies",[237] In support of this
argument Reynolds at Hampton Court referred to the Old Testament precedent of the brazen serpent which had once been good and profitable but
later became the object of idolatrous worship and had to be destroyed.[238]
The fourth argument was that insistence upon the sign of the cross implied
or suggested that the rite was necessary not merely as an ecclesiastical
requirement but as an essential part of the sacrament.[239] The fifth and
perhaps the most serious was that the institution of the sign meant the
institution of a new sacrament, which is proper only to Christ.[240] If the
Anglicans replied that the ceremony had no real signification, then there
was no good reason to demand it. But if it had a profitable signification, it
was a significant sign and therefore a sacrament. In any case there was no
ground for insisting upon this profitable sign and rejecting others.[241] As
Travers put it, "It is not lawful for the church to institute mysticall rites and
ceremonies, that is, with signification of doctrine attached unto them, this
being a kind of sacrament which no man maie institute".[242] Knewstubs
made a good deal of the same point at the Hampton Court Conference.[243]
The final argument was that ceremonies ought not to be enforced unless
they were necessary and scriptural.[244] Behind this contention there lay of
course the basic Puritan principle that the church ought not to ordain
anything for which there is neither precept nor precedent in the word

234. Whitgift, P.S., III, p. 125.
235. *Loc. cit.*
236. S.P.R., I, 93.
237. Whitgift, P.S., III, p. 125.
238. S.S., pp. 67 f.
239. Strype, *Whitgift*, I, p. 253.
240. Whitgift, P.S., III, p. 128.
241. *Ibid.*, p. 129.
242. S.P.R., I, 173.
243. S.S., pp. 67 f.
244. Whitgift, P.S., III, p. 128.

of God. At Hampton Court the Puritans were ready to concede that the cross might lawfully be used by those who thought otherwise, but they requested that they themselves should be excused as weaker brethren to whom it constituted a grave violation of conscience. The reply of James, that the Puritans gave very little sign of weakness,[245] did not really counter the argument. Indeed, if the Puritans had been met on this conciliatory ground, a solution to the problem might have been found. Unfortunately the authorities were not prepared for the legalized nonconformity at certain points which this compromise would necessarily have involved.

Against the Puritan arguments some of the earlier Anglicans like Grindal and Sandys had no real defence, for inwardly they agreed with their opponents. In fact, Sandys supported a demand for the abolition of the cross in the convocation of 1563. But the Queen was unmovable on the point, and, faced with the possibility that the ground already gained might be lost, he decided to accept the unscriptural but in itself indifferent ceremony in the hope that time would work in his favour.[246] The only argument with which these first leaders supported the ceremony was the half-hearted plea that it was indifferent.

But for the extreme militancy of the Puritans it is possible that their views would eventually have prevailed. But from the outset of the reign, and earlier, there was a party which was quite well satisfied with the 1552 book. From this party there emerged a more definite resistance to the radical programme. Jewel, of course, was an early leader of the Prayer Book party, but in his preoccupation with the Romanist controversy he found time only to point out that the cross did not "make anything to the virtue of the sacrament, not being any part thereof".[247] Whitgift, however, devoted himself more specifically to the debate with the Puritans. He had many points to make in favour of the retention of the cross. His arguments were both negative and positive. On the negative side, he refuted the individual Puritan objections, quoting Bucer and even Beza against the other Reformers,[248] pointing out the antiquity of the cross,[249] distinguishing it from other ceremonies by its purity and unbroken use,[250] and arguing that superstition does not arise in relation to the transitory sign but only to the permanent form of a cross.[251] Yet the case of Whitgift did not rest on these petty dialectics, for on the

---

245. S.S., pp. 67 f.

246. *Zürich Letters*, P.S., I, 75.

247. Jewel, P.S., II, p. 1106.

248. Whitgift, P.S., III, p. 123; S.P.R., I, 173.

249. *Ibid*, p. 126.

250. *Ibid*. p. 87.

251. *Ibid*. p. 131.

positive side he asserted two serious principles by which the sign of the cross could be justified: first, that the church has a right to take order in things indifferent, especially in relation to the details of administration and worship;[252] and second, that the test by which the church must select or reject the various rites and ceremonies is that of usefulness and suitability.[253]

In his development of these points Whitgift did not dispute the fundamental rule that the Bible itself is the supreme rule of faith and conduct. According to this rule, he allowed that the basic structure of baptism has been fixed once and for all by the divine institution. But he also claimed that the church has a liberty to arrange and amend the details of sacramental administration according to prevailing needs and circumstances. The only proviso was that the basic structure must remain, and that that which is ordained is not contrary to Scripture. On this principle he argued that the cross may be retained as a suitable accompaniment to the sacrament conveying a profitable signification. Excluded ceremonies could not be permitted because they fostered superstition and obscured rather than illuminated the true meaning of the sacrament. But crossing presented sharply to the recipient the moral and spiritual obligations undertaken in baptism. To claim that it constituted a new sacrament was absurd: "Every ceremony betokening something is not by and by a sacrament."[254] It was simply a significant accompaniment which the church had seen fit to order according to the liberty and authority committed to it. The inconsistency of the Puritans was proved by the fact that on the one hand "they were wont to find fault with dumb ceremonies" and on the other "they blamed, those that had any significance".[255]

The work begun by Whitgift was taken up by Hooker, who again defended the ceremony both in points of detail and also in general principle. Like Whitgift, Hooker could freely allow that ceremonies of this kind are accessory only, and that "baptism may tolerably be given without them".[256] But the whole argument of his book is that there is a sphere of things indifferent in which the Bible itself does not legislate and the church may take order according to guidance of reason, the

---

252. Whitgift, P.S., I, p. 208.
253. *Ibid.*, III, p. 128.
254. *Loc. cit.*
255. S.P.R., I, 173.
256. L.E.P., V, LVIII, 4.

requirements of the situation, and of course the overriding control of Scripture. On this rule the cross was retained because "it is a sign of remembrance to put us in mind of our duty, and a means to work our preservation from reproach".[257] The cross had no doubt been abused under the Papacy, but it had been rightly used by the Fathers,[258] and it did not minister to error like the cross which "superstition honoured as Christ".[259] It did not follow that the cross ought to be abandoned "because we live among such as adore the sign of the cross", for the true way to "remedy a superstitious use of things profitable in themselves ... is not still to abolish utterly the use thereof ... but rather if it may be to bring them back to a right perfect and religious usage".[260]

The leaders Whitgift and Hooker were supported by many lesser writers like Bridges, Cooper and Hutton, but no new points were raised. At the Hampton Court Conference the contestants merely retrod the familiar ground, and often seemed more anxious to score good debating points than to establish sound principles. However, the Anglicans were obviously eager to overcome the scruples of their opponents on this point, for the 1604 canons included a long statement on the matter (canon 30), and a rubric was inserted into the Prayer Book directing those who had doubts concerning the cross to this "true explication thereof and the just reasons for the retaining of it". The canon stated briefly the main reasons for its retention: its appropriateness as a mark of profession; the possibility of a lawful use; and its authorization by "those reverend fathers and great divines in the days of Edward the Sixth". Against misunderstandings it was allowed that the sign is no part of the sacrament, and that "the infant baptized is, by virtue of baptism, before it be signed with the cross, received into the congregation of Christ's flock, as a perfect member thereof, and not by any power ascribed unto the sign of the cross". The ground upon which conformity was demanded was laid down in the concluding paragraph, which assumed the right of the church to take order in things indifferent: "Since the ceremony is a thing indifferent, it is the part of every private man, both minister and other, to retain the true use of it, prescribed by lawful authority: considering that things of themselves indifferent do in some sort alter their nature, when they are either commanded or forbidden by a lawful magistrate, and may not

---

257. L.E.P., V, LXV, 5.
258. *Ibid.*, 10.
259. *Ibid.*, 16.
260. *Ibid.*, 21.

be omitted at every man's pleasure contrary to the law, when they be commanded, nor used when they are prohibited."

The haggle about the cross was superficially perhaps rather absurd and undignified, but as always in the Puritan controversy deeper issues were at stake. There was, for example, the whole question of discrimination in the use of ceremonies, to which the Anglican answer was not particularly logical; for, after all, the sign of the cross was not more significant or helpful than, say, the baptismal robe. But even behind the question of discrimination there lurked always the ultimate issue of authority, for it was in accordance with the alleged right of the church to take order in things indifferent that the Edwardian church had decided to retain the cross and that the Elizabethan attempted to enforce it. Up to a point, the Puritans could hardly dispute this right, for they themselves were ready to add to baptism such forms as prayer and Scripture-reading and a sermon, which do not figure in the New Testament administrations. But at three decisive points the accepted authority of the church was challenged by the Puritan revolt. First, it was asked whether that authority extended to the imposition of a ceremony which, however ancient or profitable, was not in itself scriptural – for prayer and Scripture-reading and a sermon were all scriptural forms, whereas the sign of the cross was not. Second, there was the implicit query who and what is the church which takes order in these matters, for against the Elizabethan contention that the will of the church is the will of the sovereign and convocation, the Puritans definitely stood for a greater representation of the clergy and laity, especially in and through the lower house of Parliament in which they had a considerable measure of support. Finally, and again implicitly, there was the question whether the church ought not from time to time to reconsider and alter those matters in which order has already been taken. Even on Hooker's principle, the fact that the Edwardians had decided for the cross did not mean that the Elizabethans had no power to decide against it. If the church had this authority at all, it was a living authority. The Puritans had as much right to press for a new exercise of it as had their predecessors in the days of Henry or Edward. The fact that the Puritans did not concede the principle enunciated by Hooker obviously limited them in the use which they could make of this argument, but it did not prevent them from demanding that the church should again revise its ceremonial according to the strict if binding demand of scriptural precept and precedent.

A full discussion of these various points would clearly take us far from the doctrine of baptism, but it is evident that some very deep and modem problems underlay the surface controversy. In the seventeenth century these problems led ultimately to open conflict, and even then they failed to find any real or adequate solution. Indeed, so long as there was the demand for a perfect conformity, with no possibility of tolerated dissent on matters of principle, it is obvious that no solution was possible. If there had been as much of conciliatoriness, forbearance and toleration as there was of self-sacrifice, pertinacity and devotion to principle, the worst evils of the controversy might have been avoided or mitigated; but for a complete settlement a new approach as well as a new spirit was needed.

(4) Circumstances

As at so many points of administration, the New Testament had no very clear guidance to give with regard to the time and place of baptism. Indeed, in apostolic times the converts seem to have been baptized at the earliest possible moment irrespective of circumstances. The Ethiopian eunuch and Cornelius are both instructive examples. But quite early, it was appreciated that this spontaneous and *ad hoc* method of administration could not continue indefinitely. The growth of the church created a need not only for the more careful sifting of candidates but also for more formal arrangements in actual administration. The one need was met by the catechumenate, the other by the fixing of a definite time and place for baptism, when the sacrament could be given with the greatest solemnity and the majority of existing members of the congregation could be present.

Of course, the development of an orderly ritual was not the work of a moment. Even in the second century, when the church was still comparatively small, baptism could be given where and when it was needed.[261] But by the end of the second century more careful attention was being given to the external circumstances of administration. Tertullian laid it down that if possible the sacrament ought to be administered at one or other of the two great festivals most intimately associated with its signification and effects: Easter or

---

261. Cf. Justin, *Apology*, I, 61.

Pentecost.[262] This was not an absolute rule, for every day was the Lord's, but baptism at these particular times did acquire a new solemnity and meaning. In accordance with this requirement the catechetical course was timed to culminate in the special period of Lenten preparation. Churches were also being built at this period, and this meant a transferring of the rite from any place where there was water to the specially constructed baptistry. By the third century it could definitely be laid down in the liturgies that baptism ought to take place in a solemn service at Easter or Pentecost on the completion of the special Lenten course of instruction and fasting.[263] Clinical baptism could still be given anywhere and at any time, but it was felt that this was in some way inferior. Augustine could recommend that even in cases of danger the sacrament ought to be administered in church if at all possible.

In the Middle Ages the theory with regard to the administration of baptism did not change, but in the christianized lands of Western Europe there was a considerable alteration in practice. A first point was the replacement of the baptistry by the font, which was usually situated at the door of the church, to underline the initiatory aspect of the sacrament.[264] A more important change was the abandonment from about the eighth century onwards of the earlier restriction of the time to Easter and Pentecost. The reasons for this step were mainly practical. The majority of recipients were now infants, and the incidence of infant mortality was high. Therefore, and especially in view of the supposed absolute necessity of the sacrament, it was essential that there should not be any avoidable delay even in public administration. In Saxon England it became an actual offence to delay baptism beyond a specified period, usually thirty nights,[265] although the Northumbrian priests allowed only nine days, probably on the Old Testament model.[266] If there was immediate danger, baptism would be administered at once and privately. Otherwise the child had to be brought to the church for open and ceremonial baptism by the priest, often in conditions of semi-privacy. From time to time attempts were made to return to the primitive custom except in cases of emergency, but the reforms never came to anything.[267] Indeed, in England the people not only refused to wait for the canonical days, but "some, deceived by the

---

262. Tertullian, *De Bapt.*, 12.
263. Neil and Whilloughby, *The Tutorial Prayer Book*, pp. 390 f.
264. Daniel, *op. cit.*, p. 410.
265. E.R., p. 192.
266. E.R., p. 196.
267. E.R., p. 191.

devil, suspected danger if their children were baptized on those days".[268]
The point is that the coincidence of the high rate of infant mortality
and a supposed absolute necessity of the sacrament made it nonsensical
and impossible to insist upon circumstances which had been drawn up
primarily for adult converts. Life was too precarious and the stakes were
too high for ecclesiastical legalism of this type. The Schoolmen were
acutely conscious of the dilemma, for on the one hand the primitive rule
was clear and incontestable, but on the other the absolute necessity of
the sacrament demanded its almost universal infringement. All that the
theologians could do was simply to state and justify the rule and then to
point out that it did not apply where there was danger to life.[269] Far from
establishing the rule, the exception actually became the rule, and the rule
the exception.

By the sixteenth century solemn baptism at the two appointed
seasons had fallen into almost complete disuse. It could still be required
in the case of adult converts,[270] but even in their case baptism was
permissible at any time if an emergency arose. In the case of infants
it was ordered that baptism ought on no account to be deferred, the
faithful being earnestly exhorted "to take care that their children
be brought to the church as soon as it may be done without danger,
and baptized with solemn ceremonies".[271] In an emergency, they were
to be baptized privately at home, and without the usual ceremonial.
It was a concession to ancient practice that the consecration of the
water was to take place at the two great festivals,[272] but even here
fresh consecration would often be necessary during the course of the
year. In fact, no workable means could be devised of harmonizing the
primitive practice of the church with the uncompromising dogma of
an absolute necessity.

On the Protestant side, Luther had no objection to a private administration in cases of real need. To him the sacrament itself was of far
greater account than the details or circumstances of its administration.
At the same time Luther saw a need to bring constantly before the people
the evangelical meaning and responsibilities of baptism. To that end he
aimed to make the service as public as possible. As the Lutheran orders
stated, it was not practicable to restrict baptism again to the traditional

---

268. E.R., p. 204.
269. Lombard, IV, *Dist.* 6 F; S., qu. 68, 3.
270. C.T., II, 2, qu. 35.
271. C.T., II, qu. 33.
272. Cf. *Rituale Romanum.*

seasons, but in all normal circumstances it ought to be given only in a public place, the church, and at a public time, during congregational worship either on Sunday or a holy day. Even sick children were to be brought to church if at all possible, and private baptism was allowed only in extreme necessity.[273] In this way it was hoped to invest the sacrament itself with greater dignity, to create opportunities for systematic baptismal instruction, and to bring out the significance of the rite as a public entry into the whole body of the church.

Similar regulations to the Lutheran were at first adopted in the Swiss centres like Zürich[274] and Berne,[275] but on different grounds two groups did not regard them as satisfactory. On the one hand there were the Anabaptists, who aimed to go back beyond primitive practice to the *ad hoc* baptisms of the New Testament itself.[276] On the other, there were the followers of Calvin, who wished to enforce absolutely the rule of public administration. The Anabaptists, of course, argued quite simply and plausibly from the binding nature of scriptural precedent. But Calvin was more impressed by general theological considerations. As he saw it, the fact that there was no absolute necessity of the sacrament destroyed the case for justifiable exceptions. Again, the public reading and preaching of the word were of the very essence of the sacrament, and these were impossible in a private administration. Finally, the covenant of which baptism was the mark was by its very nature a bond of fellowship between all its members. Therefore the giving of the mark was a matter of concern to all external or internal participants in the covenant. In accordance with this view, Calvin and Farel attempted to prohibit private baptisms even in 1538.[277] The later *Ecclesiastical Constitution*[278] and the *Genevan Order of Service* laid it down that "infants are to be brought to baptism either on the Lord's day, at the time of catechizing, or at public service on other days, so it may be performed in the presence and under the eyes of the whole congregation".[279] All the disciples of Calvin emphasized the need for public prayer and preaching,[280] and claimed that according to the divine institution the sacraments were not "to be used in privat corners as charms and sorceries, but left to the congregation".[281]

---

273. Cf. Jacobs, *op. cit.*, pp. 252 f.
274. C.R., IV, p. 707.
275. D.C.R., p. 556.
276. Murait, *op. cit.*, p. 27.
277. D.C.R., p. 581.
278. D.C.R., p. 597.
279. *Tracts*, II, p. 113.
280. Cf. B.P.S., p. 35.
281. Cf. Knox, IV, p. 186.

In this as in so many matters the policy of the Reformed school was far more radical than that of the Lutheran, being based upon theological principles which were more sharp and clear-cut. And quite naturally, in spite of their basic identity of aim, the two policies could not exist concurrently. Wherever they met, a collision was inevitable and a decision had to be made. Nowhere does this emerge more clearly than in England, where the Lutheran principles which had shaped the Anglican approach in the formative Edwardian period were challenged under Elizabeth by the more revolutionary doctrines which emanated from Geneva.

In basic theology, of course, there was little enough difference between the two schools. Neither of them regarded the sacrament as absolutely necessary to salvation, and under Edward, and even earlier, the value of a public administration had been fully appreciated. Tyndale, for example, had shown the need for public instruction and a public witness,[282] and Cranmer in the 1549 book had ordered that baptism should normally take place in church and on Sundays or holy days in order that "the most people" *may* come together to witness the ceremony and to be reminded of their own baptism. But Tyndale had always allowed private baptism in cases of dangerous sickness, and Cranmer in his *Answer to the Men of Devon* could point out that far from prohibiting private baptism "our book teacheth you the contrary, even in the first leaf, yea the first side of the first leaf of that part that treateth of baptism".[283] Ridley, too, defended private baptism, not because he thought that want of the sacrament would condemn, but because he thought that it ought to be administered if at all possible.[284] It is to be noted that no great emphasis was laid upon the exception, which was to be treated strictly as an exception and not as the rule. Indeed, a writer like Becon could complain bitterly of administration in private corners.[285] He pointed out that since baptism is "a sinew and bond between Christian people" it ought to be given "only when the faithful do most assemble and meet together".[286] In the difficult circumstances of Mary's reign there were some Protestants who apparently preferred the simple private administration to public baptism after the traditional style.[287] With the death of Mary, however, the Reformers reasserted the principle

282. Tyndale, P.S., III, pp. 72, 171.
283. J., IV, p. 222.
284. Ridley, P.S., p. 534.
285. Becon, P.S., I, p. 11.
286. Becon, P.S., II, p. 200.
287. e.g. Woodford (Foxe, VIII).

of a normal public administration, a view popularized in the translations of Bullinger's *Decades*.[288]

Unfortunately, the controversies of Elizabeth's reign tended to obscure the very real agreement on the norm, and to focus attention upon the disagreement concerning the exception. For, convinced by their Reformed mentors abroad, the Puritans quickly voiced a demand that none but public baptisms should be permitted. Their protest was not merely against private baptisms by laymen, or laywomen, which many of the Anglican leaders were equally anxious to suppress, but against private baptisms as such: for it was argued that even ministers ought not to be allowed to administer the sacrament privately.[289] In the decisive words of Sparke, no baptism ought to be private, whether in respect of place, persons, or doctrine.[290]

The main arguments against private baptism were stated briefly in the *Admonition* and elaborated by Cartwright in the controversy to which it gave rise. The first was a rather hazardous appeal to Scripture, which on the face of it did not seem to give the Puritans a great deal of support. In fact, Cartwright had some difficulty with the New Testament precedents. He had to admit that many baptisms took place "in the houses of private men", but he argued that they were in the presence of the congregation, and that therefore "the private houses which received the congregation were not for the time being to be counted private houses".[291] Even if this was true, it could still be replied that in private baptism there are two or three gathered together in the name of Christ, and therefore the private house is temporarily the church. The appeal to the "open meetings" of John the Baptist was also not very helpful,[292] for if the example of John was followed, baptism ought not to take place in any building but by the riverside. Another scripture sometimes quoted was the conjunction of preaching and baptism in Matthew and Mark,[293] but this had little direct bearing on the place or time of baptism. In any case the Prayer Book enjoined a public reception with teaching when the infant privately baptized survived. A second and more successful argument was from the example of the Reformed churches abroad. Here of course the Puritans had the weight of authority, for Beza, Calvin, Bullinger and Gualter could all be quoted in

---

288. Bullinger, P.S., IV, p. 365.
289. S.P.R., I, 166.
290. S.P.R., I, 177.
291. Whitgift, P.S., II, p. 512.
292. *Ibid.*, p. 208.
293. P.M., pp. 20 f.

their favour as against Bucer and Zwingli on the Anglican side. The third argument was the theological one, that since baptism is "a public entrance, a matriculating of us into the bodie of the church, an enrolling of us into the number of the citizens of the holie citie",[294] to administer it in private is to overthrow its essential character as a corporate act. Finally, it was argued that there is no real sense in private baptism unless it is based upon a presumed absolute necessity and "the conference of grace for the deed done".[295] If the Anglicans did not accept the implication, they had no right to preserve the hurried administration which undoubtedly maintained and fostered these false ideas.

Now we have seen already that the Anglicans themselves agreed that the only necessity of baptism is that of precept, and that many of them accepted the principle that baptism ought not to be given except by the ordained minister. There can be no doubt that their anxiety to make these points clear hampered them in their defence of the private administration. In points of detail, they could appeal to the private administrations of the New Testament, and also to the example of Zwingli, but their main argument was that the accepted necessity of precept must take precedence over the rules of administration and order. As Whitgift was at pains to point out, he was not claiming an absolute necessity,[296] nor was he defending baptism by a private person, "upon which he suspended judgment".[297] He was contending that the circumstances of administration are only incidental, and not something which is "of necessity to the sacrament".[298] Normally, baptism ought to be given in public, as the Prayer Book demanded. But if a choice had to be made between private baptism and no baptism at all, it was better to fulfil the commandment of Christ than to insist upon ecclesiastical order. Of course, ecclesiastical order was important. For that reason private baptism must not be given except in "extreme necessity of sickness, peril, death and such like".[299] But where these exceptional circumstances did arise, the sacrament itself was to be regarded as more important than the normal rule of administration.

The discussion at Hampton Court did not add anything new, except that the abandonment of lay-baptism helped to make clear the

---

294. S.P.R., I, 180.
295. Travers, *Ecclesiastical Discipline*, p. 25.
296. S.P.R., I, 177.
297. Whitgift, P.S., II, p. 540.
298. *Ibid.*, p. 509.
299. *Ibid.*, p. 513.

distinction between private baptism in respect of time and place and private baptism in respect of the minister. This reform was useful, perhaps, in that it removed certain possible misconceptions, but it did not meet the basic Puritan criticisms. By the new Prayer Book, the Puritan minister was still obliged to administer privately in case of need, and the 1604 canon (69) prescribed heavy penalties for any failure "or of set purpose, or of gross negligence" to fulfil the injunction. Not, perhaps, without a certain irony, prospective dissenters were forbidden by canon 71 either to preach or to administer the communion in private houses, so that the Puritan who refused to conform might well be convicted for doing the very thing which he had refused to do.

There can be no doubt that in the last analysis the difference between the Puritans and Anglicans was one of policy rather than of doctrinal principle. The policy of the Puritans was the more logical, and for that reason the more practical and effective. By emphasizing ecclesiastical order, and enforcing a strict rule of public administration, they ensured a solemn and edifying service, excluded all possibility of superstition or the revival of error, and added to the dignity and significance of the sacrament. From the point of view of Protestant statesmanship they were undoubtedly right. A vigorous and ruthless reorganization of the church was essential if the Reformation was to be secured against disintegration and ultimate collapse. The Anglicans, on the other hand, declared for what was a more dangerous method of retaining as much as possible of the existing system within a reformed framework. The policy offered certain immediate advantages. It enabled both priest and people to adapt themselves to the changes made, and reduced the possibilities of civil disturbance to a minimum. But in the long run it left scope not merely for the evasion of reform, but even for the reintroduction of discarded doctrines. In both respects the history of the Church of England has proved that the apprehensions of the Puritans were not entirely groundless.

Yet even if it was not attained and never could be attained, the ideal of the Anglicans did perhaps preserve a better theological balance. With all their doctrinal correctness, with all the logical application of their principles, the Puritans were in danger of losing the evangelical freedom in a new and evangelical legalism. Even in this matter of private baptism, the "substance" of the sacrament became subordinate to its external "accidents", to adopt and apply the phraseology of the

Schoolmen. To that extent the Anglican attempt to retain a private administration did stand for something fine and worthwhile. It has no doubt failed in practice, but it can still lay claim not merely to sympathy but also to respect.

4

The Grace

(1) Effects

From the very outset the sacrament of baptism has been associated with certain moral and spiritual results, attributed not merely to the psychological impact of the rite but to the inward and, in the last resort, supernatural work of the Holy Spirit. In the New Testament itself baptism was certainly regarded as much more than a "naked" sign, and throughout the history of the church the majority of theologians have found it necessary to ascribe some efficacy to it. The Reformers, as we have seen, laid a greater proportionate emphasis upon the signification than the effects, but they too could assert quite categorically that baptism not only means something but actually does something.

At the very lowest level baptism is the pledge of an individual decision for Christ, and of the corresponding entry into the new life of grace. As a pledge of this kind, it constitutes a constant reminder and permanent challenge to the Christian to be that which he ought to be. This is the first and obvious sense of the famous passage in Romans 6 in which the apostle exhorts his readers to fulfil their baptismal profession. The operation of baptism along these lines is in some sense, of course, moral and psychological. As such it did not attract a great deal of attention in the Middle Ages, which preferred to think of a habitual virtue infused into the soul at baptism.[1] Baptism did indeed carry with it "a noble train of all virtues",[2] but by a purely supernatural rather than a psychological activity, by a work done rather than by a challenge made. The baptized person retained a freedom of response. He could determine the use which he himself made of the grace infused. But it was as a once-and-for-all operation rather than as a continuing call or sign that the sacrament had its effect.

With the coming of the Reformers, however, there was a return to the Pauline insight and emphasis. Luther could still speak of an infusion of grace, the reconstitution of the sinner in righteousness,[3] but this infusion was only the beginning of renovation. In the Christian

---

1. S., III, qu. 69, 4.
2. C.T., II, 2, qu. 50.
3. W.A., II, p. 730.

life of sanctification baptism had still a great work to do as a constant summons to mortification and renewal. As Luther saw it, the threefold vow made by the Christian in baptism was a higher and more solemn obligation than any subsequent ecclesiastical or monastic vows.[4] Of course, baptism had other effects, but it was an important part of its work to engage the Christian to a life of holiness and faith.[5] The charge of Antinomianism, as, for example, in Henry's *Assertio* ("O most impious doctrine ...")[6] reads somewhat strangely in the light of this clear and energetic teaching.

The Reformed theologians did not emphasize quite so strongly as Luther this aspect of pledge or profession. But we find it clearly in Zwingli. Zwingli compared the external sign of baptism to the badge worn by patriotic supporters of the Confederation. Indeed, he refused to ascribe to it, as an external sign, anything more than the psychological value of a reminder and profession.[7] His successors, however, were more concerned to work out the difficult question of the supernatural operation of the Holy Spirit in baptism, and they could almost take for granted its effect as a call to Christian discipleship. Yet they did not entirely ignore this element. Calvin, too, pointed out that it is one of the benefits of the sacrament to show us our mortification and to bind us to the Christian life which we profess when we receive it. But if he avoided altogether the notion of an infused grace or virtue, it was not merely because he regarded the effect as purely psychological, but because he could not allow that it is so supernatural as to be magical, or so inward and invisible as to be purely fictional.[8] All the Reformers, of course, agreed wholeheartedly with Luther that the great baptismal vow renders all monastic vows superfluous and even impious.

In England it was the earlier group of Reformers which concentrated attention upon the moral working of baptism. As Tyndale put it, the fulfilment of baptism is "the lifelong job of a Christian."[9] That job will be done only as the Christian has "the profession of baptism in the heart", and the knowledge "of the law of God" and "of the promises of mercy which are in our Saviour Christ".[10] The operation is psychological to the

4. W.A., II, p. 736.

5. Jacobs, *op. cit.*, pp. 314 f.

6. *Assertio*, p. 97.

7. C.R., IV, pp. 210 f.

8. Cf. *Instit.*, IV, 15, 13.

9. Tyndale, P.S., I, p. 500.

10. *Ibid.*, II, p. 136.

extent that it is dependent upon an understanding of the sacrament, although ultimately a true and inward operation is itself the work of the Holy Spirit. Becon made much the same point when he claimed that those who have made the baptismal confession ought to "answer and to live agreeable to it".[11] The preacher Latimer made full use of the moral appeal of the sacrament, demanding a careful study of its meaning,[12] exhorting to a reception of Christ "with a pure heart" and a readiness "to go forward in all goodness according to His will and commandment",[13] and warning of the severe judgment of God upon those who refuse to fulfil the obligations of baptism and are therefore "worse than the Turks and heathen".[14] Many of the later writers could still find a place for this aspect. Bradford, for example, described baptism as the sacrament of "sanctification and holiness",[15] and he called upon "his dear sister Joyce Hales" to deny herself and to take up her cross "in fulfilment of the baptismal vow".[16] Coverdale, too, asked where was that "abrenouncing and forsaking of the world and the flesh, which we sware in our baptism".[17] In the opening passage of the *Catechism* children were reminded not only of the meaning and privileges but also of the obligations of baptism: baptism itself being regarded as the witness and challenge to personal repentance, faith and service. The superfluity of other vows was emphasized in the book *The Summe of the Holye Scripture,*[18] and in the later period Pilkington argued that "all vows following, which are contrary to that of baptism, not only may and ought to be broken, but it is wicked to keep them".[19]

Up to a point, of course, the work of baptism in this way was purely human and natural. Baptism was a visible sign to which the baptized person could be referred. It was a significant sign which carried its meaning in itself and could exercise its power by means of it. It was a sign which was also a pledge, laying upon those who accepted it certain definite and agreed obligations. But although like the word itself baptism worked in and through the mind and conscience of the recipient, in the last resort its efficaciousness even along these lines depended upon the supernatural operation of the Holy Spirit. Everyone could perceive outwardly the meaning and obligation of the sacrament

---

11. Becon, P.S., II, p. 200.
12. Latimer, P.S., II, p. 133.
13. *Ibid.*, II, p. 342.
14. *Ibid.*, I, p. 346.
15. Bradford, P.S., I, p. 121.
16. Bradford, P.S., II, p. 203.
17. Coverdale, P.S., II, p. 234.
18. Folio vii.
19. Pilkington, P.S., p. 621.

but not everyone could perceive it inwardly, and to a genuine spiritual profit. The effect was human and natural, but it could not be explained only in religious and psychological terms. It was also divine and supernatural, not as a magical act, but as a moral and religious process applied in a new way and to a new end by the constraining and guiding action of God the Holy Spirit. Even when baptism was regarded as a call or a pledge, its real effect lay in the internal rather than the external sphere.

But, of course, the moral work of baptism did not by any means exhaust its power or efficacy. Apart from its value as a challenge or incentive, baptism had always been connected with that inward cleansing from sin which it outwardly pictured. It was in and through the sacrament that the Holy Spirit was thought to apply to the soul the benefits of the Passion and to seal to the recipient the divine gift of forgiveness. In the early church forgiveness was always regarded as the primary effect of baptism.[20] Indeed for many of the Fathers "baptized" and "cleansed" were almost synonymous terms.[21] It was not merely that the external sign symbolized the internal work. Even in the New Testament the relationship had obviously been much more vital than that. And for the early writers the sign itself accomplished the inward cleansing, effecting an actual sinlessness which had then to be maintained. In other words, the baptized person emerged from baptism actually cleansed from all the pollution of sin. As Augustine observed, if there was a logical time for suicide it was immediately after baptism, when "being cleansed by the washing of holy baptism, we have remission of all our sins".[22] Even Pelagius could find the same effect of cleansing in adults who were guilty of actual sin.

In the Fathers, as in the New Testament itself, the close interrelating of sign and effect was to some extent still figurative and even rhetorical. The Schoolmen gave to the idea a more precise dogmatic formulation. For Lombard, baptism was by definition an actual purging of the soul, with the accompanying remission of all eternal penalties.[23] Thomas considered the possible objections to such a view, but he concluded that baptism does cleanse the soul and that in it all penalties are remitted by the communication of Christ's passion and by divine grace.[24] It may be noted that the remission was different

---

20. H.D., II, p. 140.
21. Cf. the references gathered by Stone, *Holy Baptism*, pp. 43-50.
22. Cf. Cary, *op. cit.*, on Art. 27.
23. Lombard, IV, *Dist.* 4 E.
24. S., III, qu. 69.

from the cleansing, and rested upon it, but in any case the baptized person was set free from both the stain and the guilt of sin. A work had been done within him as well as for him. If the theologians did not forget that ultimately this work is accomplished by the death and resurrection of Jesus Christ, amongst the ignorant it came to be associated almost exclusively with the rite itself. It was the mere administration of baptism which transformed "the image of the fiend and brand of hell" into a child of God.[25] The popular notion was not altogether false, for baptism was at least the instrumental cause of this justification, or making just, and it accomplished its effect by virtue of the correct administration except where prevented by some obstacle. The moment that baptism was given, original sin was completely purged, and so too was all actual sin committed prior to the administration. As Henry VIII put it, quoting Hugo de Sancto Victore, "the sacrament of baptism cleanses internally".[26] Or, as Stephen Gardiner stated, its function is to dispense to the baptized the effects of the Cross,[27] baptism having all the efficacy of the most precious blood of Christ.[28] Or, as Watson claimed, baptism literally accomplishes inwardly that which it symbolizes outwardly, washing the soul from all the defilements of existing sin.[29]

The Reformers, too, saw a close interconnection between baptism and forgiveness, as their loyalty to the New Testament demanded. For obvious reasons, however, they could not accept the quasi-material notions of the Schoolmen and their successors. Luther did indeed retain something of the traditional phraseology,[30] but his understanding of it was revolutionized by his new conception of justification. According to Luther, the soul is not actually cleansed from sin, either in baptism or at any time in this present life. It is rather that sin is not imputed. Negatively, the baptismal cleansing is a non-imputation of original and actual sin. Positively it is an imputation of the perfect and all-sufficient righteousness of Jesus Christ.[31] For Luther baptism was still the sign of remission, and under the Holy Spirit it could still be the instrument of justifying faith, but his whole conception of the relationship had broadened and deepened. It had broadened: for the remission could now

---

25. Cf. Manning, *op. cit.*
26. *Assertio*, p. 100.
27. J., III, p. 523.
28. J., III, p. 240.
29. Strype, *Cheke*, pp. 101 f.
30. Cf. W.A., XXX, 1, p. 215; XLVI, p. 175.
31. Hamel, *op. cit.*, pp. 86 f.

extend to the whole life of a Christian. And it had deepened: for it was a remission in spiritual rather than in quasi-material terms, in the terms of a righteousness of faith rather than a righteousness of sight and works.

The contribution made by Zwingli and the Anabaptists was on the whole the negative one of attacking the prevailing notion that the external element could itself accomplish an internal cleansing.[32] The Anabaptists in particular had no very positive doctrine to substitute for the rejected teaching. Although they maintained with truth that it is the blood of Christ which cleanses from sin,[33] they did not think of baptism as in any way a means of grace, but only as a sign of grace, and more especially as a sign of individual conversion.[34] Zwingli did not altogether share this view. As he saw it, baptism in the full sense embraces the inward baptism of the Spirit as well as the outward baptism of water. Where the two are conjoined in true believers, the effect of baptism is a genuine inward purgation. If Zwingli erred, it was in his too harsh divorcing of the two aspects or "natures" of the sacrament. The union which he envisaged was only an incidental union suspended entirely upon an operation of the Spirit which was sovereign and unpredictable. At this point the sacramental theology of Zwingli betrays both the strength and the weakness of his doctrines of providence and the incarnation.

The later Reformed theologians attempted to steer a middle course between the blatant assertions of the traditionalists and the perhaps excessive denials of the sacramentarians. Calvin started from the axiom "confessed by all the pious, that in baptism the remission of sins, as well as the grace of the Holy Spirit, is offered and exhibited to us".[35] But Calvin expressed himself with caution. In relation to baptism he preferred to speak of the benefits rather than the effects, and of the assurance of the deletion of sins rather than the deletion itself.[36] Baptism itself was not the gift of grace, or the work of grace, but the means of grace. Like every means, it was subordinate to the one who used and applied it. The great need was to concentrate, not upon the instrument, but upon the true sources of forgiveness in the death of Jesus Christ and the inward operation of the Holy Spirit. Not that the sign itself

---

32. C.R., IV, pp. 215, 627.
33. B.R.N., II, p. 280, IV, p. 44.
34. Muralt, *op. cit.*, p. 40.
35. *Tracts*, I, p. 73.
36. *Instit.*, IV, 15, 1 f.

was naked and empty, for in it, as Beza pointed out, "there be offered spiritually and truly those things which be outwardly represented by them".[37] To the non-elect the things were only offered. For that reason there could not be an automatic or *ex opere operato* efficacy. But to the elect they were applied and sealed by the gracious working of the Holy Spirit. To that extent the sacrament itself was also a means to fulfilment.

The position in England was complicated. The earlier formularies used the language of medieval theology,[38] and even the Prayer Book and Article might suggest a traditionalist understanding. The Article, for example, described baptism as an instrument, and referred to forgiveness as one of its benefits. But there is evidence that from quite an early period the baptismal forgiveness was understood by the Reformers in a Lutheran or Reformed sense rather than the Scholastic. The *King's Book* is perhaps the one exception which confirms the general rule. Even the formularies themselves make this plain. The *Ten Articles* ascribe the forgiveness primarily to Christ Himself,[39] and the Baptismal Office speaks of the benefits rather than the effects of the sacrament, and relates them in the first instance to the author of grace, and only secondarily to the means. The *Homilies* have exactly the same emphasis, for although it is boldly stated that baptized infants are washed from their sins, the washing is by virtue of the sacrifice of Christ and not of the sacrament.[40] The Article certainly describes baptism as an efficacious sign, but it then shows clearly that its efficacy is not to cleanse from sin, but to sign and seal the divine promise of forgiveness. In the last resort the baptismal cleansing is only the cleansing of promise, not of fact. Baptism is one of the ways in which the believer apprehends the promise and in that way enjoys its truth.

The individual Anglicans were all anxious to maintain the traditional connection between baptism and forgiveness. It appears in almost every writer from Tyndale to Hutchinson. But at the very outset Tyndale pointed out that the true cleansing is the cleansing in the blood of Christ, or of the Holy Spirit.[41] Again, as Becon perceived, it is the cleansing of imputation rather than of an actual work or effect: "We take Christ upon us with all His holiness and righteousness."[42] Baptism is in

---

37. B.P.S., 88.
38. Lloyd, *Formularies*, p. 233.
39. *Ibid.*, *The Ten Articles*.
40. *Homilies*, p. 25.
41. Tyndale, P.S., I, p. 424.
42. Becon, P.S., II, p. 201.

fact "our removing from that fierce judging place into the court of mercy and the throne of grace."[43] Nowell laid great stress upon the inwardness and secrecy of true baptismal grace.[44] Coverdale related it directly to Jesus Christ Himself: "Having once forgiveness through the grace and gift of Christ."[45] Cranmer, like Zwingli, perceived that there is both an outward work of baptism and also an inward, but that the true baptism will include both: "Through baptism, in this world, the body is washed, and the soul is washed: the body outwardly, the soul inwardly: the work is one."[46] Hooper took up the point that the forgiveness or washing is by imputation rather than by an actual work: "Baptism is a seal and confirmation of justice, either of our acception into the grace of God: Christ his innocency and justice by faith is ours, and our sins and injustice by his obedience are his: whereof baptism is the sign, seal and confirmation."[47] For Jewel, baptism was a means of grace because it was "a means to assure us of the death and merits of our Lord and Saviour Christ".[48] But the efficacy had to be ascribed, not to the rite itself, but to the operation of the Trinity to which it testified. As Hutchinson put it, "in that bath of holy baptism we are regenerate, washed, purified, and made the children of God, by the workmanship of the three persons".[49]

The Reformers clearly accepted the fact, not only that baptism and forgiveness are related, but that in some way baptism is a means, if not to convey, at any rate to sign and seal that forgiveness to us. But they departed radically from the Schoolmen and the sixteenth-century traditionalists not merely by ascribing the efficacy to the blood of Christ, for their predecessors and opponents could also do that, but by thinking of forgiveness as a non-imputation by promise rather than as a washing which effected actual righteousness. This meant that forgiveness was not an actual work accomplished in the soul by the act of baptism or even by a concomitant grace. It was a forgiveness of promise which the sacrament itself plainly attested and declared and which under the Holy Spirit was appropriated by the faith which the sacrament evoked or confirmed. This was the reason why the work of baptism could not be divorced from its signification. Even at its deepest level the operation

---

43. Becon, P.S., II, p. 635.
44. Nowell, P.S., p. 86.
45. Coverdale, P.S., I, p. 410.
46. Foxe, VI, p. 457.
47. Hooper, P.S., II, p. 88.
48. Jewel, P.S., II, p. 1106.
49. Hutchinson, P.S., p. 11.

of the sacrament was not wholly supernatural or magical. It was a work of God in and through the natural, the conferring of forgiveness by the open proclamation of the divine promise. Yet it was still a supernatural work. The faith by which the forgiveness became actual and personal could not be awakened or assured except by the operation of the Holy Spirit in and through the sacrament. Where the Holy Spirit did use the sacrament to that end, it could be said with truth that the baptized man was a forgiven man, not because the baptism itself had effected a quasi-material purgation of the soul, but because he was accounted righteous by faith in Jesus Christ. And understanding the sacrament as the attestation of the divine promise in Christ, he could rest upon the assurance which it carried with it. But this was possible only where there was the inward perception and faith which is not the product of ordinary human intelligence but of the sovereign operation of the life-giving Spirit.

In the Reformed understanding the old connection was still maintained, and the sacrament was still given its supernatural as well as its natural aspect. But the new conception of forgiveness and the new emphasis upon the free and elective sovereignty of the Spirit liberated the Reformers from those notions which had dominated the medieval mind. They acquired a new and proper sense of the twofold nature of the sacrament as both a natural and a supernatural work, conjoined into the one divine-human act only where there was the activity of the Spirit quickening the external act and evoking the inward response of a genuine faith and assurance.

The remission of sins was as it were the negative grace or benefit of the sacrament, corresponding both to the signification of death and also to the prerequisite of an individual repentance. But baptism was also related to a positive grace corresponding to the signification of resurrection and the prerequisite of individual faith and obedience. This was the supreme baptismal grace of regeneration. Already in the New Testament baptism had been most closely connected with regeneration, as we may see from texts like John 3:5 and Titus 3:5, as well as the much-quoted Romans 6. And although Tertullian connected the new life with the descent of the Spirit rather than the baptismal washing,[50] the majority of Fathers identified it much more closely with the washing itself. Gregory Nazianzus, for example, could describe the sacrament

---

50. Tertullian, *De Bapt.*, 6-8.

as the rectifying or amendment of our formation,[51] and Basil as the rectifying of our former birth,[52] the reconstitution of the sinner in the divine image.

It is perhaps worth remarking that especially with the decrease of adult baptism there was a tendency to think even of this positive grace in a negative way, as a removing of original defects, rather than as a full moral and spiritual renewal. To that extent the baptismal regeneration did not amount to very much more than the baptismal cleansing. The soul was reborn in the sense that it was cleansed from the pollution of original and actual sin. It was perhaps for this reason that the Schoolmen had nothing very significant to say about regeneration except that it meant incorporation into Jesus Christ, an entry into the church of Jesus Christ, and the possibility of moral renewal by the infusion of habitual virtue.[53] The truth seems to be that although regeneration was assumed to be the chief grace and effect of baptism, the concept had been so emptied of meaning that it could hardly stand as a separate entity. Indeed, in the Tridentine statements regeneration was not mentioned separately: it emerged only incidentally in the list of other graces.[54] The baptized person was regenerate in the sense that he made a fresh start and was endowed with certain virtues, but neither in spiritual status nor in moral life could he be said to be born again in the full New Testament sense. Some controversialists were even prepared to minimize the baptismal regeneration in order to maintain the superior nature and efficacy of the Lord's supper. Watson, for example, argued that baptism regenerates spiritually by the Spirit, but "the eucharist, which is the true substance of Christ's flesh, quickens the flesh".[55] The speculation foundered because in many cases the baptismal regeneration has to suffice without any reception of the eucharist, but it is interesting in that it shows how attenuated the concept had become. Only the doctrine of infused virtue preserved it from virtual obliteration.

The restoration of regeneration to much of its original meaning and honour as the chief grace of baptism was largely the work of Martin Luther. Luther did it by relating regeneration directly to the resurrection of Jesus Christ and the entry of the Christian believer

51. Cf. Wall, *op. cit.*, I, p. 82.
52. *Ibid.*, p.111.
53. S., III, qu. 69, 5.
54. C.T., II, 2, qu. 47 f.
55. Strype, *Cheke*, p. 107.

into that resurrection. The Christian was cleansed because by virtue of the death of Christ his sins were no longer imputed, the old life was dead. The Christian was also regenerate because by virtue of the resurrection of Christ a new life was imputed and already begun by faith: he was alive again from the dead. It was not that the believer actually became Christ Himself, as some of his early critics seem to have imagined.[56] It was rather that by the faith which is the work of the Spirit the Christian began a new life in which he was identified with Jesus Christ in the resurrection from the dead. Regeneration was not merely a removal of existing defilements, with a little supernatural help. It was a reconstitution of the whole man in positive righteousness. If it was objected that a full regeneration of this kind cannot be presumed in the baptized because it is not manifested, the reply was that in this life, even in the true believer, the reconstitution is complete only by promise and by faith. The whole course of the Christian life is its progressive realization under the impulsion of the Holy Spirit and of the faith which is the gift and work of the Spirit. The point is that the very emphasis of the traditionalists upon a work done, a cleansing and regeneration already effected, meant that in face of the hard teaching of reality they had to minimize the nature and especially the extent of the effects which they presumed. But Luther was under no such restraint. With his deep and scriptural insight that in this life both forgiveness and regeneration are by faith and promise, he could relate the sign to the whole work of God, and not merely to the imperfect manifestations of it in actual Christian discipleship.

The far-reaching nature of this reinterpretation may be gathered from the fact that in the later Reformers regeneration was no longer considered within the context of remission, but remission within that of regeneration: "Baptism is a sacrament ... whereby we are regenerated and engrafted into Christ for the remission of sins and eternal salvation."[57] The thinking of Calvin was very much along these lines. As he put it: In baptism "Christ Himself with all His gifts is offered to all in common". Those who received the sacrament rightly received Christ, and in Him the new life of righteousness and the forgiveness of all sin.[58] The regeneration and remission were still by faith

---

56. Cf. Warham's condemnation in E.R., pp. 397-398.

57. Quoted from Peter Martyr in E.B.I., p. 175.

58. *Tracts*, II, *Mutual Consent*, 18.

and promise, for they could be enjoyed only in Christ, and therefore
only by faith in Him. That is why a right reception was necessary if
the benefits of the sacrament were to be perceived and known.[59] But
the remission of sins was no longer the outstanding benefit of which
regeneration was a shadowy concomitant or consequence. The final
end signified and sealed in baptism was the new life in Christ already
begun in faith and one day to be completed with the resurrection
from the dead. It was in this new birth in righteousness that the baptismal death or remission necessarily culminated.

As in the case of remission, the first English statements in the reign
of Henry were couched for the most part in strictly traditional terms,
although it is interesting that in the *Ten Articles* there is a reference to
the offer rather to the work or gift of grace: "That all by baptism have
the remission of sins and the grace and favour of God offered them".[60]
Even in this early period Lutheran influences were strongly at work,
especially through the writings of Tyndale, who pointed out that the
main function of the sacrament is that of "testifying and exhibiting to
our senses the promises signified".[61] During the early part of the reign
of Edward, the Lutheran understanding found clear expression in the
translation popularly known as *Cranmer's Catechism*, which related
baptism directly to the regenerating activity of the Holy Spirit: "The
Spirit works in faith and baptisme to make us new men agayne."[62] In
baptism the old life comes to an end with the identification of the believer
with Christ's death and the non-imputation of sin. But in baptism, too,
a new life begins with the identification of the believer with Christ's
resurrection and the imputation of the whole righteousness of Christ:
"Baptism delivereth from death and the power of the devil, and gyveth
salvation and everlastynge lyfe to all them that believe."[63]

The effect of the Lutheran infiltration is seen in the revised baptismal
orders in which the chief stress falls upon the positive benefit of regeneration rather than its negative complement in remission. The prayer
which is made is primarily for spiritual regeneration. The thanks-giving
is for the blessing of the new life and incorporation into Christ according
to the covenanted promises. There is also a final prayer for a constant

---

59. *Instit.*, IV, 15, 5.
60. Lloyd, *op. cit.*, *Ten Articles*.
61. Tyndale, P.S., I, p. 357.
62. *Cranmer's Catechism*, p. 122.
63. *Ibid.*, p. 189.

entry into the death and resurrection of Christ by daily mortification and renewal. We find exactly the same emphasis in Ponet's *Catechism* and also in the Article, which was first drafted in the reign of Edward. In Ponet's *Catechism* baptism is primarily the sacrament of regeneration, pointing to the new birth by the Spirit of God and also to membership not merely of the external church but also of the communion of saints.[64] The Article defined baptism as the sign and instrument of our new birth and grafting into the church of Christ.

The individual writers expressed themselves in very much the same way. Becon, for instance, regarded baptism as the sacrament of deliverance: "We receive manumission and freedom so soon as we are regenerate and born anew by the honourable sacrament of baptism and the Holy Ghost."[65] Bradford, too, rejoiced in the positive side of baptism: "As thou, O God, dost regenerate us, and as it were engraft us into the fellowship of the church, and by adoption make us thy children."[66] Nowell,[67] Hutchinson,[68] and Jewel[69] all linked together the baptismal remission and the baptismal entry into newness of life in Christ and in the church of Christ. The emphasis is important, because it marks a return in Anglican teaching to the scriptural and patristic doctrine, and a rejection of the quasimaterial conception of cleansing. Baptism was not merely an obliteration of past sin, but the giving of a new and divine life, an entry into the resurrection. The baptismal forgiveness was not as it were a literal washing of the soul from sin and its endowment with new grace and virtue. It was a forgiveness, and accompanying renewal, by identification in faith with the crucified and risen Redeemer.

The true grace of baptism was, in fact, the new, creation of God in which by the divine promise and faith the old things are passed away and all things are become new. It was a genuine and full regeneration, an incorporation into Christ with all the benefits which that implied and involved. It was more than the formal uniting with Christ, or the change in external status, which might be presumed of all those who received the outward sign. For although the Reformers distinguished between the first regeneration of faith and the process of moral renovation in which we become by sight that which we are already by faith,

---

64. Ponet's *Catechism*, B.R., p. 72.
65. Becon, P.S., I, p. 178.
66. Bradford, P.S., I, p. 260.
67. Nowell, P.S., p. 86.
68. Hutchinson, P.S., p. 11.
69. Jewel, P.S., I, pp. 140-141.

regeneration itself was a deep and inward operation of the Holy Spirit; not a bare ontological change, but a renewal of the whole life by saving faith in Jesus Christ. It had to be admitted, of course, that this kind of new birth could not honestly be presumed of every recipient of the sacrament. But the Reformers solved the attendant difficulty, not by abstracting from the meaning of regeneration, but by replacing the static conception of the relationship between grace and sign by one which was living and dynamic.

In addition to the three chief effects already mentioned, the call to a moral life, the remission of sins, and regeneration, baptism had traditionally carried with it many subsidiary and supplementary graces. With a rhetorical flourish Chrysostom had referred to a thousand benefits, and of these he listed ten, the majority of which were the different forms of implanted virtue.[70] The most important of these effects was the presumed infusion of faith, although this had greater significance in the case of infants and will be better discussed in that connection. The Reformers rejected this view, but with the exception of Zwingli they could all describe the sacrament as a seal or "sealed instrument, to assure us of the deletion of all our sins", "to elevate, nourish and confirm our faith".[71] This aspect appeared in *Cranmer's Catechism*, which described it as "the work of baptism to quieten the conscience and to make us glad and merie";[72] in the thanksgiving of the Baptismal Office, which was bold to accept the divine promise attested in the sacrament; and in the Article (25), which referred to the sacraments as "sure witnesses, and effectual signs of grace ... by the which he doth not only quicken, but also strengthen and confirm our faith in him".

Two other benefits alleged in the Middle Ages and by the sixteenth-century traditionalists were physical healing and spiritual "character". The first need not detain us. It was not discussed by the Reformers, and in any case it could never be more than a special and additional gift.[73] Behind it there lay the not untrue perception that the physical and the spiritual are closely interconnected, but in practice it could and did give rise to the grossest of superstitions, that it is unlucky not to have the baby "done", and that a child will thrive only after it has received the sacrament.

---

70. Cf. Wall, *op. cit.*, I, pp. 118-120.
71. *Instit.*, IV, 14-15.
72. *Cranmer's Catechism*, pp. 186-187.
73. Cf. S., III, qu. 69, 8.

The doctrine of a spiritual character rested upon the distinction made by Augustine between those who merely received the dominical mark and the elect who received sacramental grace.[74] Thomas contended that this mark was an indelible impress made upon the soul which would always differentiate even the unfaithful baptized from the non-baptized.[75] The teaching was no doubt based upon the real truth that everyone who is baptized has received at least the external sign, and to that extent is marked off from other men. But as developed by the medieval theologians it involved all kinds of ambiguities and perplexities, especially in relation to the supposed impress upon the substance of the soul.[76] In its developed form it seems almost to have been an effort to find some real effect even in the case of those who opposed an obstacle to baptismal grace. It is therefore not surprising that it was rejected by critics of an *ex opere operato* efficacy. Wycliffe had had no place for the doctrine of "character"[77] and the later Reformers dismissed it as meaningless and artificial. The English attitude was summed up by Tyndale, when he described "character" as "one of those feigned words with which the Papists make merchandise".[78] The only possible truth in the conception was stated by Cranmer when he suggested that those who have received the sacrament are sacramentally regenerate,[79] i.e. they have the sign of regeneration. But obviously this was something quite different from the impress supposedly made upon the soul itself. The majority of the English writers simply ignored the idea, although Calfhill rejected the similar contention in relation to orders.[80]

The doctrine of character was not acceptable to the Reformers partly because it was not scriptural, but partly too because in its traditional form it was not even intelligible. Indeed, unless "character" is related only to the external sign, it is difficult to see what place or meaning it can possibly have. It is not potential grace, for even the unbaptized are possible recipients of future grace. And it is less than a real change in spiritual status, for there cannot be a change in status where there is an obstacle to the inflow of grace. But if we say that it relates only to the form of grace, or to a change in ecclesiastical status, the concepts

---

74. Cf. Beckmann, *op. cit.*, p.75.
75. S., qu. 66, 9.
76. T.B., p. 349.
77. *Trialogus*, pp. 157-159.
78. Tyndale, P.S., I, p. 342.
79. Cf. Cranmer, P.S., I, p. 150.
80. Calfhill, P.S., p. 12.

"character" and "spiritual impress" are hardly necessary: indeed, they are definitely harmful in that they inevitably give rise to confused and superstitious notions. The Reformers had, therefore, good reason both to oppose and to exclude them.

(2) Efficacy

Baptism was fairly generally admitted to be not merely a sign, but an efficacious sign, that is, a sign which is itself a means as well as an attestation of grace. But how can the spiritual grace be conferred or even offered through the sign? Is it by means of a purely natural operation? Is the sign itself of such a character that it necessarily produces the effect of grace? Or is it by means of a purely supernatural operation? Does God take the external sign, and in a way which transcends all human possibilities use it as an instrument of His own divine and wholly miraculous work? Or is it perhaps by means of an operation which is both natural and supernatural, a work of man, and yet also and at the same time a work of God?

The traditional answer to these questions was that the operation is wholly and altogether supernatural. It was pointed out that even in the New Testament the sign and the grace had been brought together in the closest possible way, so that the mere administration of the rite carried with it an inexplicable but unmistakable divine work. It is true that repentance was demanded in the recipient, that the sovereignty of the Holy Spirit was safeguarded, that sometimes the grace could precede the external administration, and that the grace manifested itself in open forms which left no room for doubt. But there could be no question concerning the reality and the depth of the connection. If this was true of the New Testament it was even more true of the early Fathers, who had so identified the sign and the grace that they could use the term "regeneration" as a synonym for baptism. At first, of course, the baptisms were mainly adult, so that the profession of faith was still demanded, and therefore some testimony to the baptismal grace remained. But with the increase of infant baptism, the absence of any evident faith or spiritual endowment made it necessary to presume the internal operation: and what may be presumed of one child may equally well be presumed of all. The most that could be said in relation to infants was that they did not offer any definite obstacle to baptismal grace. But if this were so, it could be taken for granted that in every case the external sign was accompanied by the internal and miraculous work. The Augustinian doctrine of election confirmed rather than checked this view, for not only did Augustine think that some grace was conferred upon all the baptized, but he regarded baptism as the proper medium for the conveyance of irresistible grace to the elect. The twofold result of this development was the static interrelating of sign and grace and the strict circumscribing of the grace which are so characteristic of Scholastic and Tridentine theology.

Of course, even the Schoolmen did not identify sign and grace absolutely. There were always exceptions, as was clearly recognized by Lombard. Martyrs, for example, received the grace signified by water-baptism apart from the external sign of water. On the other hand, the hypocritical, insincere, and unbelieving received the external sign without partaking of the internal grace.[81] With Thomas, too, lack of sincerity or faith constituted insuperable obstacles in the case of adults, although in all cases baptism did confer character, and where the unbelief or insincerity ceased, the removal of the bar automatically meant the inflow of baptismal grace.[82] The latter point is important, for it makes it clear that Thomas is thinking always in static rather than dynamic terms. The supernatural grace of baptism may in some cases be temporarily or even permanently held up, but the grace and sign are always conjoined. Even where there is an obstacle the minimal grace of character is irresistibly conferred. In fairness to Thomas it must be allowed that his view is no theological abstraction, but an attempted interpretation in sacramentalist terms of the actual facts of spiritual life. But from first to last his conception is dominated by the static relating of sign and grace and the causal understanding of baptismal efficacy. When he comes to the case of infants, the direction of his thinking emerges with even greater clarity. By their nature infants cannot oppose any obstacle, and are therefore excellent objects for the efficacious working of the Holy Spirit. The only and not very logical qualification is that they must have professing sponsors. Granted this condition, they receive both the sign and the grace with no possible impediment. The efficacy of the sacrament is guaranteed by the supremacy of the divine grace.[83]

But while the Schoolmen agreed that the sign and grace necessarily concur except where prevented by insincerity or unbelief, they did not all jump to the conclusion that the grace is actually in the sign. Certainly,

---

81. Lombard, IV, *Dist.* 4 A.

82. S., III, qu. 69, 9-10.

83. S., III, qu. 6.

a miraculous work is done when the external sign is administered. By virtue of the divine institution and the passion of Christ the baptismal sign and the baptismal grace do almost automatically concur. But there was room for definite disagreement concerning the way in which that concurrence took place. The majority of medieval scholars, and many of their sixteenth-century admirers and successors, inclined to the most obvious and simple view that God had given to the water itself a regenerative force: the grace, or virtue, was in the water. Thomas himself favoured this view, for which he could cite Augustine and Bede as venerable guarantors.[84] In the sixteenth century it found an exponent in Henry VIII, who claimed that the "force of spiritual life has been infused into the corporal element".[85] But there were other thinkers who favoured the less blatantly materialistic theory of concomitance, in which the external washing is accompanied by an internal which is directly the work of God Himself. In so far as God has ordained the external sign, the concomitant operation of God is in all cases guaranteed. To that extent there is still an indissoluble union between sign and grace. But the power of God is not actually identified with the material element. To that extent grosser and more superstitious conceptions of the sacramental operation are carefully excluded.

It is worth noting that prior to the Council of Vienne in 1311 the church was not dogmatically committed to any doctrine of automatic efficacy,[86] although the trend of patristic and especially scholastic thought was all in that direction. Even after that council the Nominalistic emphasis upon the divine will and sovereignty constituted something of a barrier against a purely static view. Baptism had this effect of grace only because God had willed and decreed that it should do so, not by virtue of any power inherent in baptism itself. But by the sixteenth century the more materialistic explanation of the mechanism of baptismal operation had gained a firm hold. Water and grace were not merely associated but strictly identified. It needed, therefore, a more revolutionary impulse than that of Nominalism to shake the supremacy of this view and to replace the whole static conception by a free and dynamic.

The impulse did not come until Luther saw his way to the doctrine of justification by faith, and it is significant that the demand for faith provoked a vigorous reaction on the part of his traditionalist opponents.

---

84. T.B., pp. 344-346.
85. *Assertio*, p. 100.
86. E.B.I., p. 32.

Henry, for example, suggested that "it is more safe to allow something to the sacrament than, like Luther, to attribute so much to faith as to leave neither grace, nor the efficacy of a sign, to the sacrament".[87] Cajetan could see a certain necessity of faith as a preliminary disposition, but he thought it a serious error to subordinate the whole efficacy of the sacrament to this disposition.[88] In the Bull *Exsurge Domine*[89] and later at the Council of Trent it was insisted that only the absence of unbelief is unnecessary,[90] that "the sacraments of the New Law contain the grace which they signify,"[91] that "grace, as far as God's part is concerned, is given through the said sacraments always, and to all men",[92] and that it is conferred through the act performed, not obtained by faith in the divine promises.[93] By these enactments the Tridentine church committed itself to a thoroughgoing doctrine of *ex opere operate* efficacy in which the material and spiritual elements in the sacraments were so interconnected that the presence of the one necessarily meant the presence of the other. Even where obstacles were opposed, the grace was still there. An impress was made upon the soul into which the grace could as it were flow as soon as the obstacle was removed. A certain liberty still remained in respect of the mechanism of operation, but the theory that the sacramental grace is miraculously enclosed in the element formed the most suitable and attractive explanation, and George Carpenter of Emmerich could be condemned for denying that "the very element itself in baptism doth give grace".[94] Where this view predominated, the static conception reached its full power, enslaving the life of the church under a sacramentalist yoke.

Of course, even in the fourteenth century automatic theories had been opposed by such thinkers as Wycliffe, who had separated between the external baptism of water and the inward purgation of the Holy Spirit, which "God Himself must do".[95] Walter Brute, too, had argued that faith is much more important than the sign, for faith is "the spiritual water, with which the faithful patriarchs baptized before the law".[96] But it was Luther who gathered these criticisms into a single force and made the decisive break-through with his new doctrine of justification. Rather

---

87. *Assertio*, pp. 103-104.
88. Cristiani, *op. cit.*, p. 60.
89. D.C.R., p. 76.
90. C.T., II, 2, qu., 39.
91. C.D., Sess. VII, *Bapt. can.*, 6.
92. C.D., Sess. VII, *Bapt. can.*, 7.
93. *Ibid.*, 8.
94. Foxe, IV, p. 374.
95. Arnold, II, p. 4.
96. Foxe, III, p. 168.

strangely, Luther continued to use expressions which suggest an *ex opere operato* efficacy, for he had a strong sense of the objectivity of the divine grace and work.[97] But at three points he broke definitely with the traditional dogma. First, as we have seen already, he pointed out that the true work of baptism is a work of faith and promise, not of sight. Second, and as a necessary corollary, he claimed that faith is indispensable to the operation of the sacrament,[98] for faith is itself the fulfilment of baptism,[99] the response of the soul which enables the sacrament to have its effect.[100] Thus the baptismal remission and regeneration is not a naturalistic or mechanical process, but an intensely personal matter in which the divine promise is held out on the one hand, and faith is the appropriation and fufilment of the promise on the other. Third, and finally, Luther did not find the power of baptism in the element, but in the baptismal word, which gives to the external sign its true signification, declaring the promises.[101] Baptism could achieve its effect only as the word of baptism was perceived and understood, and the response of faith evoked. But to say that was to suspend the efficacy of the sacrament upon the free and sovereign Spirit of God who disposes of both word and sacrament. The work of baptism was not done through the water alone, nor was it done through the Spirit necessarily acting with the water. If it was done at all, it was done only in so far as the Spirit Himself worked in, with and under the water, and sign and grace came together in the one creative act by which faith is born and the soul renewed by promise.

The Lutheran doctrine maintained a genuine unity of the divine and human aspects of the sacraments, although without that absorption of the one into the other which had characterized the traditional teaching. In Switzerland, however, more radical tendencies appeared which threatened to disrupt the two aspects, as with some of the medieval rebels. Zwingli himself distinguished so sharply between the baptism of water and the baptism of the Spirit that he seemed to make the former only a sign and the latter a free work of God which was not only unpredictable but independent of the outward act. His view was clearly dominated by the all-consuming anxiety to rebut the existing doctrine that the external element itself can confer spiritual

---

97. W.A., XXX, 1, p. 218.
98. *Ibid.*, p. 216.
99. W.A., VI, p. 532.
100. W.A., II, p. 315.
101. Cf. Wernle, *Luther*, p. 38.

grace. But, in effect, he came near to denying any possible union between sign and grace; a position which is quite consistent with his denial of secondary causes and his almost Nestorian Christology.[102] Whether Zwingli actually drew this conclusion is perhaps open to debate. The Anabaptists certainly did, for although Zwingli argued that they were confusing the two baptisms by attempting to make them simultaneous,[103] there is no doubt that they envisaged the external rite purely as a sign, and that it was not in any way, except the psychological, a means of spiritual grace.[104]

It was the task of Bucer and Calvin to purge the Reformed doctrine of its extremist tendencies and to restate the Lutheran view in a way which "did not affirm more of the sacrament than was fit".[105] Bucer could not agree either that the sacraments are "naked and bare signs",[106] or that they are "such instruments or channels of grace as that they bring grace with whatever mind or faith you partake of them".[107] They have a real, instrumental efficacy, but that efficacy is dependent upon two interrelated facts: first, the divine election, and second, the faith of the individual recipient. Sign and grace together constitute the one true baptism where the Holy Spirit uses the means of grace and the response of faith is either evoked or confirmed.

The teaching of Calvin was not dissimilar. Like Bucer, he repudiated the traditional "enclosing of the grace and virtue of the Spirit by the external sign".[108] But he avoided the opposite extreme of denying that there is any connection between the sacraments and the grace which they signify.[109] He emphasized three main facts: first, that God has ordained the sacraments as means of grace; second, that repentance and faith are indispensable to their proper use; and third, that their efficacy depends ultimately upon the divine election.[110] The sacrament of baptism does have a real effect, but only as it is sovereignly used by the Holy Spirit and received and understood in faith.

It may be noted that there are many affinities between the doctrine of Calvin and that of the Schoolmen, for they started from the same fundamental principles. But they applied the principles in very different

---

102. C.R., II, p. 203, IV, p. 223.
103. C.R., IV, p. 620.
104. B.R.N., II, p. 280.
105. Peter Martyr, in Strype, *Cranmer*, III, p. 162.
106. Lang, Art. in *Evangelical Quarterly*, I, 2, pp. 159 f.
107. E.B.I., p. 167.
108. *Tracts*, II, p. 574.
109. *Ibid.*, p. 87.
110. Beckmann, *op. cit.*, p. 96.

ways and with widely divergent results. On both sides, for example, it was held that God Himself is the true and sole author of baptismal grace. But while the Schoolmen deduced from this that God will inevitably operate through the means which He Himself has instituted, Calvin contended for His continuing freedom and sovereignty as "the internal master".[111] Again, both sides could admit the indispensability of repentance and faith, but whereas the Schoolmen conceived of repentance and faith narrowly and negatively, and argued that even the insincere and unbelieving will receive at least a spiritual impress, Calvin regarded repentance and faith positively as themselves the creative work of the Holy Spirit by which baptism has its effect and without which it can never be more than the external sign.[112] And although he did not dispute that in baptism an offer of grace is made to all, and that "the grace of baptism may resume its place" at any time when there is true repentance, he could not accept either the artificial concept of a baptismal character or the view that grace itself is present even when obstructed by insincerity or unbelief. As Calvin saw it, "the promises are common to all, but the ratification of them is the gift of the Spirit".[113]

Perhaps the true root of these differences was the different conception of grace, which the Schoolmen seemed to picture as a spiritual energy or substance, but which Calvin referred solely and directly to Christ Himself.[114] For Calvin, baptismal grace was not a spiritual medicine, but the divine favour and promise as we have it in the person and work of Jesus Christ. The office of the sacrament was the same as that of the word: to declare Jesus Christ. In the one no less than the other, Jesus Christ was proffered indiscriminately to all. The unbelieving certainly received the sign, and various external benefits. But they missed the true grace of baptism, and the sign itself testified to their unbelief. With the believing the case was different. As they received the sign they perceived Christ Himself, and therefore they enjoyed the grace. In the normal course, it was the specific function of the sacrament to confirm the faith in Christ already evoked by the word, but in the case of infants baptism could be a powerful adjunct to the word even in the evocation of the faith by which its benefits were subsequently received and enjoyed.

---

111. *Tracts*, II, p. 214, *Instit.*, IV, 14, 9.
112. *Ibid.*, p. 343.
113. *Tracts*, II, pp. 342-343.
114. *Ibid.*, p. 85.

Along lines such as these Calvin was able to hold a definite doctrine of sacramental efficacy without slipping into that static conception which meant an automatic efficacy and a practical denial of the free sovereignty of the Holy Spirit. The presentation of his doctrine varied to some extent with his successors, but not in any important particular. Beza, for example, emphasized the fact that the grace of baptism need not be simultaneous with the administration, but that "the fruit shall be shewed to the elect when it pleaseth God,"[115] "the effect beginning from that moment in which faith begins."[116] He pointed out that although the one "syne is received by a corporall and naturall maner, as well of the faithfull as of the unfaithfull", it is "to divers ends and purposes", for "the faithfull receiving the syne and the thing signified with the syne, perceive augmentation and increase of faith, the unfaithfull receive the bare syne to condemnation".[117] The reason for the distinction is that Jesus Christ Himself is the grace of the sacrament, and it is only by faith that He can be received: "He that bringeth not true faith cannot receive Jesus Christ, but he that bringeth faith receiveth him trulie and effectually, but spiritually by faith."[118] The lesson had been well learned that although there is a sacramental union of sign and grace it must be understood in a dynamic rather than a static sense, related on the one hand to the sovereign freedom of God, and on the other to the individual faith of the recipient.

It is hardly surprising that in the earlier stages of the English Reformation there were conflicting views and tendencies on this question of the baptismal efficacy. The traditionalist doctrine was clear enough. It was firmly stated not only by Henry but by writers and disputants like Fisher, More, Gardiner and Watson. Traces of this teaching may be found in an official formulary like the *King's Book*, which spoke of a real effect and virtue of the sacrament in infants and believing adults.[119] Yet the Lutheran leaven was already at work, for the *Ten Articles* referred to the need for genuine repentance and faith. Even the *King's Book* could say that "the sacrament hath its effect… by virtue and force of the working of Almighty God and the promise annexed and conjoined unto the same".[120]

It is sometimes assumed that the Baptismal Offices imply a traditional understanding of the efficacy of the sacrament, but, quite apart from

---

115. B.P.S., 34.
116. Q.R.C., 111.
117. B.P.S., 46.
118. *Loc. cit.*
119. K.B., p. 41.
120. *Loc. cit.*

the fact that they are liturgical rather than doctrinal documents, this is an obvious exaggeration. It is true that there are definite assertions with regard to the effects or benefits of the sacrament, but these assertions can be paralleled in the similar Lutheran and even Reformed statements, and may be interpreted hypothetically, or sacramentally and evangelically. In any case, the Prayer Book does not say anything at all about the mode of efficacy: there is no necessary interconnection of the benefits proffered or conferred with the actual administration of the water. The impression sometimes given that the Prayer Book reflects an *ex opere operato* conception is in fact purely superficial.

The Article, too, seems at a first glance to share something of the uncertainty or confusion of the earlier statements and possibly of the Baptismal Offices. It describes the sacrament quite categorically as an instrument to engraft the recipient into Jesus Christ. Some commentators like Stone[121] and Smithen[122] take it that this implies an *ex opere operato* view of the efficacy after the Scholastic manner. But certain points tell strongly against this conclusion. First, the opening sentence rejects the Anabaptist rather than the Reformed view, and it does so only on the ground that it is inadequate, not that it is false. Second, the statement that baptism is an "instrument" or means may be understood just as well in a Lutheran or Reformed as in a Scholastic sense. Third, the very term "instrument" was used by Reformers like Bucer and Calvin, although not necessarily in the sense of effective cause.[123] Fourth, when it is said that those who receive the sacrament "rightly" will enjoy its benefits the Latin word is not *rite* but *recte*, which suggests the need for a right disposition as well as a correct administration. Fifth, the Article must be set in the context of the general sacramental teaching of Article 25, which speaks of a wholesome effect or operation only in the worthy recipient, that is, the one who receives by faith and rightly (in this case *rite*). Sixth, the language of the article approximates closely to that of the parallel Reformed confessions. This is tacitly admitted by Stone, who in a weak analysis of the allegedly confused and inconsistent Reformed teaching notes that there are in the confessions phrases of a more satisfactory kind.[124] We may conclude, then, that it is only an

---

121. Stone, *op. cit.*, p. 61.
122. Smithen, *Continental Protestantism and the English Reformation*, p. 209.
123. e.g. *Tracts*, II, p. 84, 214.
124. Stone, *op. cit.*, p. 58.

arbitrary and unhistorical criticism which will read into the Article a static interrelating of the baptismal sign and grace.

When we turn to the individual writers, we find ample confirmation of the fact that first a Lutheran and later a Reformed conception did completely replace the traditional and Scholastic. An early attack on the identification of the grace with the element was made in the book *The Summe of the Holye Scripture* which stated quite categorically that there is no virtue in the water.[125] Tyndale was of the same mind. The Holy Spirit does not work in the water, but "accompanieth the preaching of faith, and with the word of faith, entereth the heart and purgeth it".[126] Latimer, too, denied that the baptized are necessarily regenerate.[127] One of the reasons why Lambert was martyred was that he would not admit that the sacraments of themselves can give faith.[128] The emphasis in these earlier writings was all upon the Lutheran doctrines, that faith is indispensable to true reception, that the power is in the word and promise, and that the grace is only from God. In the words of *Cranmer's Catechism*, "it is not the water, but the almightie worde of God, which receyveth God's worde and promise".[129]

The swing-over to a Reformed interpretation did not mean any shift in the basic position. It was still denied that the grace or virtue of the sacrament can in any way be attributed to the external sign. In the *Reformatio Legum*, for instance, there was a passage ridiculing those who regarded the sacrament "with so much awe and wonder as to believe that the Holy Spirit emerges from the external element itself, and that his influence, power and virtue, by which we are new created ... swim in the very waters of baptism".[130] Becon, too, stated firmly that "baptism itself bringeth not grace, but testifieth unto the congregation".[131] Again, it was still insisted that faith is indispensable to a true reception. Turner made this point in his comparison of the new learning (Romanism) with the old (historic and reformed Christianity): The new learning thought "that it is enough and sufficient to receive the sacraments effectually and with fruit, to have no stop nor let of deadly sin", but the old "that faith is necessary to be had in him that receiveth the sacrament

125. Foxe, V, p. 592.
126. Tyndale, P.S., I, pp. 423-424.
127. Ryle, *Bishops and Clergy*, pp. 110-111.
128. Foxe, V, p. 193.
129. *Cranmer's Catechism*, p. 190.
130. Cardwell, *A History of Conferences,*p. 18.
131. Becon, P.S., II, p. 220.

with fruit".[132] Bradford argued that "baptism requireth faith",[133] and Grindal that the water is powerful only "to the faithful receiver".[134] Many writers stressed not merely the futility but the danger of receiving the sacraments where there is no faith: "To use the sacraments without faith profiteth not, but rather hurteth."[135]

It was perhaps by way of this demand for worthy or faithful reception that the Anglicans arrived at what was substantially a Reformed understanding of baptismal efficacy. The true work of baptism was not the outward washing of water, but, as both Cranmer and Ridley perceived, the corresponding inward washing by the Holy Spirit.[136] This work was the miraculous work of God: "God worketh wonderfully by His omnipotent power in the true receivers, not in the outward visible signs."[137] There was no automatic efficacy: the sacrament was a means of grace only as God used it as such to those who received it in faith. The water did not cleanse from sin, or give new life, or infuse faith and other virtues, but to the elect and therefore the faithful it was a confirmation of faith, and to that extent a means of cleansing and new life, which in this world are by faith and promise. Of course, a general offer of divine grace was made to all those who received the sacrament externally, but in the words of Rogers salvation was given "only if they do believe".[138] The external and internal aspects did not need to be coincident in time: "Some have faith afore they receive any of the sacraments ... some neither afore, nor at the instant, nor yet afterwards."[139] The outlook of the Anglican Reformers was perhaps summed up by Whitgift when he wrote: "It is a certain and true doctrine to all such as profess the gospel, that the outward signs of the sacrament do not contain in them grace, neither yet that the grace of God is of necessity tied unto them, but only that they be seals of God's promises, notes of Christianity, testimonies and effectual signs of the grace of God."[140]

The Puritans, of course, did attempt to find traces of the medieval teaching in the retention of private baptism and the rubric concerning the salvation of baptized infants dying in infancy. But their objections were met by the firm statement that "the book did not mean to affirm

---

132. Turner, *The Old Learning and the New*, Folio A 4.
133. Bradford, P.S., I, p. 121.
134. Grindal, P.S., p. 62.
135. Coverdale, P.S., I, p. 411.
136. Cranmer, P.S., I, p. 341, Ridley, P.S., p. 275.
137. *Ibid.*, p. 341.
138. Rogers, p. 267.
139. *Ibid.*, p. 269.
140. Whitgift, P.S., III, p. 382.

that the sacrament did of itself confer grace *tanquam ex opere operato*,
but that by these words [i.e. the rubric] it only dissuaded from the the
opinion which the Papists had of their confirmation, called Bishoping".[141]
And the lesser writers of the Elizabethan period make it plain that the
Reformed view propagated by the leaders was the commonly accepted
one in the church of the time. Cooper, for example, marked off the
Anglican from the traditional teaching: "Yet we do not attribute the
operation hereof to the water, or outward element, but to the might of
God's Word and the power of the Spirit."[142] Alley and Some both saw a
need of faith to receive the grace or benefits of the sacraments.[143] Prime
asserted the sovereignty of God Himself over the sacraments which he
had appointed: "God is not so bound that He must work with, or cannot
work without those means, by his Spirit, the salvation of those whom he
had chosen and predestinated to eternal life before all worlds."[144] Willet
related the sacraments primarily to the divine promises,[145] and Haddon
would not "attribute so much to the sacraments as that through them,
as through channels, from the mere work wrought, the grace of God
should be necessarily imparted to us."[146]

A more difficult question is that of Hooker's teaching, which at least
in phraseology seems to mark a definite recession from the dynamic to
a modified form of the static conception. Hooker was prepared to assert
an instrumental necessity of the sacrament in all ordinary cases.[147]
He argued that in the case of infants, who could not believe, but also
"could conceive nothing opposite", "that grace was given which is the
first and most effectual cause out of which our belief growth".[148] But
Hooker, too, perceived that the proper office of the sacrament is to
present Christ.[149] In so far as grace is offered, it is not quasi-materially
in the element, but spiritually in Christ Himself.[150] Even his assertion
with regard to infants could be interpreted in an evangelical sense, that
the work of divine calling is begun in baptism. The difference, such as

---

141. Strype, *Whitgift*, I, p. 257.
142. Cooper, *Sermons*, p. 30.
143. Alley, *Praelecions upon 1 Peter*, fol. 133; Some, *Treatise on the Sacraments*, C2.
144. Prime, *Treatise on the Sacraments*, B 1.
145. Willet, *Synopsis Papismi*, pp. 538-541.
146. Haddon, *Contra Hieron., Osorium*, I, 2, fol. 38-39.
147. L.E.P., V, LXVII, 6.
148. L.E.P., V, LXIV, 1.
149. L.E.P., V, LXVII, 6.
150. *Loc. cit.*

it was, was mainly one of phrasing and emphasis. But it was an important difference all the same, for it pointed forward to the replacement of the Reformed teaching by the High Anglican compromise of the seventeenth century.

The Anglicans as a whole, however, stood for all the basic truths represented by the Continental Protestants. And there can be little doubt that in the light of New Testament teaching their dynamic conception of sacramental efficacy was much nearer the truth than the static view of their traditionalist opponents. On the traditionalist side it could be argued that God does in fact make use of material means to accomplish spiritual ends, and that the very primacy of God demands an automatic efficacy so long as no definite obstacle is opposed. The Reformers could accept the two presuppositions, that God does work in and through the material, and that He is sovereign in all His operations. But they did not come to the same conclusions. They could not endue the material itself with spiritual power. And they felt that to tie the grace of God indissolubly to the means is in effect to bind the divine sovereignty, and incidentally to exalt the human administrator who disposes of the means.

The Reformers did not deny the union of sign and grace. But they understood it in terms of the similar union which we find both in Christ Himself and also in the word which attests Him. On the one side there is the human action, corresponding as it were to the human nature of Christ, and to the word spoken or written which is the medium of the divine utterance. On the other side there is the divine and inward action, corresponding to the divine nature of Christ, and to the word which God Himself speaks by the Holy Spirit. The two conjoin in the one act, which is the true baptism. But the conjunction does not mean that the human action is either obliterated by the divine or absorbed into it, nor does it mean that a perceiving and receiving of the human aspect necessarily carries with it a perceiving and receiving of the divine. In an ultimate sense, it is no doubt true, and the Reformers themselves would admit it, that where the external act is performed, the internal grace is always offered, and therefore present. The presence of Jesus Christ as a man means always His presence as God. The word of the Gospel is always the word of grace and promise, and to that extent the word of God. But the point which the Reformers wished to make is that the divine aspect cannot be perceived or operative in man naturally, by the mere performance of the act. It is only by the Holy Spirit that Jesus of Nazareth is known as the Christ of God. It is only by the Holy Spirit that the word of the

Gospel can do its work as the living word of God. It is only by the Holy Spirit that the external administration can be quickened to a true and living baptism. And that means that the efficacy of the sacrament is dependent, not upon a correct performance of the outward rite, but upon the inward and sovereign action of the Holy Spirit manifested in the perception and faith of the recipient. Just as it is possible to meet Jesus of Nazareth and not to know His true nature and power: just as it is possible to hear the word of the Gospel and not to receive it as the word of life and power: so, too it is possible to receive the external baptism of water, and yet to miss the genuine and inward baptism which is forgiveness and renewal. The baptismal promises are always declared, and to that extent the grace is present. But the promises are perceived and known, and therefore effective, only where there is the inward operation of the Spirit in the heart of the recipient. The true grace and efficacy of baptism is therefore dependent upon the free activity of the Holy Spirit impelling not to indifference and unbelief but to repentance and faith.

For the Reformers, then, there was a very real baptismal efficacy. But it was the efficacy, not of the means, but of the Holy Spirit disposing of the means. The sacrament was not a cause which had a definite effect because God had ordained that it should have that effect. Nor was it a cause which was accompanied always by an effect which God had appointed. If the means had been committed outwardly to men, it did not in any way or for any moment cease to be God's means. The Holy Spirit was always the "internal master", and baptism accomplished its work only as God Himself used and applied baptism according to the election of grace. The objectivity of the sacrament was fully safeguarded. Even the faith by which its promises were believed and effective was itself the operation of the Spirit, not a free choice or disposition on the part of the recipient. But the dangers of a mechanistic and even magical conception of the divine operation were effectually avoided.

(3) Infants

From an early period the full effects of baptism had been postulated of infant no less than adult recipients. Infants received the necessary remission of sin, for even if they were not guilty of actual sins, they shared the general sin of the race. They were also "regenerated and reformed back again from wickedness to the primitive state of their nature".[151] As Augustine put it, baptism was necessary to infants "in order that they who by their generation are subject to condemnation, by regeneration may be made free from it".[152] All the more important effects of the sacrament applied equally in the case of infants. The demand for faith was met either by the faith of the sponsors or by the absence of definite unbelief in the infants themselves. It is interesting that even Pelagius did not abandon infant baptism. He postulated a forgiveness of such childish sins as peevishness, and the elevation of baptized infants to a higher state than that which they enjoyed by natural creation, as heirs of the divine kingdom.[153]

It was primarily the teaching of Augustine which determined the medieval attitude to the case of infants. Like their master, the Schoolmen applied to all infant recipients the graces of remission of original sin, regeneration, and the infusion of habitual faith and other virtues.[154] But the Schoolmen were conscious of the difficulty that we cannot ascribe to infants the minimal faith normally required for baptismal efficacy. Thomas stated the possible objections with his usual fullness: Infants cannot have faith, they have no free will, and their parents often bring them with the purely carnal intention of physical healing. But against these objections he pointed out that the lack of faith is due only to physical incapacity, that they do believe in the faith of their sponsors or the church, that the carnal intention of sponsors does not constitute an impediment, and that infants themselves do not oppose any obstacle. Thomas could not accept the suggested compromise, that infants receive a spiritual impress which may lead later to good works, but he claimed for them the full graces of remission and regeneration.[155]

The doctrine of the Schoolmen was repeated by the traditionalist party in the sixteenth century, although sometimes with a greater emphasis upon the infusion of faith, which seemed to meet the Lutheran demand for personal faith in the recipient.[156] It was still maintained that original sin is always remitted in baptism. That was why the Bull

---

151. Quoted from Ambrose in Wall, *op. cit.*, I, p. 114.
152. Cf. Wall, I, p. 147.
153. Wall, I, pp. 197, 241.
154. Cf. Lombard, IV, *Dist.* 4 H.
155. S., III, qu. 69, 6.
156. Cf. Foxe, VIII, pp. 351 f.

Exsurge Domine could state that infants have already received the grace of justification.[157] It was also the basis of Gardiner's surprise at the difficulties concerning justification when obviously "infants are justified and saved in baptism by virtue of Christ's baptism".[158] The canon of the Council of Trent pointed out that "the merit of Jesus Christ is applied, both to adults and to infants, by the sacrament of baptism rightly administered".[159] Although infants have not committed any actual sin, "they are truly baptized for the remission of sins, that in them they may be cleansed away by regeneration which they have contracted by generation".[160]

The traditional teaching was necessarily opposed by Luther, who denied an *ex opere operato* efficiency of the sacrament and insisted upon the need for faith. Yet Luther did not draw the conclusion that there are no effects of baptism in infants, for as we have seen he maintained boldly that infants do have faith, and he challenged his opponents to prove the contrary.[161] What this faith was for Luther it is difficult to say with any precision. Sometimes he spoke of it rather as the absence of a hostile disposition, or even as an infused gift.[162] Whatever it was it enabled infants to enjoy the baptismal benefits of remission and regeneration. The benefits themselves, however, were understood evangelically as remission by non-imputation and the regeneration of faith, so that no place was left for the familiar causal conception. The same was true in the case of Melanchthon, who in reply to the Anabaptists claimed for infants a definite remission of original sin by virtue of the sacramental ministry. But again the remission was understood evangelically as non-imputation.[163]

For a more radical approach to the question we have to turn to Switzerland, where the Anabaptists denied that baptism can have any effects in infants, or that infants have any right to receive the sacrament even as a sign. According to their view infants have neither faith nor original sin: therefore they do not qualify for baptism and it cannot either mean anything to them or accomplish anything within them.[164] Zwingli himself agreed that the external administration itself cannot

---

157. D.C.R., p. 76.
158. Foxe, VI, p. 50.
159. C.D., *Original Sin, can.* 3.
160. C.T., II, 2, qu. 31.
161. W.A., VI, p. 538.
162. Cf. W.A., VI, pp. 537-538.
163. C.R., XXXIII, pp. 295, 859.
164. C.R., IV, p. 617.

effect anything, that infants have no faith, and that for the children of Christians there is no guilt of original sin. But he did not deny that infants may enjoy the inward baptism of the Holy Spirit which is the true grace of the sacrament, and he thought it presumptuous on the part of the Anabaptists to try to equate in time the external ordinance and the internal work.[165] In a word, the real objection of Zwingli was to the view that it is the external action itself which conveys the internal grace. He did not deny that infants may actually enjoy the grace according to the divine election and operation.

It was this possibility of an inward baptism which dominated the teaching of Calvin, who emphasized more clearly than Zwingli the positive side. According to Calvin the work of baptism in infants did not greatly differ from the work of baptism in adults. It had, of course, a powerful psychological effect as the infant grew in years, for the whole life of the child was lived under the sign of the Gospel, with all that that implied both as a promise and as a call to repentance and faith. The purpose of infant baptism was "to enable children to receive and produce the fruits of their baptism on acknowledging its reality after they have grown up".[166] But the psychological impulse was itself the operation of the Holy Spirit, and it merged into the more direct and supernatural work. To infants baptism was a seal of the covenant blessings of remission and regeneration "of which they were previously partakers" by the election.[167] The sign did not actually confer the blessings, although it could always be a means either to call or more particularly to confirm. But it did testify to the fact that the elect are heirs of the benefits "sacramentally" given in baptism, and by the faith which it evoked or confirmed the Holy Spirit accomplished inwardly the work signified by it, sometimes in infancy, more generally in adult life. Calvin did not shrink from the conclusion that this inward fulfilment may very well take place in infancy, or that in all the elect there is planted at baptism a seed of repentance and faith which will one day come to fruition in the definite act.[168]

The apparent concessions made by Calvin are not the result of muddled or inconsistent thinking, as his many critics have suggested. They proceed naturally from his evangelical understanding of forgiveness and regeneration, his firm doctrine of the freedom of God in the divine

---

165. C.R., IV, pp. 215, 620.
166. *Tracts*, II, p. 89.
167. *Tracts*, II, p. 319.
168. *Instit.*, IV, 16, 18-20.

election and calling, and his high sense of dignity of the sacrament as a means of grace. Without any embarrassment he could associate baptism with the forgiveness of original sin, not because baptism accomplishes a quasi-material purgation of the soul, but because it declares and seals the divine forgiveness by non-imputation or promise. Again, he could associate it with the first work of regeneration, not because new life is given in or with the water, but because baptism is a pledge of the divine purpose of renewal, and may under the Holy Spirit be a means to its initiation or fulfilment. But with infants as with adults it was the secret election of God and the sovereign freedom of the Spirit which determined the efficacy of the external seal and declaration.

It was the perception of this dependence of baptism upon the election which enabled Calvin's Reformed contemporaries and successors to ascribe to the sacrament the same high value as did Calvin himself, even in the case of infants. Bucer made it plain that it is only the elect who truly receive baptism, although this included many children, "of whom by far the greater number were snatched hence in childhood, who I make no doubt are saved by the mercy of Christ".[169] Elect children might be said to enjoy the presence of the Spirit, who led them "so far as suffices for their age and condition".[170] Beza, too, thought that the elect had "the seed and the spring of faith by virtue of the promise which was received and apprehended by their elders". He did not doubt that "by this marke (joined by the prayers of the church which is their assistant) God doth seale the adoption and election in those which He hath predestinate eternally".[171] It was not that external baptism any more than the external word could of itself make the baptized the children of God. Infants were baptized, not to make them God's but because they were God's already.[172] Behind the means of grace there stood the eternal purpose of God in election upon which the baptismal promises and benefits were securely based. In point of time, the personal calling of the elect might not coincide with the moment of external baptism. But baptism was still the seal of the promised grace. Under the Spirit it could be a means to evoke or strengthen the faith by which the grace was apprehended. To that extent it might properly be described as an effectual sign of grace even when the recipient was an infant.

---

169. E.B.I., p. 169.
170. *Loc. cit.*
171. B.P.S., 48.
172. Bullinger, P.S., IV, p. 382.

In the Anglican writings, especially of the earlier phase of the Reforma-tion, the traditionalist, Lutheran and Reformed views were all represented. The statements in the *Bishops'* and *King's Books*, and perhaps in the *Ten Articles*, reflected the medieval teaching. Baptism was necessary to infants because it conferred the remission of original sin.[173] But it may be noted that the interconnection of baptism and the remission of original sin could bear a Lutheran interpretation, as in Melanchthon's defence of infant baptism. Again the actual grace and purgation were attributed not to the water but directly to the Holy Spirit who is received in baptism. The *King's Book* definitely asserted the salvation of baptized children dying in infancy.[174] In this respect it was followed by the *Homily*, although in the *Homily* the washing and adoption were referred to the sacrifice of Christ and not to the external administration of the sacrament.[175] In effect, the *Homily* did not teach more than Calvin himself, who could regard death in infancy as a mark of election and postulate a special work of the Spirit to apply the atoning sacrifice of Christ to the infant soul.

The reigns of Henry VIII and Edward VI saw a steady inflow first of Lutheran and later of Reformed teaching on this subject. On the Lutheran side baptism was thought to carry with it real remission and endowment with the Spirit by virtue of the divine promises and the faith of the recipient. Becon was one of the main protagonists of this doctrine. He claimed that "forgiveness of all sins is granted at the very moment of baptism".[176] By all sins Becon did not merely mean original sin and sins already committed, but all the future sins of adult life. When the baptized fell into actual sin, "he fell from the grace of baptism and lost the Holy Ghost".[177] But the baptismal forgiveness was not forfeited completely, as in the traditional scheme. Baptism was a refuge to which penitent sinners could always return: "Those who through frailty and ignorance again offend and break the law of God have always in their baptism an holy anchor to fly unto."[178] The point was that for Becon the forgiveness was not an actual purgation, which would obviously be negated by a fresh act of sin. It was a non-imputation according to the baptismal promise. "God does not save us for the outward baptism, but for his gracious promise."[179] That is why

---

173. See Lloyd, *op. cit.*
174. *Op. cit.*, p. 254.
175. *Homilies*, p. 25.
176. Becon, P.S., I, p. 399.
177. *Ibid.*, II, p. 206.
178. *Ibid.*, I, p. 339.
179. *Ibid.*, II, p. 216.

there could be a re-entry into baptismal grace, without any need for a new sacrament of forgiveness. And at the back of all Becon's teaching there lay a strong doctrine of election. Infants could be regarded as believers and inheritors of the kingdom until they actually showed the contrary. In baptism the gifts of cleansing and renewal were proffered to all. Although there were many who would later reject the gifts, to the inwardly elect the promises were definitely sealed. However far they might wander from God, they would always return to the grace attested by their baptism. And they would always find in the seal an assurance of their pardon and adoption.

The views of Becon seemed to be shared by many of the early Protestants, as we may see from statements made in the Marian examinations. Haukes argued that infants were washed from original sin by virtue of the representative faith of their parents.[180] Woodman thought that infants had a genuine faith of their own, which would persist in those who were truly called of God.[181] Something of the same teaching may be found in the *Homily of Salvation*, which envisaged a forgiveness of original sin which would avail for the whole life in the case of those who repented of actual sins and turned their thoughts to Christ.[182] A variant of the doctrine appeared later in Davenant, who maintained of infants that they all have by baptism that forgiveness and grace which is appropriate to their childhood state. In the case of those who die in infancy nothing more is required. Those who grow to years must enter into the fuller remission and regeneration which come with adult repentance and faith.[183] It may be noted that all the Reformers accepted a non-imputation of original sin to the children of Christians. Many of them would extend the privilege to the children of heathen as well, although only as a probability.

The Baptismal Offices have often been thought to reflect a view similar to that of Becon, and it may be allowed that all children who receive the sacrament are regarded as in some sense justified and regenerate. But we must always remember that when the Reformers spoke of these blessings they were not thinking of actual effects in the soul, but of imputed blessings grounded upon the work of Christ and the divine election and promises. Repentance and faith were certainly presumed to be necessary in the case of those who grew to adult life, as

---

180. Foxe, VII, p. 193.
181. *Ibid.*, VIII, p. 356.
182. *Homilies*, p. 25.
183. E.B.I., p. 300.

may be seen from the *Catechism* and the confirmation service. For the rest, the offices may easily be given a Lutheran sense and all infants regarded as regenerate according to their infant state. But they may also be given a Reformed sense, and the infants regarded as regenerate only "sacramentally", the enjoyment of the inward grace or benefits being dependent upon the prior election of God and the corresponding operation of the Holy Spirit.

There can be no doubt that it was in this latter sense that the Reformed party interpreted and approved the services. At root, the view was not greatly different from that of the Lutherans. But it avoided some of the less satisfactory features. No actual faith was ascribed to infants, and there was no alternation between the enjoyment of grace and its forfeiture through new acts of sin. Hooper was one of the first advocates of the Reformed teaching. He emphasized the fact that the baptismal forgiveness is a forgiveness of non-imputation.[184] Nowell pointed out that although the promised grace belongs to the elect from all eternity and is visibly signed and sealed in the sacrament, yet its fulfilment is only with individual repentance and faith, according to the providentially ordered working of the Holy Spirit.[185] Bradford interpreted infant baptism to mean that "infants and babes are taken and accounted of as members of Christ's mystical body, wherein they are received and sealed".[186] They are not "made" members of the body of Christ in the cruder sense of the term, for the Holy Ghost and the pardon of sins do not "lie lurking in the water."[187] They are regarded as having that status because they have the sign and seal of the covenanted blessings. To use the phrase of Whitaker, "infants are baptized, not to make them the children of Abraham, but because they are the children of Abraham".[188] Rogers thought that it was a definite error to see in baptism the cause of the salvation of infants. Although original sin was not imputed to them, the true cause was the electing grace of God, and the true work of baptism would often not be done until much later, "by the help of God's word read and preached, which engendereth faith".[189]

Looking at them in this way, even the Puritans were not altogether dissatisfied with the Baptismal Offices. They saw that baptism is

---

184. Hooper, P.S., I, p. 129.
185. Nowell, P.S., pp. 87-88.
186. Bradford, P.S., I, p. 82.
187. Bradford, P.S., I, p. 89.
188. E.B.I., p. 299.
189. Rogers, P.S., pp. 249-250.

the seal of the divine promise and election. Therefore its confident pronouncements need not be equated in time with the individual calling to a state of grace. This being the case, the infants of Christians could well be described as the children of God and heirs of the kingdom of God. That is what they were externally by the divine covenant and sacramentally by the administration of the sign. The only statement which aroused misgivings was the categorical assertion concerning the salvation of the baptized, which seemed to contradict the plain fact that "many which have been circumcised and baptized have dyed out of God's favour".[190] But as we have seen, the rubric was included in order to counteract erroneous teaching concerning the supposed necessity of confirmation. In any case most of the Reformers took it that baptized infants dying in infancy were assured of salvation.

The Article made no special pronouncement upon the effects of baptism in the case of infants. It simply stated the effects generally, with the implication, perhaps, that the case of infants did not differ materially from that of adults. As Goode realized so clearly, the sacramental theology of the Reformers constituted a single whole. Hence the distinction in subjects did not give rise to any distinction in operation, except where it was a distinction between the believer and the unbeliever. Indeed, we may go further, as the Reformers themselves did, and say that the efficacy of the one sacrament did not differ from that of the other. The point is important, for it means that if causal or mechanistic conceptions were excluded at one point, they were excluded at all points.

The Reformed view may be summed up in the following way. By virtue of the atoning work of Jesus Christ, the remission of original sin was sealed to infants in their baptism, not by an actual purgation, but by non-imputation. But to the elect there was also sealed the forgiveness of all sin, and new life in the Spirit, according to the predestinating will of God declared in the evangelical promises. This forgiveness and new life was proffered to all recipients in so far as baptism testified to them the divine grace and salvation in Jesus Christ. Finally, baptism was a means used by the Holy Spirit to evoke or confirm in the elect the personal faith by which they entered personally into the promised grace. In the case of children dying in infancy this work was perhaps done by a special inward enlightenment. In others, baptism was as it were the seed out of

---

190. S.P.R., I, p. 72.

which faith eventually grew. In the counsel of God and in Christ, the work was already accomplished: that was why the sign and its fulfilment did not need to be identified in time. But in individual life, the full entry into the benefits proffered and sealed in baptism could not come even with inward conversion, but only with the dissolution of the body, and the resurrection to eternal life.

If this is a true interpretation of the Reformed and Anglican teaching, the emphatic language of the Prayer Book does not point to a work done, in the Scholastic and Tridentine sense, but rather to a promise made. The promise can be counted upon as already fulfilled because it is the promise of God who sees the end from the beginning, a promise vicariously realized in Jesus Christ. To say that, of course, is not to say that the Prayer Book statements cannot be understood in other ways. Goode could point out that there are at least six permissible readings, none of which does real violence to the language.[191] But it is to say both that the Reformers themselves had a fairly definite conception in mind, and that the statements ought to be interpreted in accordance with the general evangelical principles for which they were clearly contending.

In any case, there can be no doubt about one point, and that was that they resisted strongly any idea of a mechanistic or quasi-material renovation. There can also be no doubt that their resistance at this point was justified. It is true that mechanistic and quasi-material notions cannot finally be disproved, for the processes of the soul cannot be submitted to empirical investigation. But it is also true that the whole scheme presupposed by such notions is artificial and unreal. A great and miraculous work is done when the infant is baptized but in terms of actual life it seems to make surprisingly little difference whether the infant is baptized or not. Neither spiritually nor morally can the recipient of the sacrament be readily distinguished from the non-recipient. The objection prevails against every form of *ex opere operato* teaching. To argue that there is an ontological change, or the implanting of a first seed of spiritual life, when all the time there is no appreciable difference, is simply to build theological castles in the air, and to discredit the true benefits of the sacrament.

The Reformed answer to the question is in fact the only satisfactory answer. It admits that the renewal sealed in baptism is only by promise.

---

191. E.B.I., pp. 1-26.

We are righteous not because we are made righteous but because God counts us righteous. The baptismal forgiveness and regeneration is not a work done, except in so far as it is already accomplished in Jesus Christ. It does not require to be demonstrated, for the entry into it, and therefore its demonstration, is the lifelong work of the true Christian. If there is a real work of baptism, it is not indiscriminate, nor is it necessarily revealed or fulfilled at the moment of administration. In Christ, and by faith, the work has been done from the very beginning. That is why baptism may be administered just as well to infants as to adults if they have the external qualifications. But in individual life it is fulfilled only with a true conversion to God, a continuance in the Christian life, and the consummation in literal death and resurrection. Where there is no conversion and continuance, and therefore no final consummation, the proffered benefits of baptism are clearly rejected. There is, therefore, no effective operation of the Holy Spirit, and no true baptism.

The two criticisms which may be brought against this view are, first, that the doctrine of imputation seems to be no less unreal than that of *ex opere operato* efficacy, and second, that a high conception of the divine election and sovereignty is necessarily presupposed. The answer to the first criticism is that there is no genuine unreality in imputation except where it is artificially separated from the vicarious work of Christ and the effectual calling of the Holy Spirit. To the second it may be replied that a consideration of the election as an eternal election in Christ may perhaps remove some of the difficulties created by the harsh and unlovely doctrine of a preexistent and somewhat arbitrary decree of individual election. In addition, it must be remembered that the Reformed understanding does have three definite advantages: it refuses to postulate purely imaginary effects which are not borne out by actual life; it allows for a truly supernatural operation in which God Himself has the primacy; and it maintains its "sacramentalism" within a genuinely evangelical interpretation of the work of God. If a balanced and healthy doctrine of the sacrament is to be worked out to-day, it must surely be along the general lines of the Reformed understanding.

(4) Post-baptismal Sin

At a very early date, although an effect of real purgation and restoration was ascribed to baptism, it was perceived that sin is not in fact eradicated from the baptized. In theory, those who are baptized ought not to commit fresh sin. In practice, however, there cannot be the slightest doubt that they do so. This continuance not merely of the attraction of sin but of its actual commission gave rise to a twofold problem: the problem of its forgiveness and the problem of its explanation. On the one hand, it had to be asked whether there could be fresh remission for the more serious of post-baptismal offences. On the other, it had to be asked how this persistence of sin was to be explained.

The first problem involved a bitter and protracted struggle between the rigorists who denied all hope of remission and the more lenient who evolved a system of penitential readmission. On the side of rigour were groups like the Montanists and later the Novatianists and Donatists who took their stand upon such Scriptures as Hebrews 6 and 10 and 1 John 5:16. Tertullian seemed to incline to the same view, for he advocated what was for a while a common practice, that of postponing baptism until the last possible moment in order to gain the maximum possible benefit and to avoid the greater risks of an early administration.[192] On the side of leniency Hermas emerged as the prophet of at least one chance of post-baptismal repentance, and the popes of the second and third centuries made provision for the readmission of even the most serious of offenders. The harshness of the penitential discipline was a safeguard against the dangers of moral laxity which their opponents not unnaturally suspected. The hands of these advocates of leniency were strengthened by the scandal of death-bed baptisms and the wild excesses of the Donatists. In the fourth century great Fathers like Basil,[193] Chrysostom[194] and Jerome[195] could all advise early baptism and hold out hope for the forgiveness of post-baptismal sins.

But if baptism effected an actual purgation of the soul, it obviously could not purge away sins which were not yet committed, and baptism could not be reiterated. Therefore those who pleaded for a second forgiveness after baptism had to find some fresh means of spiritual cleansing and renewal.

---

192. Tertullian, *De Bapt.*, 18.
193. Basil, *Orat. de Bapt.*, 40.
194. Chrysostom, *Hom. de Pœnit.*
195. Jerome, *Dial. adv. Pelag.*, I, 3.

The answer to the problem was what subsequently became the fully developed sacrament of penance, the so-called second plank which could still save the soul from shipwreck even when the first had been carelessly abandoned. If the efficacy of penance was more limited than that of baptism, it had at least this advantage, that it could be repeated indefinitely. It was as a practical provision for the continuance of the Christian life that the new sacrament assumed such a tremendous importance in the Middle Ages, and the Schoolmen found considerable exercise for their ingenuity in working out the various and complicated problems which it posed.

But the Schoolmen were also interested in the second problem, that of the persistence of sin even in the baptized. For after all, if in baptism the soul was purged thoroughly from original sin, why should the baptized even have a desire to sin? The question could be answered only by a sharp distinction between original sin on the one hand and concupiscence on the other. Concupiscence had to be defined negatively. It was a weakness which God had left for the purposes of discipline. It was one of the temporal penalties of the Fall with which baptism did not deal except by way of mitigation. It was not in itself sinful, but if not resisted it could and did give rise to definite acts of sin. In a word, although original sin was abolished in baptism, concupiscence remained. The grace of God was well able to restrain it, but there was always the possibility that the baptized would yield to its promptings and therefore commit fresh sin.[196]

In the sixteenth century, when the traditionalists were opposed by the new Lutheran interpretation, they held fast by the medieval doctrine and practice. One of the heresies condemned in the Bull *Exsurge Domine*[197] and again at the Council of Trent[198] was the assertion "that the whole of that which has the true and proper nature of sin is not taken away, but only rased [cancelled] or not imputed". In line with Scholastic teaching, the Holy Synod of Trent could admit that concupiscence remains as "an incentive to sin … left for our exercise", but this "the catholic church has never understood to be called sin, as being truly and properly sin in those born again, but because it is of sin and inclines to sin".[199] As the *Catechism* explained, concupiscence was one of the temporal consequences of the Fall which had been left "for

---

196. Cf. Mackinnon, *Luther*, IV, p. 84.
197. D.C.R., p. 76.
198. C.D., *Original Sin*, can., 5.
199. *Loc. cit.*

the purposes of probation". It could not be equated with original sin which had been effaced or destroyed by baptism. It was as it were the innate predisposition which gave rise to acts of sin, the combustible material which was not itself the fire but constituted the fire.[200]

If concupiscence still explained the possibility of post-baptismal sin, penance continued to provide the only and obvious remedy. To discuss all that was involved in penance would require an independent treatise, but the broad outlines of sixteenth-century teaching are clear enough. Penance was still regarded as the second plank to which the sinner must cling if all hope of salvation was not to be abandoned.[201] Strictly, "the remission offered in penance concerned only mortal or grievous sins", although it was extended in some sense to "the lighter sins which are called venial" as well.[202] Penance did not absolve from the necessity of making satisfaction, nor did it remove the scars of sin, nor did it remit the definite temporal punishments of the offence. But it was at least reiterable. That meant that those who forfeited salvation by the commission of mortal sin after baptism could still find eternal forgiveness, and therefore an ultimate redemption, by way of this sacrament.[203] Without penance, they would be ineluctably lost except in those rare cases where there was perfect contrition.[204]

This, then, was the teaching which prevailed in traditionalist circles and against which the Reformers made a necessary and decisive protest. At a first glance, it is true, the earlier teaching of Luther did not seem to differ greatly from that of his contemporaries. He could allow that penance itself was a sacrament. He also made a clear distinction between original sin and concupiscence. The latter was regarded as a temporal penalty of the Fall, to which no inherent guilt attached, and which had been weakened although not destroyed in baptism.[205] But the doctrine of justification by faith revolutionized the whole approach of Luther to this problem of original sin. For if sin is forgiven because it is not imputed, not because it is effaced, there is no reason why the root of sin should not be said to persist in the regenerate, even if in the mercy and by the promise of God it is no longer reckoned. But if this is the case, then we

200. C.T., II, 2, qu. 42.
201. C.T., II, 5, qu. 1.
202. C.D., XIV, *can.* 20.
203. *Can.* 12, 61.
204. C.T., II, 5, qu. 1.
205. Cf. Hamel, *op, cit.*, p. 17.

can say that original sin exists as a fact, although not as guilt: and original sin and concupiscence can be brought into a much closer relationship.[206] The baptized do not need to fear the divine wrath, for they have already begun to live in purity and innocence.[207] But concupiscence remains within them, and as the consequence of original sin it is itself sinful by nature, as well as giving rise to definite acts of sin.[208]

This novel conclusion of Luther was resisted for two reasons: first, because it destroyed the whole reality of the baptismal purgation; and second, because it seemed to render nugatory all efforts at moral reform. If the baptized were still sinners, and necessarily so, then baptism itself had no value, and there was no obvious reason for not continuing in actual sin. Luther himself had a twofold safeguard, that there is a real forgiveness by grace and promise, and that this forgiveness is known only by that true faith which is a work of the Holy Spirit and which issues in works of righteousness. But this safeguard could not even be understood by those who thought exclusively in sacramentalist terms.

But Luther's doctrine of justification also revolutionized his whole approach to the problem of penance. If sin is forgiven because it is imputed, not because it is effaced, there is no reason why it should not avail for concupiscence and indeed for all sin, quite irrespective of the moment when baptism is administered. Being a remission by promise, the baptismal remission need not be restricted to pre-baptismal sin. It extends to the whole life of the believer. And that means that there is no need for penance as a second plank of salvation when the baptismal remission has been forfeited. Baptism is not a first plank which may be frustrated by the very first act of mortal sin.[209] It is the one ark of salvation, completely trustworthy, firm and unshakeable, the abiding and indestructible refuge of the sinner.[210] Penance may be retained for its pastoral value, but its only meaning is as a renewing of baptism, a returning to the power and faith of that sacrament by the forsaking of sin and doing penance.[211] It is itself a sacrament only in a derived and secondary sense, not conveying a new grace, but renewing that forgiveness which is already enjoyed by virtue of the great and primary sacrament. The heart of penance

---

206. Hamel, *op. cit.*, p. 17.
207. W.A., II, p. 730.
208. Cf. *Formula of Concord*, Art. 1.
209. W.A., VI, p. 529.
210. Wernle, *Luther*, p. 33.
211. W.A., VI, p. 529.

is not the external rite, but that inward penitence, the hatred of sin and the trust in God for forgiveness, which constitutes it a genuine re-entry into the grace and power of baptism.

The objections brought against Luther's doctrine of concupiscence applied with equal force against his rethinking of the post-baptismal forgiveness. But again they were based on a complete misunderstanding of what he was really saying. For Luther did not believe at all that non-imputation meant an automatic forgiveness of all sin quite apart from the inward state of the sinner. Nor did he think that the Christian life made no demand for striving or penitence. On the contrary, it was only the man of faith who knew the divine forgiveness. And for that man the inward penitence of the heart was a lifelong vocation. Behind it all there did not stand an artificial process of salvation but the divine word and the divine grace: where sin abounded, grace did much more abound. It was upon that rather than upon a sacramentalist system that Luther based both his thinking and his faith.

It was perhaps inevitable that the reforming movement should involve at some point a revival of the rigorist conceptions of the early church. With their crude literalism of New Testament interpretation, their contempt for church history, and their ideal of a pure and gathered church, the Anabaptists were logically predestined to develop unbalanced views of this nature. It has been suggested that the Anabaptists taught an actual sinless perfection of all true believers. Certainly, Zwingli believed that this was their teaching, for he says categorically that they would not allow adults to be baptized unless they knew that they could live without sin.[212] The same charge was made against the Anabaptists in the Confession of Augsburg,[213] and according to Rogers the Family of Love taught that "in the regenerate sin is cut away, as with a razor, so that the godly cannot sin".[214] There can be little doubt that some of the Anabaptists must have been perfectionists or near-perfectionists, although of course they attributed their sinlessness to the blood of Christ, not to the baptismal cleansing. On the other hand, the majority were perhaps holding out perfection only as a possibility, or as the Christian ideal, an ideal which could be fully attained only by the few, and not without serious and constant striving. In other words, the baptized ought to know

---

212. C.R., IV, pp. 210 f.
213. Augsburg, XII.
214. Rogers, P.S., pp. 141 f.

that they can live without sin, but not that they will necessarily or actually do so.[215]

Whether perfection was regarded as a fact or only as a possibility, it is still the case that the Anabaptists were rigorist in outlook. Any departure from the accepted standards was treated in the sharpest possible form by the application of the ban. The details of the ban and its working need not concern us now, but underlying it there was the definite thought that the offending brother was cut off not merely from ecclesiastical fellowship, but from all hope of ultimate salvation. Directly or indirectly, the Anabaptists were denying two cardinal points in Reformation teaching: first, the continuance of concupiscence even in the regenerate, and second, the extension of the baptismal remission to even the most serious of post-baptismal sins. On the Anabaptist view, sin after baptism meant "abandonment to the inexorable judgment of God".[216] Their particular view of the church inclined the English Separatists to the same point of "seeming to take away, with Novatus the wicked heretic, all hope of salvation from those which offend of knowledge willingly".[217] It need not be supposed that the Separatists and Anabaptists necessarily withheld from even the excommunicate the possibility of repentance and restitution. But the severity of the ban, combined with the doctrine of perfection and unhealthy speculation on the unforgivable sin, did lead in some cases to an equation of the sin against the Holy Ghost with some grave and wilful sin committed after baptism. The classic example in Elizabethan England was "the elder Bolton, who being convinced that God neither could nor would forgive him, was driven to complete desperation and committed suicide".[218]

It was not merely the particularism of the Anabaptists but their radical Pelagianism and subjectivism which led them to this conclusion. By their Pelagianism they were driven to deny original sin and the persistence of concupiscence, thus clearing the way for at least a serious possibility of Christian perfection. By their subjectivism they were driven to suspend the salvation of the Christian upon his own decision either to believe and obey or to disbelieve and disobey. The Reformers could agree, of course, that personal faith is necessary. But just as they

---

215. Cf. Muralt, *op. cit.*, p. 36.
216. Cf. Calvin's discussion and refutation in the *Institutes*.
217. Rogers, P.S., p. 141.
218. *Ibid.*, quoting from Gyfford, *Reply to Barrowe and Greenwood*.

avoided too close an identification of the work of God with the external sign, so they avoided too close an identification of it with the human consciousness of faith. In the purpose of God in Christ the elect believer was always forgiven, even though for a time he might live in open sin and be quite destitute of faith. On the other hand the non-elect never had remission of sins at all, even though he might for a time have the consciousness of faith, and perhaps make a public and up to a point a sincere confession of it.

The Anabaptists had, in fact, a praiseworthy longing for holiness. They made an equally praiseworthy effort to maintain righteousness and discipline in the church. But in face of the deeper problems of concupiscence, the fact and forgiveness of post-baptismal sin, and the whole assurance of salvation, they lacked the perception and balance which the Reformers owed to their high sense of the divine sovereignty and election. It was because of this that they came to insist upon impossible standards, to concentrate upon the human choice which is reversible by nature, and to lose the only sure grounding of salvation, in the love and purpose and activity of God Himself. The penalty which they had to pay was a tortured preoccupation with the problem of unforgivable sin, the harsh application of disciplinary measures, and a lack of that wider charity which alone can save the church from pharisaism and schism.

Against both the traditionalist teaching on the one hand and the Anabaptist aberration on the other the Reformed school developed its view of concupiscence and post-baptismal remission very much along the lines already laid down by Luther. It was Calvin, perhaps, who stated the Reformed doctrine with the greatest force and lucidity. On the basis of the Pauline reference, he declared roundly that concupiscence has the very nature of sin even in the baptized. To argue that it is merely the source or penalty of sin is to set the verse at variance with its context. To say that it is sin before baptism but not after is an absurd contradiction. Concupiscence, as Calvin understood it, is always hateful to God, and therefore "of its own nature it is truly sin".[219] This is still the case even in the regenerate, although then "it is not imputed, and the guilt is abolished by the grace of Christ".[220] He thought that this understanding was confirmed by "many passages of Ambrose and Augustine which admitted of no doubt as to their meaning".[221]

---

219. *Tracts*, III, pp. 87 f.
220. *Loc. cit.*
221. *Loc. cit.*

But if the sin of concupiscence was not imputed to the believer, that meant that there was no real problem of post-baptismal remission. The whole of the so-called sacrament of penance was therefore superfluous and unnecessary. It was only in the sense of inward penitence that penance could be described as a second plank. Penitence was the true means to repair the garment of innocence received in baptism when damaged or rent by sin. But it was "impious" to suggest that penance or even penitence was supplementary to baptism, as though baptism had been completely effaced by fresh sin. For baptism itself was the sacrament of penitence and faith. Therefore its remission extended to the whole life of the Christian, and all penitence was a re-entry into baptism.[222]

As regards the Anabaptist teaching, Calvin accepted the need for a firm ecclesiastical discipline. But he could not agree that the divine pardon is so tied to regeneration or baptism that the post-baptismal lapse must rob the Christian of all hope of salvation. The forgiveness of God was a continual forgiveness graciously extended to those who always "carried about with them the remains of sin, and could not continue one single moment were they not sustained by the uninterrupted grace of God forgiving their sins". The office of the church was certainly to exercise discipline, but primarily it was to hold out the divine promises. The keys were not only for unbelievers "who should be converted from impiety to the faith of Christ". They were also for believers who after their baptism fell into sin, but turned again in repentance. Excommunication was no doubt necessary in certain cases both as a warning and also for the purifying of the church. It was also the church's duty to warn the wilful and impenitent of the great danger and condemnation in which they stood. But the church had no authority to anticipate the final judgment of God. To that extent it had constantly to hold out the promise of baptismal remission to those who were ready to return with a true penitence and faith.[223]

In England the obvious traditionalists like Shetler and Gardiner insisted upon the necessity of penance,[224] and regarded concupiscence only as "the scarce of originall synne", but not itself "to be accompted our synne".[225] But the reforming party followed very closely the

---

222. *Instit.*, IV, 19, 17.
223. *Instit.*, IV, 1, 23-28.
224. Strype, *Cranmer*, I, p. 257.
225. Quoted from Gardiner by MacLear and Williams, on Art. 9.

teaching of the Lutheran and Reformed schools. Tyndale was a pioneer of the typically Lutheran thought that the Christian "fight against the appetites" is "the fulfilment of our baptism".[226] This implied both a continuance of concupiscence and an extension of baptism to the whole life of the believer. The thought was taken up by Cranmer, who in Article 6 of the *Thirteen Articles* stated that the guilt of original sin is abolished, but that the corruption of our nature, which he equated with concupiscence, remains.[227] The Article was cautiously worded, but it certainly reflects the view that the actuality of original sin continues, although the guilt is not imputed. At a more official level, the *Ten Articles* had seen in inward penitence the only requirement for the forgiveness of post-baptismal sin: "Such men which after baptism fall again into sin … whensoever they convert themselves, shall without doubt attain remission of sins". The phrase "attain remission of sins" seems perhaps to imply a new forgiveness rather than a re-entry into the baptismal remission. On the other hand the sacrament of penance is pointedly ignored, and there is a definite movement towards the understanding of the baptismal remission in relation to the whole Christian life. The same emphasis upon the need for a sincere inward repentance, with faith in the divine promises, may be discerned both in the *Homily of Salvation*[228] and also in the General Confession and Absolution introduced into Morning and Evening Prayer in 1552. The prayer of confession gives the opportunity for a movement of genuine penitence in relation to past misconduct. In the prayer of absolution the minister exercises the power of the keys by "declaring and pronouncing" to those "who truly repent and unfeignedly believe" that forgiveness which is already promised by Holy Scripture and sealed in the sacrament of baptism.

Rigorist or perfectionist views seem to have penetrated into England in the later forties. The Statute 32 Henry VIII *cap.* 49 expressly condemned a new error, "that sinners after baptism cannot be restored by repentance", Again, in 1549 some London tradesmen were reported to hold the curious view that "the regenerate cannot sin inwardly"[229] – the "inwardly" is perhaps a concession to the apparent facts of external experience. The connection between the two opinions is that if

---

226. Tyndale, P.S., I, p. 500.
227. Cranmer, P.S., II, p. 474.
228. *Homilies*, p. 23.
229. E.M., I, 1, p. 291.

the regenerate cannot sin, those who do so prove themselves to be hypocrites and are therefore rejected and condemned. The doctrines were firmly resisted by the Anglican leaders and they were never held in sufficient strength to be of great importance. The same is true of the more serious outbreaks under Elizabeth, when the Separatists took up the rigorist cause, and the Family of Love emerged as the exponents of perfectionism.

Of the more orthodox Reformers Becon calls for special mention, for he developed the Protestant teaching with great fullness and power. In Becon's view the one and only source of Christian forgiveness is Jesus Christ Himself. Jesus Christ is the Saviour not only before and in but also after baptism. The baptismal blessing has, therefore, a value which is not limited or exhausted by the baptismal act. As something which is grounded in the patient loving-kindness of God in Jesus Christ it cannot be destroyed by even the vilest of post-baptismal sins: "Though we sin after baptism never so grievously, yet doth not God straightway take vengeance on us, and cast us headlong into hell-fire ... but he patiently abideth our conversion."[230] The forgiveness to which Becon referred was, of course, a forgiveness by non-imputation. It extended to concupiscence, which according to Becon was left in the regenerate for the exercise of faith, and was even of itself sinful.[231]

Other writers who had occasion to deal with this matter were Jewel, Fulke, Calfhill and Sandys. Jewel defended the teaching of the Article that concupiscence has the nature of sin. His arguments were almost identical with those of Calvin.[232] He could point out that the Protestant remission was even fuller than the so-called perfect remission which his opponent Harding ascribed to the sacrament: for "it is a remission of all manner of sins, and that not in half or in part ... but full, whole and perfect of all together".[233] In Fulke there is rather a strange reference to the "plucking up even of the root of sin" in baptism. The context makes it clear that this was not a doctrine of perfection. Fulke agreed that concupiscence remains. He was not thinking of the immediate effect, but of the ultimate relevance of the baptismal forgiveness, which covers all the sins of believers "to our eternal salvation".[234] Calfhill was of the opinion that penance may be gathered out of baptism in so far

---

230. Becon, P.S., I, p. 178.
231. *Ibid.*, II, p. 204.
232. Jewel, P.S., III, p. 464.
233. *Loc. cit.*
234. Fulke, P.S., II, p. 388.

as baptism constantly moves the soul to repentance and faith "by the promise exhibited".[235] Sandys condemned those deathbed baptisms of the early church which obviously rested on the false assumption of a perfect but restricted efficacy. To combine the maximum enjoyment of sin with the maximum baptismal grace was a misguided and cynical stratagem which God Himself would finally "mock".[236]

The Anglican teaching found its clearest and most definite expression in the two Articles which treated of the subject, Articles 9 and 16. Some commentators have suggested that Article 9 derives from the similar Article in the Confession of Augsburg. This may be true in a general way; it is more nearly akin to the statement in Reformed confessions like the Belgic and Gallican. The main points made by the Article are that concupiscence continues in the regenerate, that it has the nature of sin according to the teaching of the apostle, but that it is not imputed to the believer. The fact that concupiscence is said only to have "the nature" and not "the true and proper nature" of sin – the doctrine condemned at Trent – does not have quite the importance that some commentators have tried to give it (e.g. MacLear and Williams). As Jewel and Harding both understood, the Anglican teaching cannot be reconciled with the Tridentine. For the Tridentines concupiscence cannot strictly be described as sin at all – it is called sin only out of deference to St. Paul and in a loose and improper sense. Since it is not in itself sin, there is no need to refer to the non-culpability of it by virtue of the person and work of Jesus Christ.

The second of the two Articles, Article 16, is a repudiation of the rigorist opinion that wilful sins committed after baptism constitute the unforgivable sin. Against that teaching the Article asserts that the forgiveness sealed in baptism extends to all subsequent sins provided there is a genuine repentance and faith. Rather perversely, attempts have been made to read into this Article an attack on the Reformed doctrine of final perseverance (cf. Browne and MacLear and Williams). The true historical reference is sufficiently obvious to make this interpretation quite fanciful and even nonsensical. Against it we have also to consider the following points. First, the doctrine of final perseverance did not imply a licence to commit sin, to which reference was made in the corresponding Article of the Augustana (12). Second, the Reformed doctrine of concupiscence carried with it the continued

---

235. Calfhill, P.S., p. 242.
236. Sandys, P.S., p. 152.

sinfulness of the elect, for which cleansing was constantly needed. Third, the purpose of the Article was to strengthen the assurance of post-baptismal forgiveness rather than to destroy it. The attempt to turn the Article in an anti-Reformed direction probably rests upon a complete misunderstanding of the doctrine of final perseverance. It certainly had no foundation in fact, and it can be made only for the purpose of advancing partisan interests rather than the interests of genuine exposition.

The early commentary of Rogers makes it plain beyond any possible doubt that at least in the early days the Articles were understood in a definitely Reformed sense. The first point which Rogers made was that according to Article 9 original sin continues in the elect or regenerate. The adversaries to this truth were "the Papists, Giselbertus and the Family of Love, the Carpocratians, Adamites both old and new, and the Begadores in Almaine".[237] In support of his contention that concupiscence must be regarded as genuine sin he referred to St. Paul and to the other Reformed confessions. In this case the adversaries were the Pelagians, Glover the Brownist, Francis of Colen, Lombard, and the Church of Rome.[238] The possibility of actual sin in the regenerate he proved from the examples of David, Solomon and Peter, and from the presence in the Bible of warnings and exhortations, which would be meaningless if the elect could not sin. In the usual list of adversaries he mentioned "the Catharans, Novatians and Jovinians, which think God's people to be regenerate into a pure and angelical state", the Libertines, "who held that whosoever hath God's Spirit in him cannot sin", and various papists who claimed that "the works of men justified are perfect in this life", and that "St. Francis attained unto the perfection of holiness and could not sin at all".[239] But while the elect did continue to commit actual sin, Rogers pointed out that on the basis of the promises of Holy Scripture, and again in line with the other confessions, the Article could still teach a very definite forgiveness for all those who sincerely repented. This doctrine was oppugned, first by the Papists, who wished to tie the forgiveness of post-baptismal sin to the sacrament of penance, but more particularly by the rigorists, "which leave nothing but the unappeasable wrath of God to such as do sin after baptism, the Montanists, the Novatians, Melchior Hoffmann,

---

237. Rogers, P.S., pp. 100 f.
238. *Loc. cit.*
239. *Ibid*, pp. 138 f.

the German Anabaptists and the Barrowists".[240] In this connection
Rogers cited the terrible example of the "desperate, whose sins being
either infinite or abominable, they think how God He neither can nor
will forgive them, Cain and Judas, Franciscus Spira, Doctor Kraus and
the elder Bolton".[241]

The position of Rogers was perhaps an extreme one. Yet the evidence
proves that all the leading Anglicans of the period accepted his main theses
concerning concupiscence and post-baptismal forgiveness. On the Puritan
side Travers claimed that concupiscence has to be considered truly sin in
the regenerate,[242] and Hooker stated that the very thought or tendency
to sin is no less sinful than the act itself.[243] Again, Willet emphasized the
unlimited reach of the baptismal remission, which included sins done after
the administration of the sacrament as well as before.[244] It was only with
the general abandonment of a Calvinistic theology that the Anglicans
began to drift from these well-established principles and to seek a post-
baptismal forgiveness first in the eucharist[245] and later in a revived system of
auricular confession and priestly absolution, speciously introduced under
cover of the provision at the end of the first Communion Exhortation. But
the teaching of the Articles as of the individual Reformers is so plain that
those who take a contrary view can do so only by straining their meaning
or openly or tacitly disavowing their authority.

Taking into account the fact of Christian life as well as the teaching
of Scripture, we can hardly dispute the conclusion that the Reformed
interpretation was a great advance on that of the Schoolmen and the
sixteenth-century traditionalists. The medieval and Tridentine scheme
did form a logical and consistent whole, but it was open to severe criticism.
Not only did its postulating of a necessary effect of baptism expose it to
the worst evils of sacramentalism, but its definitions were all speculative
and artificial. A whole series of baptismal effects was invented which did
not make the slighest difference in real life. Concupiscence was weakened
in the baptized, but the baptized still succumbed to it. Concupiscence
itself was not sin, but almost inevitably it resulted in sin. The baptismal
remission was a tremendous and miraculous blessing, but it was forfeited

---

240. Rogers, P.S., pp. 138 f.
241. *Loc. cit.*
242. Travers, *Answer,* p. 237.
243. Hooker, *Discourse on Justification,* VII.
244. Willet, *Synopsis Papismi,* p. 579.
245. Waterland, *Works,* IV, pp. 644-646.

so quickly that it ceased to have any very practical value. The traditionalist explanations of reality had in fact no contact with reality. They left the ordinary believer in a sacramentalist and sacerdotalist maze from which there was no exit except at death.

As against that, the Reformers accepted the fact that sin is not eradicated by baptism or regeneration, that even in the elect the sinful nature remains, and that the Christian life is a life of constant vigilance and warfare. But they could still maintain a continuing forgiveness for those who truly repent and believe, not because God abolishes sin or ignores it, but because by virtue of the death and resurrection of Jesus Christ He sees the elect as they are in Jesus Christ, and not as they are in themselves. This forgiveness does not involve any change in temporal nature, except in so far as the Holy Spirit begins the work of regeneration and transformation into the likeness of Christ. But it does involve a change in standing before God. According to the actuality of temporal life the man of faith is always and constantly a sinner. But according to the greater actuality of the divine grace and promises he is already and eternally a new man in Jesus Christ. That means that post-baptismal sin does not create any new problem of forgiveness. If the man of faith is a man of real faith, he does not rest upon himself, but only upon the love of God and the reconciling action of Jesus Christ.

The merits of this interpretation are plain to see. It preserves a full doctrine of the divine sovereignty. It maintains the divine independence of time. If it does not start from the experience of Christian life, it also does not stray from it. It balances the temporal and the eternal aspects of baptism. And it relates baptismal grace not only to regeneration, but to the whole work of redemption from its beginning with regeneration to its consummation in the resurrection from the dead. Against the charge of a possible antinomianism it sets the inward work of the Holy Spirit which accomplishes in the temporal life of the believer that which he already is in eternity. Against the criticism that everything is suspended ultimately upon the election of grace, it may be argued that the election is not a prior and arbitrary selection of individuals, but an election of those who identify themselves with Jesus Christ. In the sense that God is the Lord of time, who sees the end from the beginning, it is always true that man's choice of God is also God's choice of man, not perhaps as a decree, but as an act, not as an election of the individual as such, but as an election of the individual in Christ.

If these points are borne in mind, many of the difficulties about election and imputation will disappear. Election and imputation are surely the eternal and final aspects of temporal and relative realities. If the Reformers and their successors did not always express themselves too happily on these matters, they did at least break through the inadequate and misleading medieval systematization, and open the way to a more satisfying and scriptural interpretation.

Conclusion

Now that the detailed investigation has been completed, it is possible to draw together some more general conclusions concerning the Anglican teaching. A first and self-evident point is that with the exception of some obviously unreformed statements under Henry the Anglicans of the Reformation period were no less decisive than their fellow-Reformers abroad in their repudiation of the traditional doctrine. This repudiation was not merely a vaguely indicated and loosely expressed disapproval, but a specific and detailed controverting of current views. It was not merely a disagreement at a few small and comparatively insignificant points, but a serious divergence on every major issue. It was not merely a rejection of some popular misconceptions or corruptions, but an express denial of the accepted theological formulations. It found utterance not merely in the extensive doctrinal and devotional writings, but in outline at least in the more official catechisms, articles and other formularies. It pointed ultimately not merely to a divergence in sacramental teaching, but to the fundamental disagreement between a sacramentalist conception of the Christian faith and an evangelical.

A second and equally self-evident conclusion is that within this repudiation the formularies themselves do not bind the Anglican to a single line of baptismal understanding on every issue. Even in the sixteenth century there were three permissible interpretations; the Lutheran, the Reformed and the embryonic High Anglican. The Lutheran was not specifically represented in the later formularies. It had few exponents amongst the more eminent post-Edwardian Reformers. But it had certainly left its mark upon the ceremonial and devotional character of the Baptismal Offices, and it was never definitely excluded, as was the Lutheran doctrine of the Lord's supper, The Reformed was, of course, the predominant interpretation. Not only the Puritans but from the reign of Edward onwards the majority of Anglican divines accepted a kinship with other Reformed communions on all the main doctrinal questions. The High Anglican marked a cautious retrogression towards the traditionalist view. But as represented by Hooker and Bancroft and some of the more conservative Elizabethan bishops it remained well within the limits of the official and evangelical teaching of the articles and offices.

It must be pointed out, however, that although a restricted variety of interpretation was permissible, there is little support for the view which Stone baldly asserts but does not argue, that the Articles were "drawn up, not as the complete expression of the mind of the Church of England for all her children, but as a concordat intended to facilitate the comprehension of individuals rather than to exactly define truth".[1] If by this somewhat ambiguous statement Stone means, as he seems to mean, that the Articles are meant to be vaguely comprehensive, the assertion is almost entirely devoid of historical foundation. It was clearly recognized by the bishops of the Marian hierarchy that in their Edwardian, and later their Elizabethan, form the Prayer-Book and Articles were quite incompatible with the Tridentine codification. If the majority of clergy accepted the new order, it was not because the formularies made the way easy for them. It was either because they did not understand the issue or more likely because they did not regard open resistance as worth while. At the other end of the scale the views of Anabaptists and sectarians were also excluded. Therefore prior to the development of High Anglican interpretations the only toleration was for the various shades of Lutheran and Reformed opinion. If the Article especially now appears to be vague and indecisive, it is not so in relation to the discussions of the period, but only in consequence of theological developments subsequent to its formulation. To give the impression that it is deliberately loose, or even ambiguous, is therefore erroneous and misleading.

But if in the sixteenth century the formularies were understood predominantly in a Reformed sense, then that means that there can be no possible disloyalty to the Prayer Book or Articles in contending for the same understanding to-day. It is not suggested, of course, that every single theologian of the period interpreted the formularies only in the one way. It is not narrowly asserted, as well it might be, that from the purely historical standpoint the official statements cannot be made to support a different theological formulation. It is claimed, however, that the interpretation favoured by the Reformers themselves is surely a legitimate and indeed the most probable and convincing of

---

1. Stone, *op. cit.*, p. 60.

all the suggested interpretations. Since the Gorham case, it has been fashionable in certain circles to dismiss this interpretation as in some sense a betrayal of the official teaching. But unless the Reformers did not really understand their own doctrine, or senselessly compromised it, it is obviously the one interpretation which the formularies do both state and demand, whatever others may legitimately be read into them.

And that leads us to a further point. If the formularies were generally understood in the Reformed sense, it is evident that on this issue there is nothing in the confessional statements which constitutes a doctrinal barrier to communion with either the Lutheran or the Reformed churches. That there are differences in order and discipline is obvious, but there is no need to magnify these or to regard them as of decisive theological significance. On the Anglican side they are explained and covered by Article 34. But in their basic theology of baptism the Anglicans not only agreed substantially with the Protestant churches abroad but they were proud of that agreement. And that means that a true loyalty to their work carries with it an acceptance of the kinship which they themselves both acknowledged and proclaimed. If the Church of England is to become a real bridge-church and not an island-church, and if its members are to make genuine progress towards that reunion which so many of them profess to desire, a first and very practical step is to reacknowledge this doctrinal affinity and the existing obligation of intercommunion which at one time it was thought to entail.

A final point is this. The formularies as understood by the Reformers themselves still offer an interpretation of baptism and its efficacy which may commend itself to the modern theologian who obviously cannot go back to medieval conceptions, but is hesitant to go beyond the Reformed teaching to a frankly naturalistic and immanentist view both of God and of the operations of God. The problem plainly opens up far wider issues than that of confessional loyalty or of the doctrine of baptism alone. On the one hand there is the ultimate loyalty to truth itself, on the other the interrelatedness of baptism with the basic Christian doctrines. But this much at least may be said. The Reformers did bring their doctrine of baptism into line with their general evangelical teaching. And their statement has left the way open for interesting and constructive work, especially in relation to those ultimate questions which engage theologians at the present time: the questions of history and revelation, of time and eternity, of sign and grace, of the work of man and the work of God. Naturally, the Reformed view will call for a certain amount of restatement both in contemporary language and with reference to contemporary demands. Naturally, too, it will need to be modified and corrected and amplified at not a few individual points. But the underlying principles will still show themselves to be relevant to the most pressing problems and proof against the most searching criticisms. Grounded as they are upon Holy Scripture, they will also be found capable of almost infinite adaptation in detail as new insights are gained into Christian reality and Christian truth.

Select Bibliography

Sources

The Parker Society and British Reformers Series.
A Full and Plaine Declaration of the Ecclesiasticall Discipline, 1573.
Alley, W. *Prælections upon the First Epistle of St. Peter*, 1562 (revised edition, 1571).
Aquinas *Summa*, III, qu. 60-71.
Babington, G. *Notes upon Genesis*, 1592 (ed., 1622).
Bancroft, R. *A Survey of the Pretended Holy Discipline*, 1593 (ed., 1663).
Dangerous Positions and Proceedings, 1593.
Bekenntnisschriften der Evangelischen Kirchen, Die, Göttingen, 1930.
Bellarmine, R. *Short Christian Doctrine*. Trans. ed., 1836.
Beza, T. *A Brief and Pithy Summe*. Trans. R.F., London, 1585.
Quæstionum et Responsionum Christianarum Libellus, Geneva, 1576.
Bibliotheca Reformatoria Neerlandica, Vols. I-V.
Bridges, J. *The Defence of the Government*, London, 1587.
Bucer, M. *Scripta Anglicana*, Basel, 1577.
Calvin, J. *Institutes*, Vol. IV.

Tracts

An Answere to a Supplicatorie Epistle, London, 1583.
An Apology of the Private Mass, 1562, Ed. Cambridge, 1880.
Canons and Decrees of the Sacred and Œcumenical Council of Trent. Trans. Waterworth, London, 1848.
Catechism of the Council of Trent, Ed. Donovan, Dublin.
Commentaries on the Harmony of the Evangelists, John, Acts, Romans and 1 Corinthians.
Cooper, T. *An Admonition to the People of England*, 1598, Ed. Arber, Birmingham, 1882.
Cranmer, T. *Works*, Ed. Jenkins (4 vols.).
Cranmer's Catechism, Ed. Oxford, 1839.

Formularies of the Faith under the Reign of Henry VIII, Ed. Lloyd, Oxford, 1856.

Foxe, J. *Acts and Monuments*, Ed. Townsend, London, 1844.

Gardiner, S. *Letters*, Ed. J.A. Muller, Cambridge, 1933.

Geste, E. *Treatise against the Private Mass*, 1548.

Gilby, A. *A Pleasaunte Dialogue ...*, 1581.

Haddon, W. *Lucubrationes*, London, 1567.

Harleian MSS. 6848, 6849.

Henry VIII *Assertio Septem Sacramentorum*. Trans. T.W., Dublin, 1746.

Homilies, Ed. Oxford, 1822.

Hooker, R. *Laws of Ecclesiastical Polity*, Ed. Walton, Oxford, 1865.

King's Book, Ed. T.A. Lacey, London, 1932.

Knox, J. *Works*, Ed. D. Laing, Edinburgh, 1895.

Lombard, P. *Sententiarum*, IV, Ed., 1553.

Luther, M. *Werke, Weimarer Ausgabe*.

Marprelate Tracts, The, Ed. W. Pierce, London, 1911.

Melanchthon, P. *Opera, Corpus Reformatorum*.

Prime, J. *Treatise on the Sacraments*, 1582.

Puritan Manifestos, Ed. Frere and Douglas, London, 1907.

Reformation of the Laws, The, Ed. E. Cardwell, Oxford, 1850.

Rituale Romanum Pauli V, Ed. 1614.

Seconde Parte of a Register, The, Ed. A. Peel, Cambridge, 1915 (2 vols.).

Sermons, London, 1580.

Smythe, R. *The Assertion and Defence of the Sacrament of the Altar*, London, 1546.

Some, R. *A Godly and Short Treatise on the Sacraments*, London, 1582.

Summe of the Holye Scripture, 1529-1530.

Tracts and Treatises, IV, Ed. R. Vaughan, 1845.

Travers, W. *A Defence of the Ecclesiastical Discipline*, 1588.

Turner, W. *The Old Learning and the New*, London, 1548.

Whittingham, W. *A Brief Discourse of the Troubles at Frankfort*, Ed. Arber, London, 1907.

Willet, A. *Synopsis Papismi*, 3rd ed., London, 1600.

Wycliffe, J. *Select English Works*, Ed. Arnold, Oxford, 1869 (3 vols.).

Zwingli, H. *Sämtliche Werke, Corpus Reformatorum*.

Works of Reference

Anrich, G. *Martin Bucer*, Strassburg, 1914.

Beckmann, J. *Vom Sakrament bei Calvin*, Tübingen, 1926.

Bingham, J. *Works*, VIII, 1840.

Boehmer, H. *Luther and the Reformation in the Light of Modern Research*, Trans. Potter, London, 1930.

Boudriot, N. *Calvins Tauflehre im Licht der katholischen Sakramentslehre*, *Reformierte Kirchenzeitung* LXXX, 1930.

Burnet, G. *A History of the Reformation of the Church of England*, Oxford, 1829 (3 vols.).

Burrage, C. *The Early English Dissenters*, Cambridge, 1912 (2 vols.).

Cardwell, E. *A History of Conferences*, Oxford, 1840.

Cary, H. *Testimonies of the Fathers*, Oxford, 1835.

Catholic Encyclopedia, Art. Baptism.

Cristiani L. *Du Luthéranisme au Protestantisme*, Paris, 1911.

Daniel, E. *The Prayer Book*, London, 1909.

Dix, G. *The Theology of Confirmation in Relation to Baptism*, London, 1946.

Dosker, H.E. *The Dutch Anabaptists*, 1918-1919.

Doumergue, H. *Calvin and the Reformation*, New York, 1909.

Eells, H. *Martin Bucer*, New Haven, 1931.

Ellinger, G. *Philipp Melanchthon ein Lebensbild*, Berlin, 1902.

Gairdner, G. *Lollardy and the Reformation in England*, London, 1924.
  (4 vols.).

Galle, F. *Versuch einer Charackteristik Melanchthons als Theologen*, Halle, 1845.

Garrett, C.H. *The Marian Exiles*, Cambridge, 1938.

Gee, H. *The Elizabethan Clergy and the Settlement of Religion*, Oxford, 1898.

The Elizabethan Prayer Book and Ornaments, London, 1902.

Gee, H., & Hardy, *Documents illustrative of English Church History*, London,
  W.J.1895.

Goode, W. *The Doctrine of the Church of England as to the Effects of Baptism
  in the Case of Infants*, London, 1850.

Gore, C. *The Holy Spirit and the Church*, London, 1924.

Hamel, R. *Der junge Luther und Augustin*, Gütersloh, 1904.

Harnack, A. *A History of Dogma*, Vol. II.

Hart, H. *Ecclesiastical Records*, Cambridge, 1846.

Harvey, A.E. *Martin Bucer in England*, Marburg, 1906.

Hastings' Encyclopedia of Religion and Ethics, Art. Baptism.

Heitmüller, W. *Taufe und Abendmahl im Urchristentum*, 1911.

Heppe, H. *Die Dogmatik der evangelisch reformierten Kirche*, Neukirchen, 1935.

Hirsch, E. *Hilfsbuch zum Studium der Dogmatik*, Berlin, 1937.

Hopf, C. *Bucer and the English Reformation*, Oxford, 1946.

Jacobs, H.E. *The Lutheran Movement in England*, Philadelphia, 1890.

Kennedy, W.P.M. *Parish Life under Queen Elizabeth*, Oxford, 1914.

Kidd, B.J. *Documents of the Continental Reformation*, Oxford, 1911.

Knappen, M.N. *Tudor Puritanism*, Chicago, 1939.

Köstlin, L. *The Life of Luther*, London, 1900.

Lambert, J.C. *The Sacraments in the New Testament*, Edinburgh, 1925.

Lang, A. *Martin Bucer*, Art. in the *Evangelical Quarterly*, April 1929.

Zwingli und Calvin, Bielefeld und Leipzig, 1913.

Lorimer, P. *John Knox and the Church of England*, London, 1875. Mackinnon,
  J. *Luther and the Reformation*, London, 1925-1930 (4 vols.).

Manning, B.L. *The People's Faith in the time of Wyclif*, Cambridge, 1919.

Mason, A.J. *The Relation of Baptism to Confirmation*, London, 1891.

Muller, J.A. *Stephen Gardiner and the Tudor Reaction*, London, 1926.

Muralt, L. von *Glaube und Lehre der schweizerischen Wiedertäufer*, Zürich, 1938.

Niesel, W. *Die Theologie Calvins*, München, 1938.

Pauck, W. *Calvin and Butzer*, Art. in *Journal of Religion*, April 1929.

Luther and Butzer, Art. in *Journal of Religion*, January 1929.

The Heritage of the Reformation, Chicago, 1950.

Pearson, A.F. Scott *Thomas Cartwright and Elizabethan Puritanism*, Cambridge, 1925.

Peel, A. *The Brownists in Norwich and Norfolk*, Cambridge, 1920.

Pierce, W. *John Penry, His Life, Times and Writings*, London, 1923. *Historical Introduction to the Marprelate Tracts*, London, 1908.

Pocock, N. *Troubles Connected with the Prayer Book of 1549*, Camden New Series, 37.

Pollard, A.F. *Cranmer*, Heroes of the Reformation Series.

Quick, O.C. *The Christian Sacraments*, London, 1927.

Reitzenstein, A. *Die Vorgeschichte der christlichen Taufe*, 1929.

Ryle, J.C. *Bishops and Clergy of other Days*, London, 1868.

Schaff, P. *Creeds of the Evangelical Protestant Churches*.

Creeds of the Greek and Latin Churches.

Scheel, O. *Dokumente zu Luthers Entwicklung*, Tübingen, 1929. *Martin Luther*, Tübingen, 1921-1930 (2 vols.).

Seeberg, R. *Die Lehre Luthers*, Leipzig, 1917.

Servière, J. de la *La Théologie de Bellarmine*, Paris, 1908.

Smith, R.J. *The Anabaptists*, London, 1935.

Smithen, F.J. *Continental Protestantism and the English Reformation*, London, 1927.

Smythe, C.H. *Cranmer and the Reformation under Edward VI*, Cambridge, 1926.

Stange, D.C. *Der Todesgedanke in Luthers Tauflehre*, Art. in *Zeitschrift für syst. Theologie*, 1928, IV.

Stone, D. *Holy Baptism*, Oxford Library of Practical Theology.

Strype, J. *Annals of the Reformation* (4 vols.).

Ecclesiastical Memorials (3 vols.).

Historical Collections of John Aylmer.

Life and Acts of Edmund Grindal.

Life and Acts of John Whitgift (3 vols.).

Life and Acts of Sir John Cheke.

Memorials of Thomas Cranmer (3 vols.).

Sturge, G.E. *Cuthbert Tunstal*, London, 1938.

Usher, R.G. *The Presbyterian Movement in the Reign of Queen Elizabeth*, Camden Society, 1905.

The Reconstruction of the English Church, 1910 (2 vols.).

Usteri, J.M. *Calvins Sakraments-und Tauflehre*, 1884.

Die Stellung der Strassburger Reformatoren Bucer und Capito zur Tauffrage, 1884.

Vertiefung der Zwinglischen Sakraments-und Tauflehre bei Bullinger, 1883.

Zwinglis Tauflehre, 1882.

Wall, W. *The History of Infant Baptism*, Ancient and Modern Library
  (2 vols.).

Wernle, P. *Der evangelische Glaube: Luther*, Tübingen, 1918.

Der evangelische Glaube: Zwingli, Tübingen, 1919.

Index of Names

Index of Subjects

Index of New Testament References

You may also be interested in:

Thomas Cranmer, Theologian

by G.W. Bromiley

In his important evaluation of the theological leader of the English Reformation, G.W. Bromiley charts Cranmer's doctrinal views, scriptural interpretation and liturgical composition. His nuanced position on various controversial issues of the day, not least baptism, is articulated with clarity and care, and his ecumenical sensitivity is foregrounded.

While arguably more adept as a scholar than as a creative theologian in his own right, Cranmer's writing nevertheless formed the cornerstone of future Anglican theology. Through his Articles of Religion (42, later reduced to 39) and the Book of Common Prayer, he set the parameters within which the Church of England was to operate. Perhaps most significantly, as Bromiley shows, his extensive citation of patristic sources established a precedent for his successors that continues today. Written by one of the great ecclesiastical historians of the twentieth century, Thomas Cranmer, Theologian is the essential starting point for understanding Cranmer's influence and legacy in the Anglican church.

Geoffrey W. Bromiley (1915-2009) was Professor of Church History and Historical Theology at Fuller Theological Seminary. He gained his MA at Cambridge and his PhD and Dlitt in Edinburgh, and was previously lecturer and vice principal at Tyndale Hall, Bristol, and Rector of St Thomas' Episcopal Church, Edinburgh. Among his substantial output are his *Introduction to the Theology of Karl Barth*; *Historical Theology: An Introduction*; and *Baptism and the Anglican Reformers* (James Clarke & Co.).

Published 2023

Hardback ISBN: 978 0 227 17873 7
Paperback ISBN: 978 0 227 17871 3
PDF ISBN: 978 0 227 17874 4
ePub ISBN: 978 0 227 17872 0

You may also be interested in:

The Institution of a Christian Man

Edited by Gerald Bray

Compiled during the early years of the Reformation, The Institution of a Christian Man lays out the principles of the nascent Church of England. In his definitive new edition, Gerald Bray charts the development of this text from the first version introduced by Archbishop Thomas Cranmer and his cohort of bishops, to the extensive edits made by Henry VIII himself, and finally to the version written by Bishop Edmund Bonner under the radically different circumstances of Mary I's reign.

By combining the Bishops' Book and the King's Book into a single text – rather than in sequence – Bray shows which sections were added, deleted, and retained throughout the revisions. This process allows the reader to reconstruct the texts and, at the same time, follow the process by which one was transformed into the other. Bishop Bonner's Book, which appears separately, illustrates additional changes and elaborations from the previous two books. Such a comparative study in a user-friendly and accessible style has never been published before.

> *'The three official statements of faith produced under Henry
> VIII and Mary Tudor are at last given the full scholarly
> treatment they have long cried out for. . . . Every historian
> of the English Reformation will want to keep this
> wonderfully easy-to-use edition within arm's reach.*
> – **Alec Ryrie**, Durham University

Reverend Dr Gerald Bray has a PhD from Paris-Sorbonne. He worked as Professor of Anglican Studies at Beeson Divinity School, and is now a Research Professor for the same institution. He is also Director of Research at the Latimer Trust. His other publications with James Clarke & Co Ltd include *Documents of the English Reformation* (1994; 2nd edition 2004) and *The Books of Homilies: A Critical Edition* (2016).

Published 2018

Hardback ISBN: 978 0 227 17668 9
Paperback ISBN: 978 0 227 17670 2
PDF ISBN: 978 0 227 90642 2
ePub ISBN: 978 0 227 90643 9